T0370045

The
BEST of
Reader's
Digest

Reader's
Digest
New York / Montreal

CONTENTS

INTRODUCTION

For more than 100 years, *Reader's Digest* has celebrated the enduring power of great stories—those that teach you a truth about the human experience, that move you to take a stand or reach out to someone in need, that make you feel. Showcasing work from prominent writers and leaders as well as from everyday folks with an extraordinary tale to tell, the magazine has shone a light on diverse views and experiences.

From daring rescues to funny vignettes about modern life to inspiring lessons passed from one generation to the next, this collection includes some of the most thrilling, touching and humorous articles from our archives.

You'll be on the edge of your seat as you follow the climbing guide who outraced a sudden winter storm on Mount McKinley to find two men whose tent had blown off the side of the mountain. You'll feel the pain of a father (an FBI agent, no less) when he realizes that his own son had committed a heinous crime. You'll laugh ruefully in recognition at the woman who attempts to convince her husband to part with the LPs he has no way to listen to anymore and the yellowing books he knows were once meaningful to him (even if he can't remember why). And you'll be rooting for the ragtag team of 7- and 8-year-old ballplayers determined to win their season to honor the memory of their coach, who had been killed in an accident.

In addition to these and many other timeless favorites, we've included arresting photographs, uproarious jokes and cartoons, and true stories from readers like you—plus bonus material never published in the magazine itself.

—The Editors of *Reader's Digest*

Why We Forgive

by Desmond Tutu, from the book *The Book of Forgiving*

Anger may be justified, but "getting even" won't make you feel better

There were so many nights when I, as a young boy, had to watch helplessly as my father verbally and physically abused my mother. I can still recall the smell of alcohol, see the fear in my mother's eyes and feel the hopeless despair that comes when we see people we love hurting each other in incomprehensible ways. I would not wish that experience on anyone, especially not a child. If I dwell in those memories, I can feel myself wanting to hurt my father back, in the same ways he hurt my mother and in ways of which I was incapable as a small boy. I see my mother's face and I see this gentle human being whom I loved so very much and who did nothing to deserve the pain inflicted upon her.

When I recall this story, I realize how difficult the process of forgiving truly is. Intellectually, I know my father caused pain because he was in pain. Spiritually, I know my faith tells me my father deserves to be forgiven as God forgives us all. But it is still difficult. The traumas we have witnessed or experienced live on in our memories. Even years later they can cause us fresh pain each time we recall them.

Are you hurt and suffering? Is the injury new, or is it an old, unhealed wound? Know that what was done to you was wrong, unfair and undeserved. You are right to be outraged. And it is perfectly normal to want to hurt back when you have been hurt. But hurting back rarely satisfies. We think it will, but it doesn't. If I slap you after you slap me, it does not lessen the sting I feel on my own face, nor does it diminish my sadness as to the fact that you have struck me. Retaliation gives, at best, only momentary respite from our emotional pain. The only way to experience healing and peace is to forgive. Until we can forgive, we remain locked in our pain and locked out of the possibility of experiencing healing and freedom, locked out of the possibility of being at peace.

Without forgiveness, we remain tethered to the person who harmed us. We are bound with chains of bitterness, tied together, trapped. Until we can forgive the person who harmed us, that person will hold the keys to our happiness; that person will be our jailer.

When we forgive, we take back control of our own fate and our feelings. We become our own liberators. Forgiveness, in other words, is the best form of self-interest. This is true both spiritually and scientifically.

We don't forgive to help the other person. We don't forgive for others. We forgive for ourselves.

Originally published in the July 2014 issue of *Reader's Digest* magazine.

KINDNESS COUNTS

One month after we arrived in the U.S. from halfway around the globe, I drove to Dulles airport with my wife to pick up a guest. When we came back to the parking lot, our car was dead. It was an unexpected and embarrassing accident. Since we were new here, we were kind of stuck. Fortunately, a gentleman who parked his car close by came to help us jump our car. "Next time I might be in your position," he said. "Spread the love."

—Shuai Tang, *Arlington, VA*

READING RAINBOW

As a first grade Reading Recovery teacher, I had to do assessments at the beginning of the year to determine who qualified for the program. Part of the assessment was having the students read a sheet with randomly ordered upper- and lowercase alphabet letters. One of the students I was testing came to the lowercase *m*. He looked and looked at it. Finally he turned to me and said, "I have seen that letter on M&M's, but I don't know what it is called."

—Heidi Bailey, *Tremonton, UT*

Song of Defiance

by Fergus M. Bordewich

They confronted the Nazis with the only weapon they had: their voices

Murry Sidlin was tense with anticipation as he walked through the cobbled, mist-shrouded streets of Terezin in the Czech Republic. Images kept forming in his mind of the village as it must have been 60 years before, when it was a Nazi concentration camp filled with desperate and dying Jews. They were the reason that Sidlin had traveled here from Portland, where he was resident conductor of the Oregon Symphony. But it wasn't the suffering of these Jews that brought him. It was their triumph.

The 60-year-old Sidlin, a short, powerful man with silver hair, clutched a red bound musical score in his hand: the Verdi *Requiem*. He entered one of the old barracks and made his way down a flight of dimly lit steps and then along a dank basement corridor. Finally he found himself in front of a heavy wooden door. He hesitated, then pushed it open.

The feeble light revealed a long, narrow room filled with heaps of lumber, broken chairs, old bricks and rubble. Sidlin's eyes blurred with tears. He knelt down, scraped a handful of dust from the floor and rubbed it onto the score. *Here, in this very room,* he thought, *ordinary people rose to the level of the superhuman.* His own mission now was to make sure the world would never forget them.

The slogan "Arbeit macht frei" above the gate to the camp translates to "Work sets you free."

*   *   *

Terezin had been a perverse kind of showcase. In contrast to Auschwitz, Treblinka and other extermination camps, the Nazis designed this former garrison town near Prague to fool the world. For much of World War II, Nazi propaganda suggested that Jews there enjoyed a life of leisure, even using captive Jewish filmmakers to craft a movie showing "happy" Jews listening to lectures and basking in the sun. (The filmmakers were deported to Auschwitz as soon as they finished their work.)

The reality was horribly different. As many as 58,000 Jews were stuffed into a town that had originally held 7,000. Medical supplies were almost nonexistent, beds were infested with vermin, and toilets overflowed. Each day, prisoners were fed bread delivered in the same horse-drawn hearse that had carried the previous night's harvest of corpses to the crematorium. Of the 150,000 prisoners who passed through Terezin, 35,000 died there, mostly from disease and hunger.

Yet the camp made concessions for propaganda purposes. SS troops were posted outside the fortress, while daily activity was overseen by a Jewish "Council of Elders," which turned a blind eye to inmates' activities, unless they might attract Nazi attention.

So, amid the pervasive atmosphere of death, writers managed to write, painters to paint, and composers to compose. Among them was Rafael Schaechter, a conductor in his mid-30s. Charismatic, with a striking face and wavy, dark hair, Schaechter was just beginning to make a name for himself in the rich cultural mix of prewar Prague. He had scarcely thought of himself as Jewish at all, until he was seized by the Nazis.

"They will deport your whole chorus and hang you," the Jewish elders warned.

As his months in the camp stretched into years, and more and more Jews disappeared eastward on Nazi transports, Schaechter's fury at his captors steadily grew. And then he thought of a daring plan.

He confessed his idea to his roommate, Edgar Krasa, in a single sentence: "We can sing to the Nazis what we can't say to them."

Song of Defiance

* * *

More than half a century later, in 1998, Sidlin was thumbing through a book on the Holocaust at a yard sale in Oregon when he was startled to read that inmates at Terezin had managed to stage the famous Verdi *Requiem*. *Why*, he wondered, *did those Jews risk their lives to perform music of the Catholic liturgy?* Clearly something extraordinary had taken place at Terezin.

Eager to know more, Sidlin posted a query on the internet, seeking anyone who had information about the Verdi performance or Rafael Schaechter. After weeks of waiting, he received a reply from a woman in Israel who identified herself as Schaechter's niece. "Schaechter's roommate might still be alive somewhere near Boston," she told him. "His name is Krasa." Sidlin called information, and minutes later he was talking to a man with a booming voice and a thick Czech accent.

"The *Requiem* was an act of resistance," Krasa told him.

* * *

Schaechter's dream was to tell the Nazis, to their faces, that they would one day pay for their crimes against the Jews. The slightest protest, of course, could bring fearful retribution. But music offered a shield.

Everything that Schaechter wanted to say lay camouflaged within the Latin words of the *Requiem*, with its themes of God's wrath and human liberation. Schaechter had access to no musical instruments except a broken harmonium found in a rubbish heap. Other than that, he had only human voices to work with. Throwing himself into the plan, he managed to recruit 150 singers, ranging from Krasa, who had once harmonized with a barbershop quartet, to distinguished former members of the Prague Opera.

Among the group was a brown-eyed teenager named Marianka Zadikov (now Marianka May). During her 12-hour workday, she labored at everything from scrubbing windows to making tobacco pouches for German soldiers. At night, however, she slipped away to the basement carpentry shop, where she felt lifted up by Verdi's music and Schaechter's passion. "Without Rafi Schaechter, we'd never have survived," says May, one of the

7

tiny handful of chorus members to live through the war. "He saved us through this music."

Aching with hunger, sopranos, altos, tenors and basses would take their places among sawdust-covered tables, while Schaechter pounded out Verdi's towering themes on the harmonium. Since there was only a single score, the singers had to memorize their parts, in Latin, a language that few besides Schaechter understood.

When they rehearsed the key section called "Dies Irae," or "Day of Wrath," Schaechter explained that it meant God would judge all men— including the Nazis—by their deeds. "We are putting a mirror to them," he said. "Their fate is sealed."

Although the Germans had spies among the prisoners, Schaechter managed to keep the real meaning behind the chorus's rehearsals a secret. Still, the camp's Jewish elders were upset. "The Germans will deport your whole chorus, and hang you," they warned Schaechter at a stormy meeting.

That night Schaechter told his chorus, "What we are doing is dangerous. If anyone wants to leave, you may go."

No one left.

Again and again, the chorus was depleted by deportations to Auschwitz. But Schaechter kept on, always training more to replace the ones lost. At last, in the autumn of 1943, he was ready. The first performance took place for prisoners gathered in a former gymnasium. Someone had found an old piano missing a leg and propped it on a crate. During the performance, a technician kept it in tune with a pair of pliers.

Verdi's music burned through the audience like an electrical charge, and many remember it as one of the most powerful events of their lives. "The *Requiem* was like food put in front of them," says Sidlin. "They gnawed at it from sheer hunger."

Over the ensuing months, the *Requiem* was repeated several times for additional audiences of prisoners.

By now, it was the late summer of 1944. The Germans understood that the war was lost, and they wanted to leave no Jews alive to tell about the concentration camps. Members of Schaechter's chorus disappeared almost weekly on Nazi transports.

Edgar Krasa, with Marianka May, holds the Verdi score that conductor Murry Sidlin, left, took to the site of their suffering.

Schaechter received an order from the camp's commandant to stage a command performance of the *Requiem*. This would be "in honor" of a visit by Red Cross representatives who, fooled by the Nazis, would notoriously report that the Jews were living in comfort at Terezin. There would also be high Nazi officials present—among them, an SS lieutenant colonel named Adolf Eichmann. The scene was set for a face-to-face confrontation between defiant Jews and the man behind the Final Solution.

Despite his best efforts, Schaechter could muster only 60 singers for the chorus. Emaciated, they gathered on the small stage at the former gymnasium. Eichmann sat in the front row, dressed in full Nazi regalia. The Jews looked the Nazis in their eyes, and their voices swelled as they sang:

The day of wrath, that day shall dissolve the world in ash. ... What trembling there shall be when the judge shall come. ... Nothing shall remain unavenged.

"We literally became the music," recalls May. "We wanted to shout the 'Dies Irae' at the Nazis, because we couldn't kick them or beat them."

When the performance ended, there was no applause. The Nazis rose in silence. As he left, Eichmann was heard to say, with a smirk, "So they're singing their own requiem." He never realized the Jews were singing his.

Soon after, Schaechter and nearly all his chorus members were loaded into boxcars bound for Auschwitz. Schaechter was never seen again.

Marianka May was among those freed when Allied troops reached Terezin. "I believed in nothing in that camp," says May, with a look in her eyes that takes in both the death-filled streets of Terezin and the soothing hills of upstate New York, where she now lives. "I would say to myself, 'Is God there? If so, then how could these children be dying?' Schaechter wasn't a religious man. But what was it but God that he gave us in the music?"

Murry Sidlin has the score of the *Requiem* that he took to Terezin on a shelf in his home. The dust of that basement carpentry shop still covers its pages. These days, the conductor has a new score before him, a tribute to Schaechter and his brave choir. It is a theatrical dramatization by Sidlin that will premiere soon on PBS television. Its title: *Defiant Requiem.*

When his musicians lift their instruments and the first notes sound, Sidlin knows he will feel the presence of ghosts. And he can only hope to evoke one man's remarkable will. "Rafael Schaechter was not a conductor but a man on a spiritual mission," Sidlin says. "When he raised his baton, it was like Lancelot raising his sword."

Originally published in the April 2003 issue of *Reader's Digest* magazine.

Defiant Requiem *was broadcast nationwide on PBS in the spring of 2013. It was named Best Feature Length Documentary at the Big Apple Film Festival in New York City and was the runner-up for the Audience Award in January 2013 at the Palm Springs Film Festival. In 2014,* Defiant Requiem *was nominated for two News and Documentary Emmy Awards: Outstanding Historical Documentary Long Form and Outstanding Writing.*

"My Family Is Dying!"

by Sheldon Kelly

A terrible scream in the night brought help from a stranger

J ay Sines, 24, got home from work at the local sawmill shortly after midnight, Nov. 19, 1988. He looked in on his wife, Toni, and their two small daughters. All were sleeping soundly. "Let's hit the sack, Nick," he whispered to the family puppy.

As he stepped outside to the kennel, a shrill, horror-filled scream ripped through the still, near-freezing air of rural St. Maries, Idaho. For a moment Jay thought it was a cougar prowling the looming Clearwater Mountains. Then he saw flames lighting the sky half a mile away. Hurriedly he put Nick in the kennel and ran to wake Toni. "Call the fire department! Send them to Mill Town Road!"

Seconds later, Jay was fishtailing his car down the dirt driveway to the main road. The fire raged at a small hillside complex of mobile homes. Jay slid the car to a stop and sprinted up a steep, rutted lane toward the reddening glow.

Reaching the hilltop, he saw that a 70-foot-long trailer was ablaze. Flames were snapping 30 feet into the air. A young woman in torn night-clothes was running wildly back and forth, jumping to smash at the 6-foot-high windows with her hands. "Dear God!" she screamed. "My family is dying!"

Jay felt a moment of panic. He seemed to be the only person there to help. Never had he seen such a fire! Flames were leaping out of broken windows at the far end of the trailer and coiling along the roof; the roaring, crackling noises grew louder by the second. He grabbed the woman by the shoulders. "Where are they?" he shouted.

Cindy Thaut, curly blond hair matted with perspiration, tear-streaked face twisted in anguish, babbled breathlessly. If her family could not be saved, she wished only to die with them. Jay shook her. Precious seconds were ticking away. "Talk to me!" he demanded.

Barely coherent, Cindy told him that she had escaped through one of the master bedroom windows. Her husband, Leonard, had gone for their two children. He was supposed to hand them out to her from the bedroom. But, seconds later, flames had burst from the kitchen and living room windows. Cindy began crying hysterically.

"Where are they?" Jay yelled. Cindy pointed to the smoldering end section of the trailer, where thick, black smoke poured from the windows.

*　　*　　*

From the time he was old enough to play sports, Jay Sines had learned to battle the odds. As a Little Leaguer, he had pitched a no-hitter to win the state championship for his underdog team. And in tiny St. Maries, the shy, good-natured boy's grit had earned him townspeople's respect.

Over the roaring fire, there was suddenly a strange sense of quiet. The baby had stopped crying.

Once, during a high school football game, Jay's left knee had been so severely injured that doctors told him he would be unable to play again that year. After major surgery and muscle grafting, he labored determinedly at physical therapy. Several months later, at a league-championship basketball game, Jay ran onto the court wearing a leg brace. The crowd, many of them tearful, rose to their feet in wild applause. Buoyed by such invincible spirit, the team won.

Always, Jay recalled the words of his father, Murl, a mountain logger and volunteer baseball coach: "The word *can't* never did anything for anybody. You *can* do it! Never stop trying, son!"

Jay's father's words seemed etched in his mind. A lean, muscular 6-footer, Jay bolted toward a bedroom window. Arching his body, he leaped through the broken shards of glass to land inside.

His eyes burned in the pitch-darkness. His first breath caught in his throat as if his windpipe were blocked. Then he began breathing in loud, forced wheezes. Almost immediately he stumbled over a tall, heavily built man who had fallen near the center of the room.

"The babies," the man moaned. "Oh, God! Get the babies!"

The children's cries, though muffled, seemed inches away. "Where are you?" Jay called. Then he sensed movement in the darkness. Bending over, he felt a child's arms encircle his neck.

Cradling the toddler, Jay passed him outside to Cindy. It was 22-month-old Ryan, Cindy said tearfully. There was still 6-week-old Angela. And Cindy's husband, Leonard.

Each inhalation now brought on choking spasms. Jay ripped off his sweatshirt and wrapped it around his face. Unable to see, he ran his hands along the floor until he touched the now-unconscious man's shoulders. Jay tried to lift him, but the dead-weight body barely moved. He tried again and again. Then the sweatshirt fell away, and he gagged on the poisonous smoke tearing through his lungs. *I can't breathe ...*

Jay lurched to the broken window and tumbled out to the ground. *Another second inside,* he thought, *and I would have passed out.*

By now, more help had begun to arrive. A neighbor disappeared into the smoke-filled trailer only to fall back seconds later, gagging. Inside, the baby's cries grew faint. The trailer's end section resembled a belching industrial chimney surrounded by flames. It was a scene from hell.

Then, over the roaring fire, there was suddenly a strange sense of quiet. The baby had stopped crying.

For an instant, Jay saw his own daughters, 4-year-old Crystal and 8-month-old Bri-Anna. He hesitated for a split second, listening hopefully for another faint cry. Nothing. Only the mother's agonized pleas. He inhaled deeply and plunged back inside.

Dropping to his hands and knees, Jay moved quickly, feeling bedding, clothes, furniture and the unconscious body of the infant's father. Each effort was becoming more painful. Jay's lungs seemed ready to burst. He staggered to the window, stretching to breathe in fresh air.

* * *

Holding his breath, Jay once more searched the room on his hands and knees. *Where are you, Angela? Where?* The heat inside the trailer had become nearly unbearable. Jay knew there was very little time left.

He focused his attention on the unconscious father. Discovering that Leonard's legs were entangled in an overturned recliner chair, Jay worked frantically to free him.

Exasperated, Jay jerked hard on the obstructing chair. Suddenly he felt himself falling. An instant later, he was on the floor, momentarily stunned. Somehow a section of the recliner had slammed into his head.

Critical seconds elapsed, but with the chair out of the way Jay could grab Leonard and pull him to the window. "Never stop trying!" his father had told him. "Never!"

As Jay paused by the window, Cindy handed him a flashlight, her voice breaking. "Please ..." The light's beam penetrated the dense smoke. Suddenly, Jay's heart raced. A small bundle lay where Leonard had fallen. Jay looked closer. It was Angela, wrapped tightly in a thick blanket. He felt her squirm. "She's alive!" he called.

Quickly he swept her up and handed her to the deputy sheriff, who had arrived moments earlier. Jay took another deep breath and reached for the father. *I've got to get him out,* Jay thought. *It's now or never.*

* * *

Jay seized Leonard's shoulders and with a surge of adrenalin heaved the man's upper body onto the dresser beneath the windowsill. Then he grabbed both legs and, summoning all his strength, began pushing.

"We've got him!" the deputy shouted. He and two volunteers pulled Leonard's body into their arms and scrambled to safety. Jay climbed out the window and slid to the ground, soaking wet and vomiting. His smoke-filled lungs emitted an eerie whistling sound. After a moment, he crawled away, trying to focus through swollen, stinging eyes.

Jay staggered to his feet and walked unsteadily back toward the fire. He pushed three gas-laden vehicles away from the blaze. Flames continued to gush out of the trailer's windows as volunteer firefighters and another law office arrived.

As her husband was placed in the police car to be driven to the hospital, Cindy walked over to Jay. His face was grimy and bleeding, with one eye nearly shut. He tried to smile as she embraced him, her face streaming with tears. "God bless you," she cried. "God bless you!"

A small bundle lay where Leonard had fallen. It was Angela, wrapped tightly in a blanket.

Jay walked to his car, numb with exhaustion. It was 12:55 a.m. The headlights and ignition were still on, and the battery was dead. Jay push-started the car and drove to the hospital for treatment of smoke inhalation, cuts and contusions. It was around 3 a.m. when he reached home.

Cindy and the children were rushed to the Benewah Community Hospital for similar treatment. Leonard, unconscious, was transferred by trauma-unit helicopter to Sacred Heart Hospital in Spokane, Washington, about 60 miles away.

News of Jay's incredible feat spread quickly. The local newspaper called him the ultimate hero. At the sawmill, his co-workers gave him a standing ovation, and a Spokane television station announced that "a sure tragedy had a happy ending" because of Jay's "bold, selfless efforts." Publicity-shy Jay insisted, "I was just there."

Townspeople responded to the Thaut family's plight with food, clothing and a rent-free home. Leonard's co-workers at the Reglis stud mill turned over their entire $2,200 Christmas fund.

Two weeks later, Leonard, unable to speak or see clearly and with severely damaged lungs, returned home. Now it was his turn to fight the odds. "I'm going to get well and shake Jay's hand," he wrote on a slip of paper for Cindy.

*　　*　　*

On Sept. 14, 1989, Jay welcomed the Thaut family into his sunny backyard. It had just been announced that in December he would be awarded the prestigious Carnegie Medal for heroism, and Leonard and Cindy had come to congratulate him.

Leonard's voice and eyesight are back to normal, and he is learning to adapt to his diminished lung capacity. He thanked Jay for saving their lives. "I'd want somebody to do the same for my family," Jay said after a moment's silence, and the two young men shook hands firmly, smiling, near tears.

As Leonard walked away, Jay could not help thinking that thanks were also owed to another man—the father who had told him never to stop trying. Never!

Originally published in the April 1990 issue of *Reader's Digest* magazine.

Jay, Leonard, Cindy and Angela still live in St. Maries, Idaho. Ryan Thaut moved to Reno, Nevada, where he is a miner.

Cindy and Leonard (who is on disability because of the injuries he sustained in the fire) divorced about 20 years ago. Their children, Ryan and Angela, now each have two children of their own.

Four-Wheel Dives

by Roz Warren, from HumorOutcasts

What does the condition of your car say about you?

Have you ever noticed that with some friends, when they offer you a ride and you get in their car, the first thing they say is "Sorry about the mess," even if the car's interior is so antiseptic you could perform surgery in there? On the other hand, I've been in cars that more closely resemble the inside of a hamper than a vehicle—and the owner doesn't seem to notice.

Maybe it's because I grew up in Detroit, but I believe that the condition of your vehicle says something about you. Is your car the mobile counterpart of the kitchen junk drawer, an area designated for chaos, a place to speed away from responsibility? Or is it a sanctuary from the chaos of your home, your job, your family, a self-contained space where order is easily attained and maintained? After all, cars are all about escape, starting with that first solo drive out of your parents' driveway and into the world. So I recently asked my Facebook friends: Is the inside of your car clean and tidy, or is it a disaster area? Here are some of the more telling examples from my personality driving test:

- I have four dogs, one of whom is chronically carsick. You really wouldn't want to get into my car. Unless you're a dog.

17

- I keep a duster in the door pocket and use it at lights. And I shake out my floor mats once a week. There's nothing wrong with that. There ISN'T.

- I divide people into those who brush off my passenger seat and hop right in and those who grimace, then get in with a look of determination and pity.

- I always carry lots of bottled water, just in case I break down in a desert. Even though I live in Philadelphia.

- If I ever disappear due to foul play, the cops will easily be able to trace the last six months of my life from the junk on the floor of my car.

- My car is spotless. I just wish the rest of my life were this beautiful and well-ordered.

- I think of my car as my pocketbook on wheels. It contains everything I need for daily survival.

Four-Wheel Dives

- Food wrappers. Books. Thermoses. Coffee cups. Sunglasses. Jackets. Blankets. Troll doll in a nurse uniform. Emergency apocalypse backpack. Flashlights. Hair ties. Reading glasses. Newspapers. Receipts. Grocery lists. Stuff for Goodwill …

- We call my husband's car Meals on Wheels because he has stashed so much snack food in it.

- Last week, I found a squirrel in my car.

- I'm a teacher, which means my car is full of school supplies. If times get tough, I'll just sell pens, markers and construction paper out of my trunk.

- My husband has stashed an ax under the driver's seat of my car. Yes. An ax.

Originally published in the October 2018 issue of *Reader's Digest* magazine.

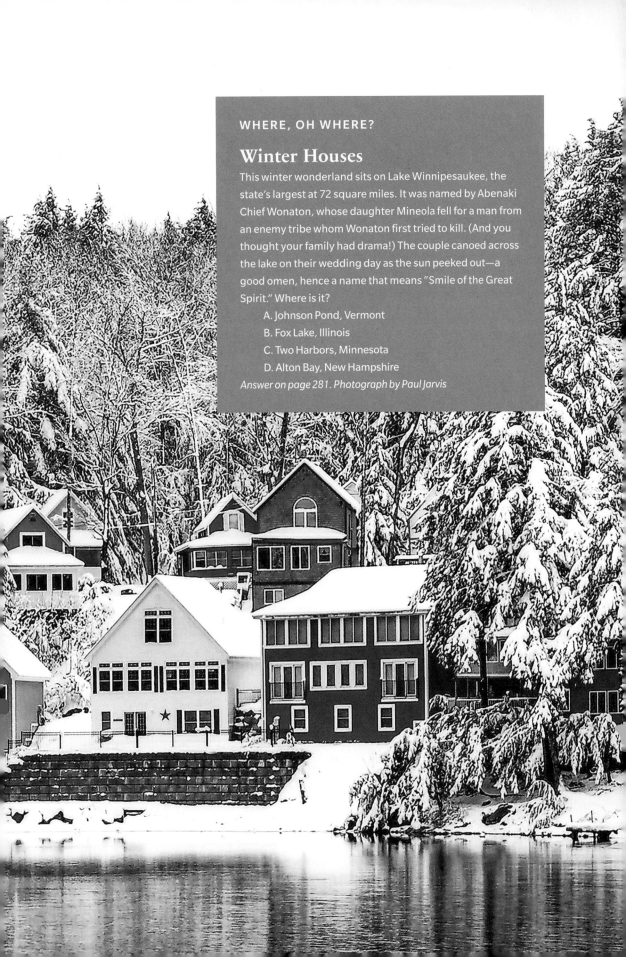

Winter Houses

This winter wonderland sits on Lake Winnipesaukee, the state's largest at 72 square miles. It was named by Abenaki Chief Wonaton, whose daughter Mineola fell for a man from an enemy tribe whom Wonaton first tried to kill. (And you thought your family had drama!) The couple canoed across the lake on their wedding day as the sun peeked out—a good omen, hence a name that means "Smile of the Great Spirit." Where is it?

    A. Johnson Pond, Vermont

    B. Fox Lake, Illinois

    C. Two Harbors, Minnesota

    D. Alton Bay, New Hampshire

Answer on page 281. *Photograph by Paul Jarvis*

Humor Hall of Fame

Whenever my family leaves the house, our Shetland sheepdog's animal instincts start to kick in. He runs circles around us and nips at our heels to keep us all together. Watching this display, my friend couldn't resist: "You always herd the ones you love."

—JOLENE HUEHOLT

Four jackrabbits are strolling in the prairie. Out of nowhere, a gang of coyotes begins to chase them. So the rabbits run under a huge cactus for refuge. Then the hungry coyotes surround the cactus. One jackrabbit says to another, "OK, should we make a run for it, or wait till we outnumber them?"

—BENITO F. JUAREZ

"Honey, the dog learned a new trick and now I owe him 12 dollars."

The Arrow That Saved My Life—Twice

by Donna Barbour

After a freak backyard accident almost kills her, a Texas woman is taken on a miraculous medical journey

It was a warm April evening in 2012, and I had gotten home from work about an hour earlier. As I often did after a long day, I went straight to my backyard and did some work in my flower garden before deciding to light the grill to make dinner for my husband and myself. I had only just walked a few steps on the patio when I suddenly felt a horrifying blow to the right side of my neck. It felt as though someone had hit me with a baseball bat. I knew that no one was in the yard with me, so no one could have hit me. Totally confused, I reached up and, to my shock and horror, realized that I had been shot—with an arrow.

I grabbed the arrow with a death grip where it had pierced my neck and ran inside, screaming my husband's name. Ed was in the back of the house talking to our daughter, Keila, on the phone. He dropped the phone and ran to me. Ed grabbed me by the shoulders to stop me from running and told me to lie down on the couch. Then he went to call 911. I lay there and prayed. I didn't know if there was any way that I could survive.

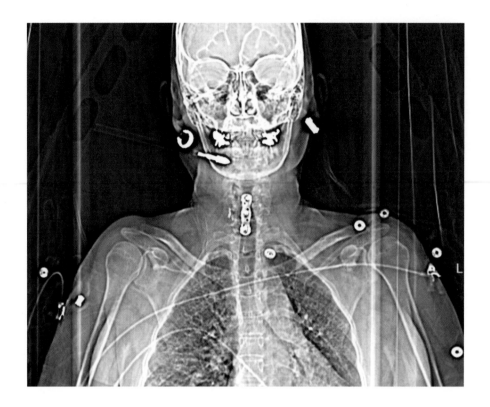

The next hour or so was a crazy, jumbled mix of events. The arrow had come from a young man practicing with a compound bow, used for hunting, in his backyard. Luckily, he was using a practice arrow, which is smooth and rounded; a broadhead arrow for hunting would have killed me. He lived across the alley and was shooting to the north. The arrow had ricocheted and turned back to the south. It went over two, possibly three, fences, through the shrubs and an oak tree's branches, between two large hanging baskets, and into my neck as I walked across the patio. A shot from a compound bow can travel up to 200 miles per hour, or 300 feet per second.

We had EMTs who were simply wonderful that evening. As they entered the house and sat down beside me, they were perfectly calm and totally focused. They called for help from the paramedics and for a medical helicopter from Amarillo, Texas, which is about 65 miles away and the closest city with a trauma center.

As the helicopter lifted off to take me to Amarillo, I felt complete peace. I had seen the large number of people outside my house, and I knew that

Donna Barbour after surviving the accident (above), and the scan showing the arrow penetrating her neck (left)

the Lord was being bombarded with prayers on my behalf. I felt certain that everything would be fine.

At the hospital, family and friends were gathering. I tried hard to reassure them. I kept telling them I was OK, but the looks on their faces told me that they weren't buying it. It was a difficult job since I had an arrow sticking out of my neck!

Soon they took me back for a CT scan to determine the location of the arrow on the inside. The doctors and nurses began telling me how lucky I was. The arrow had gone between the carotid artery and the jugular vein. That space between the two is a quarter of an inch or less. The diameter of the arrow is larger than the space it went through. It actually pushed the artery to the side—without nicking it. There was no bleeding at all. Although I didn't realize at the time how truly incredible this was, I began arguing with them that I wasn't "lucky";

I was "blessed"! This is an argument I have continued to wage ever since.

As I was being taken back to surgery to remove the arrow, my family entered a waiting room full of people—in fact, there were two waiting rooms full! Someone told my son, Kyle, that there was a post on the site texasbowhunter.com asking for prayers for me. It turns out a friend had called her son, who is a bow hunter, and told him about the accident, and he had posted the prayer request on that website.

The morning after my two-hour surgery, with my family all gathered in my room, a couple of the doctors came by to see me. After they left, the surgeon came in. He checked the wound and talked to us about what he had done. Then he told us something that rocked our world again.

He said the CT scan had revealed that I had a brain tumor. I remember going a bit numb but thinking, *God works in mysterious ways!* The surgeon said that they were almost certain the tumor was benign, but that it was located in a very difficult place. I was stunned, of course, but I felt as if it was God's plan for me to find it.

A few days later, I went in for a second opinion from another neurosurgeon. He said that it was a difficult surgery but that it had to be done. The tumor was about to cross the midline of my brain, which would have resulted in a massive stroke.

The brain surgery was successful, and in less than a week I was back home. I was discouraged and feeling horrible. I had lost a lot of blood from a bacterial infection, *Clostridium difficile,* and was extremely anemic and weak. I was beginning to have symptoms of post-traumatic stress disorder, hearing the *swoosh* and then the *thunk* of the arrow. Thankfully, that didn't last too long.

All my adventures had taken a toll, and I needed a time of healing and rest. All was uneventful for a couple of years. I continued to tell people that I was not lucky; I was blessed. I had an MRI each year to make sure that the tumor was not growing back. But in 2015, after I had my MRI, the doctor's office called and told me that I needed to come back in.

The doctor explained that there was still no sign of a tumor but that they had found a brain aneurysm. Normally, aneurysms aren't discovered until they rupture, and that is almost always too late. Again, I was facing uncertainty and dreading brain surgery. I simply do not know how people go through times like these without the Lord and the peace that comes from knowing that God is in control.

In the weeks before the surgery, I felt at peace with whatever the outcome would be. We went to Dallas for the procedure. They found that it was a very fragile and difficult aneurysm, covered with blisters and on the verge of rupturing, but the doctor successfully clipped it.

I wasn't lucky; I was blessed.

Had it not been for that arrow, I would have died from a brain tumor, a stroke or an aneurysm! And honestly, the arrow should have killed me. But it didn't.

For weeks and weeks, everyone gathered around me when I went to the grocery store or the post office. People would stop and hug me and even cry, saying how happy they were that this had happened. It strengthened everyone's faith.

Coincidences? Luck? I think not. The gentleman who wrote the last comment on the prayer-request thread on texasbowhunter.com summed it up in just two words. He simply wrote, "Amazing grace."

Originally published in the July/August 2020 issue of *Reader's Digest* magazine.

What Became of the Airlift Orphans?

by Karen Walker Ryan

Saigon was falling, and people were fleeing. Towns in South Vietnam were choked with fear. America's long, horrible experience in Southeast Asia was coming to an end.

As a stewardess for Pan American World Airways, I had an enviable job, enjoying layovers in glamorous places like Paris and Hong Kong.

But during the Vietnam War, Pan Am also flew a regular two-day-a-week schedule into Saigon. For the most part, I had seen the war as puffs of smoke 35,000 feet below. I had also seen it in the tense calm of the young men who got off our flights in Saigon, hearts pounding.

The other stewardesses and I knew that to these soldiers returning from leave, we were much more than hometown girls with warm smiles. We were the face of America—the last of their country some would see for a long time, perhaps forever.

"See you again soon," we usually said with brave smiles as each soldier stepped from the cool air of our jetliner into the hot, grubby arms of war. Then our doors would shut and we were gone.

Never did I imagine that as the conflict closed down, its smallest and

Stewardess Karen Ryan cradles one of hundreds of infants she helped spirit out of Saigon in 1975.

most innocent victims—the orphans of war—would be packed into our aircraft, transforming it into a vessel of mercy.

Our flight crew was in Hong Kong on the evening of April 4, 1975, when orders came that our next day's scheduled flight to Tokyo had been canceled. Our new mission was to board a special Pan Am charter to Saigon, pick up over 400 Vietnamese orphans and get them safely on their way to America.

If I'd had much time to think, the prospect would have been emotionally overwhelming. At 32, I was a childless woman who wanted children—a woman whose marriage was breaking up. Though I loved children, I had rarely changed a diaper. But we were women and they were babies, and somehow we were supposed to know what to do.

The giant 747 we boarded the next morning was stocked for the occasion: hundreds of baby bottles, thousands of diapers and, theoretically, a bassinet for each infant. A section had been transformed into an airborne pediatric hospital filled with syringes, intravenous feeding tubes, and all the equipment needed to keep little lungs breathing and tiny hearts beating.

On the runway at Saigon's Tan Son Nhut airfield, several old army buses chugged toward our plane—each filled with fragile lives orphaned by war.

The children were refugees from all over war-ravaged Vietnam—many from families splintered by bombs and left homeless and hungry. Others were newborns who'd been abandoned in the streets of Saigon.

For security reasons, our plane would be on the ground as briefly as possible, so we had much work to do. In a whoosh, our doors were opened and the soggy heat and smells of Saigon pushed into the cabin. Suddenly I had three screaming babies in my arms and someone was trying to hand me another.

Their bodies felt almost feverish as I placed my infants in bassinets and went back to the doorway for more. As I looked at the beautiful little faces and tried to comprehend the magnitude of what we were doing, tears filled my eyes. I tried to hide them, but then I saw the face of the stewardess who was passing the babies to me. She, too, was weeping.

What Became of the Airlift Orphans?

We were taking more than 400 human beings from their homeland into a world they could not even imagine. All we could do was hug them and coo at them—surely odd sounds coming from strange faces.

After the last of more than 300 infants were stuffed onto the plane, older children came up the ramp, many of them terrified and crying. Some were in good shape, others clearly very ill or crippled.

Among the older children was 8-year-old Hoang Van Long. His 78-year-old grandmother, with whom he had gone to live when his mother died, had relinquished him to an orphanage, hoping he would be adopted by an American family. She knew he would have far better opportunities than would come his way when the Communists took over.

A cheerful boy, Hoang took his seat beside a window so he could watch his homeland fade away. Burning in the child's mind were images of his mother and grandmother, who he knew had loved him.

Burning even more brightly in his pocket was a photo of his new family—a mother, a father, three brothers—who were waiting for him in a small town in a place called Ohio.

Like Hoang, most of the children on our flight were already assigned to families that had met the rigorous U.S. adoption standards. Most arrangements were made by the sponsor of our charter flight—the Holt International Children's Services of Eugene, Oregon, a 44-year-old not-for-profit agency specializing in adoptions.

We were taking more than 400 human beings from their homeland into a world they could not even imagine.

Our flight was one of several dozen that made up what came to be called Operation Babylift. In that bleak April alone, nearly 2,000 orphans were evacuated to the United States and another 600 to homes in other countries.

During the few moments of serenity as our plane lumbered down the runway, I ached for the women who had made an almost unimaginable sacrifice: giving up their babies with the desperate hope that they might prosper in a far-off land.

But once underway for our five-hour trip to the U.S. soil of Guam, we had no time to think about anything except the 409 children who filled the cabin. Within an hour, the plane was soaked with spilled formula and bins of dirty diapers.

During the flight, I cradled and rocked dozens of the little ones. Many had on plastic wristbands with their names—difficult names for my tongue, such as Vu Dinh Tien or Nguyen Thi Mai.

I ached for the women who had given up their babies with the desperate hope that they might prosper in a far-off land.

Still, I tried to say their names in a soothing tone as I whispered to each baby, praying for them, wishing them well. I scribbled down some of the names as best I could, thinking, I suppose, that someday I might try to find out what happened to them.

Yet something nagged at me about all of this. It wasn't just whether these children could fit in as Americans. It was whether they would even want to be Americans and have American names and live in strange places like Ohio or California or Massachusetts.

These questions weighed heavily on my mind as our pilots made a gentle landing in Guam—hardly rustling a bassinet. The small lives I had intersected with for a mere five hours were placed in the hands of a fresh crew, which would fly them on to Seattle.

From there, the children would head for every nook and cranny of the United States. They were like seeds flung across the vast landscape of America, to take root and flourish—or, I worried, to wilt and lie fallow.

I flew for a few more years, then settled down with a wonderful new husband on his family's cattle ranch in Montana. When our son Paul was born, he was the baby I had dreamed of for so long. I also started my own business, called Heartland Caregivers, which each year places 250 nannies, elder care–givers and home managers with families in need.

My only tangible connection with our orphan flight was a yellowing copy of a story I wrote about the experience for my local newspaper—a story published by *Reader's Digest* in May 1976 called "A Planeload of Babies." I had reread it many times and wondered what became of the children. But

What Became of the Airlift Orphans?

I did not think I'd ever know the end of the story. Then, one afternoon last year, an editor from *Reader's Digest* called to ask whether I was interested in finding out what had happened to some of the babies on my flight.

For a moment, the drum-tight emotion of those few hours long ago came cascading back across the years. I was thrilled.

*   *   *

Kara Delahunt was standing in the lobby of Washington's Mayflower Hotel when I saw her from across the marble floor. For a brief time, I felt as overwhelmed as when the first baby was handed to me on the plane in Saigon.

Using some of the names I had scribbled down during that flight, the Holt adoption agency had put me in touch with several of the children. In Kara's case, I had called her in Washington and asked to meet her.

I paused to collect myself. Kara is a beautiful young woman, now 25, with a grace and vitality I could sense as she stood waiting for me.

When I introduced myself, she smiled, and we embraced in a long hug. When last I had seen her, she was not even 5 months old and her name was Nguyen Thi Mai Trang. Adopted by Kati and William Delahunt of Quincy, Massachusetts, she was given the name Kara. The Delahunts also had a natural daughter nearly three years older.

Kara and I spent hours together that day and the next, visiting museums and art galleries—and talking. I was struck by just how typical her childhood had been. She'd grown up on *The Brady Bunch* and *The Cosby Show* and later MTV, and loved reading Nancy Drew and Laura Ingalls Wilder.

Despite some unsettling teenage

When Karen (right) last saw Kara, Kara was barely 5 months old, and her name was Nguyen Thi Mai Trang.

fads—including an outrageous poodlelike haircut that quickly grew out—her parents say they were never once worried about her.

Kara herself speaks with a near reverence for her adoptive parents, and her gratitude for the life they have given her. And there's something else: "They always taught me that my mother loved me so much that she gave me up." Perhaps that knowledge inspired her, in college, to spend a summer working at an orphanage in Chile.

Today Kara, a graduate of Middlebury College in Vermont, works in Washington with an international public relations firm. She has a master's degree in Spanish and is also fluent in German. She speaks not a word of Vietnamese.

In April of this year, the 25th anniversary of her leaving Saigon, Kara is returning to the country of her birth. "Vietnam is so foreign to me," she says. "Yet it is part of me. I want to go see it, and then come back and think about it."

Unlike some of the orphans, Kara doesn't feel an urgency to find her birth parents. "I'm curious about my family in Vietnam," she told me. "But to be honest, I'm really just an American kid."

*   *   *

"My dream was to be an American boy," says Matthew Steiner.

No doubt there are some sad stories too, but the Holt adoption agency says most of the children have fit remarkably well into American life.

Among those I spoke with from my flight was Hoang Van Long, the friendly 8-year-old who had sat by the window trying to imagine his life to come. He was adopted by James and Mary Steiner of West Liberty, Ohio, where Dr. Steiner had a family medical practice.

"My dream was to be an American boy," Matthew Steiner says. "And that's just what happened."

In high school Matthew played sports and was co-valedictorian of his class. From there, he went to Goshen College and then to medical school. Today he is an emergency room physician in Charlotte, North Carolina.

"I grew up in a wonderful family," Matthew says. "We were taught that what matters most is how much you can help others."

In 1995 he returned for a visit to Vietnam, and he has been on medical missions to Latin American countries. He and his wife, Laura, also a physician, are expecting their first child this month.

In the case of another infant, given the name Chris Brownlee, I found myself weeping with his father as he told me about the night he and his wife met their new son at JFK Airport—and the unimaginable joy they felt.

Chris is a graduate of Ohio Wesleyan University with a degree in psychology. He works in Boston at a home for troubled youngsters and loves music and martial arts.

Chris told me that in a few years he wants to go back to Vietnam. "But first I want to understand who I am here before I try to find out who I was there."

On a hazy afternoon earlier this year, Kara Delahunt and I walked along the valley of the dark walls of the Vietnam Veterans Memorial. As my eyes swept the rows of names of the more than 58,000 Americans who died in Vietnam, I wondered how many were young soldiers I might have spoken to, or even hugged, as they got off my plane in Saigon.

My sorrow was deep as I thought of so many brave men—all boys of my generation—who should have been our husbands and the fathers of our children. Instead, their names stared silently from this wall.

As always, I wondered whether any good whatsoever had come from that long and savage nightmare.

Chris Brownlee counsels troubled youths.

Then I glanced at Kara. She stood pensively, the Washington Monument over her shoulder in the distance. Kara's dark eyes seemed full, brimming with emotion.

Looking at her, I thought of the thousands of people touched by the lives of these orphans. Then Kara caught my glance and smiled gently.

Yes, I thought. This is the good that came from Vietnam: In these orphans, Americans received a gift even greater than the gift of freedom we offered them. For Kara and the others have only strengthened and renewed this country's culture. And with their success has come a powerful affirmation—that the human spirit, which beat so vigorously in those tiny hearts long ago, can never be extinguished.

Originally published in the May 2000 issue of *Reader's Digest* magazine.

PAPA BEAR

I was surprised to learn the sleeping arrangement at the log home we were sharing with my in-laws for the week, specifically that my young daughter had agreed to sleep in a downstairs bedroom by herself. As we settled in, we discussed the number of deer we had spotted on our way up to the log home. My wife shouted, "I hope we see a bear or two this week!"

At bedtime, my wife and I retreated to the upstairs loft and my in-laws headed for a bedroom downstairs. My wife and I were about to doze off when our daughter appeared in our room with a worried look on her face. She said a bear was scratching at her window. I decided it would be best if I slept downstairs and my daughter shared the loft with my wife.

On my way down, I passed my father-in-law, asleep in front of the television. I was in bed only a couple of minutes when I heard a tap ... tap on the window. Something was indeed out there, but it wasn't a bear—at least that's what I told myself.

Some time later, I was awakened again, this time by a loud, low-pitched growl. I saw a large figure in the doorway and froze as it inched closer to me. I realized what it was—only after my father-in-law leaned in to give me a goodnight kiss. I blurted out in my deepest voice, "It's David, not Marissa." My father-in-law jumped back. We both laughed nervously at the awkward moment, and I explained the bedroom switch. I told him that the only thing scarier than a bear attack was Papa Bear coming in to kiss me goodnight. He growled in agreement!

—David Warren, *Miamisburg, OH*

The Coldest Case

by Mary A. Fischer

Forty-six years after two cops were brutally murdered, an L.A. law enforcement team nabs the killer

Whaen the cold case unit was formed in Los Angeles, detectives faced a daunting backlog of 9,000 unsolved murder cases dating back four decades. But killings don't get any colder than the 1957 murder of two young cops during a routine traffic stop. Investigators had all but given up on the case—one of the oldest unsolved homicides in the country—when modern technology finally caught up with justice.

The story begins 48 years ago, on July 21, in a desolate area of an oil field in Hawthorne, California. With its view of the ocean and glittering city lights, the spot made a perfect lovers' lane, which is where, around midnight, two teenage couples in a 1949 Ford were parked. They weren't alone for long. Out of the darkness, a man in his 20s, with a pompadour hairstyle, approached the car and, in a distinct southern drawl the teenagers would never forget, said all he wanted to do was rob them. He pointed his .22, told the frightened youths to hand over their watches and cash, then made himself out to be a liar.

Snapping off pieces of both duct and surgical tape to strap over their eyes and mouths, he forced three of them, two boys and a girl, into the backseat, while he raped the other girl in the front. Terrified, the youths figured they'd be killed so there would be no witnesses. Instead, the intruder ordered the teenagers to take off everything but their underwear, and left them, nearly naked, in the middle of nowhere as he sped away in their Ford.

Two miles to the west, in the city of El Segundo, officers Richard Phillips, 29, and Milton Curtis, 25, were patrolling the streets when they saw a man in a Ford run a red light. It was 1:30 a.m. They pulled the car over and noticed clothes—a yellow sundress, a slip and a man's sport shirt—strewn across the backseat. The officers ordered the driver out of the car, and as Curtis used his radio to call headquarters, the man pulled out his .22 and shot Phillips three times in the back. Then he pointed the gun inside the patrol car where Curtis was sitting and fired three more times, striking him in the chest.

Phillips managed to discharge his service revolver three times in the direction of the man—who by then was climbing back behind the wheel of the Ford—before he fell to the ground. With both officers down, the driver took off. Four blocks away, he abandoned the car and fled on foot.

Back in the oil field, the teenagers eventually stumbled upon a security guard and asked for help. Still dazed when the police showed up, the youths struggled to recall physical details of the perpetrator in hopes a composite sketch would lead to his arrest.

Clothes—a sundress, a slip and a shirt—were strewn over the backseat.

The young rape victim was examined, but in the 1950s, says Darren Levine, the deputy district attorney assigned to the case in 2002, "the way they handled a rape case was much different from today. They gave back the girl's semen-stained underpants and slip, so we never had that forensic evidence to work with later on."

*   *   *

Keith Curtis, now 53, was only 5, and his sister 2, when he heard a knock on the door at 4 a.m. "I was awakened by voices and my mother's crying," he recalls. His mother was so rattled she couldn't get the front door unlocked. "What's wrong?" she called to the El Segundo police chief. "Is my husband hurt?"

"No, it's worse than that," said the chief, who, at a house a mile away, had just delivered the same devastating news to the widow of Officer Phillips and his three young children.

"I was confused for a while," Curtis says. "My mother kept saying my father had just gone away on a trip. Finally, she told me he'd gone to heaven and couldn't come home."

The killing of the policemen made headlines in Southern California for months. In the abandoned Ford, detectives found three bullet holes from the shots Phillips fired—two in the rear window and one in the trunk—but located only two projectiles. Where was the third? The answer would eventually stun them. Also in the Ford, torn clothing and pieces of tape were found, along with three partial fingerprints on the steering wheel and a car panel. But with no computer databases against which to check the prints, police simply sealed and stored them.

Over the next few years, as detectives worked the case, bits of evidence surfaced. A month after the murders, a woman gardening in her backyard near where the Ford was abandoned found a man's watch but made no connection to the crimes. Two years later, her husband was clearing brush in the yard when he discovered a piece of a .22-caliber handgun but, like his wife, didn't think much about it and put it on a shelf in the garage.

In 1960, the couple's son was working outside when he found the revolver's rusty cylinder. The boy's father, having seen news stories about the officers' deaths, put two and two together. He reasoned that, with his house located close to the crime scene, the suspect had tossed the incriminating evidence in the backyard as he fled. The man phoned police.

When a ballistics check confirmed that markings from rounds fired by the gun were consistent with bullets removed from Curtis's and Phillips's bodies, elated police finally had their first break. Investigators were able to trace the murder weapon to a Shreveport, Louisiana, Sears store, where records indicated it had been purchased three days prior to the killings. But because identification wasn't necessary for the purchase, the customer had simply signed the receipt, "G. D. Wilson," in wide-spaced lettering.

Investigators located the clerk who handled the transaction. Amazingly, he recalled that the purchaser was a man with a pompadour who seemed in a hurry to get out of town. But the trail went dead when those leads led nowhere, sending the case into cold storage for another 42 years.

*   *   *

The backlog of cold cases grows longer each year. Of the more than 560 homicides committed annually in Los Angeles, almost 50% go unsolved.

Lisa Kahn, head of the DA's forensic sciences division, and David Lambkin of LAPD's cold case unit, are leading the effort to crack the city's cold cases by using modern technology, including tracking software, DNA evidence (blood, hair and semen) and computerized databases of fingerprints and ballistics records. The work began in 2001 with a $50 million state grant to cover the costs of examining DNA in unsolved sexual assault cases. The grant allowed detectives to review cases using a state database containing 300,000 DNA samples from known offenders. To date, investigators in L.A. have solved 28 cold cases and are hopeful of solving another 50 this year.

Kahn first became fascinated with forensics when she tried a double rape case in the late '80s. It was the first case in L.A. County in which DNA was entered as evidence, and it introduced Kahn to the world of genetic profiling. Because the rapist wore a mask, his victims could not identify him. Kahn obtained blood samples from the suspect that, when tested against semen left in the victims' bodies, produced a DNA match.

"I look at an old case like a big forensic puzzle," says Kahn. "You can tell a lot from DNA testing—whether there were multiple perpetrators, for example, or whether a victim was killed, or dumped, at the scene."

Not all cold cases are solved using DNA. Fingerprint evidence can be a helpful tool, and it would prove key in the El Segundo officers' murder case. Before computerized fingerprint databases were developed in the mid-'80s, detectives had to come up with a suspect and then compare prints on file, often with limited results.

With advances in technology, however, fingerprints can now be scanned

Los Angeles County Sheriff Leroy Baca, Howard Speaks (who lifted the fingerprint on July 22, 1957, at the crime scene), and the Chief of the El Segundo Police Jack Wayt (left to right), speak at the press conference after the court proceedings for the murders of officers Curtis and Phillips.

directly into huge computer systems. "We can take a fingerprint from a crime scene, process it and search it against prints in the database," says Lambkin, "which can tell us who the suspect is instead of vice versa."

That's precisely what happened in the 1957 case, which was reopened in the fall of 2002 after investigators, out of the blue, received a tip. A man dying of cancer informed police that his kid brother, years earlier, had boasted of killing the El Segundo officers. When detectives checked out the kid brother, they determined that he wasn't credible.

"He took credit for all sorts of crimes," says Deputy DA Levine, "including killing Robert Kennedy. But the tip, though irrelevant, stirred up interest in the case."

By then, fingerprint analysis had come a long way. In July 1999, the FBI completed compiling its Integrated Automated Fingerprint Identification System (IAFIS), a nationwide fingerprint database containing some 40 million prints of known offenders. Detectives assigned to the 1957 case ran its composite of the prints from the Ford through the database, then waited expectantly to see what would come back.

"I'll never forget the moment when I got the phone call from the crime lab analyst who said we had a match," recalls Lt. Craig Cleary, head of El Segundo's detective unit. "I thought he was kidding. 'Are you sure?' I asked."

"I'm certain," the analyst said.

The print belonged to a man named Gerald F. Mason who lived in Columbia, South Carolina. In 1956, a year before the officers' killings, a then-22-year-old Mason had been arrested in South Carolina for commercial burglary (the only other crime on his record), so his fingerprints were on file in that state. But those prints did not make their way to the national database until many years later.

Detectives began tracking Mason and soon learned more details about him. He was 68, weighed 195 pounds, had been married for 40 years, and had two grown children and several grandchildren. After working in gas stations in his youth, he had eventually bought a service station chain, an investment that made him a wealthy man. In fact, he was well known and respected in Columbia. Upon retiring a few years earlier, he had begun spending much of his time bowling and playing golf.

The first call Cleary made after identifying Mason was to the family of Officer Milton Curtis. "I was intrigued but wary," says Keith Curtis, who today works for a heavy equipment company, is married and has a 19-year-old daughter. Cleary also phoned Richard Phillips's family. By then, his widow was in her 70s, and his three children were middle-aged. "I talked to her son, and he almost hung up on me," Cleary says. "He thought it was a prank call. But the more I talked, the more he realized this might be true."

Gerald Mason wipes away tears after pleading guilty to the 1957 murders in March 2003.

"I'm not a religious guy," explains Deputy DA Levine, "but this was one of those cases where you feel someone above is watching over you. All the stars aligned to make it work."

Still, Levine wanted more evidence. "I wanted to make sure, 46 years later, before arresting someone who is a pillar of his community, that we had a rock-solid case that would go to trial and end with a conviction." Investigators tracked down as many witnesses as they could, but several, including the 16-year-old boy who had owned the Ford, had died.

One witness—the Sears clerk with the excellent memory—was not only still alive, but he had risen through the ranks to become a vice president of the retail chain. All those years later, the man still remembered Mason, his southern accent and that he appeared in a hurry. Having learned that Mason had been living at a YMCA in Columbia when he was arrested in 1956, detectives began checking other YMCAs to see if they could place him near the Sears in Shreveport, where the murder weapon had been purchased.

Sure enough, on the registry of a YMCA right across from the store, they spotted the signature of one "George D. Wilson." Detectives compared the signature with the one on the gun sales form and with Mason's signature on a recent business document. All three matched.

"We knew we had him then," Levine says. Detectives are still not exactly sure why Mason had come west to California, but his journey across the United States, possibly to deal with a legal matter involving his mother, fit the time period of the crimes.

It was daybreak on Jan. 29, 2003, when a group of eager officials, including Deputy DA Levine and Lieutenant Cleary, came to Mason's front door. "He had the deer-in-the-headlights look," Cleary recalls.

"We want to talk to you about the murder of two El Segundo police officers," one of the detectives said.

"He didn't deny it," Cleary says, "but we could tell he was shocked we'd solved the case after all these years."

Officials searched Mason and found a circular scar, the size of a dime, on his back. In a later admission, Mason finally provided the answer to a question that had baffled investigators for decades. Phillips's third bullet, which police could not find no evidence of at the scene of the crime, had struck Mason just below the right shoulder blade, and he still had the scar.

In March 2003, after waiving extradition, Mason was brought to Los Angeles, where he pleaded guilty to two counts of first-degree murder. He was not charged with rape and robbery because the victims didn't want to go through the ordeal of a trial. Sentenced to two life terms, Mason, as part of his plea agreement, is serving out his days in a South Carolina prison.

Mason declined to be interviewed for this story, but during his plea hearing he offered officials some insight, however credible, into his motive for the killings. "It wasn't premeditated at all," Mason told the officials. "[One of the officers] started pressing me … I was scared they came. I was really fearful."

As for robbing the teenagers and raping the 15-year-old girl, alcohol appears to have had an influence. "I really don't have an explanation for why this happened to them. I wish I did," Mason said. "I'm still trying to just figure out how I got there [in the oil field]. I do recall being in Vegas. I feel like I have a memory of a liquor bottle in that field somewhere, [which] I left empty." What Mason seemed to imply was that the deadly events of that night in 1957 had occurred while he was in some kind of alcohol-induced haze.

In contrast, Keith Curtis's memory of his father has always been crystal clear. "I never gave up hope," he says. "I missed not having my dad around, and he missed a lot too. I just could never accept that someone had simply gotten away with his murder."

Originally published in the September 2005 issue of *Reader's Digest* magazine.

Gerald Mason died in a South Carolina prison on Jan. 22, 2017, at age 82. The cold case unit was eliminated in a 2018 downsizing, but resurrected in 2020 as an all-reserve unit. It is now staffed by 12 retired detectives along with several volunteers. The new cold case unit has solved seven homicides, soon to be eight, according to supervisor Mitzi Roberts.

The Gift of Understanding

by Paul Villiard

*The confidence of childhood is
a fragile thing. It can be preserved or
destroyed in an instant.*

I must have been around 4 years old when I first entered Mr. Wigden's candy shop, but the smell of that wonderful world of penny treasures still comes back to me clearly more than a half-century later. Whenever he heard the tiny tinkle of the bell attached to the front door, Mr. Wigden quietly appeared to take his stand behind the candy case. He was very old, and his head was topped with a cloud of fine, snow-white hair.

Never was such an array of delicious temptations spread before a child. It was almost painful to make a choice. Each kind had first to be savored in the imagination before passing on to the next. There was always a short pang of regret as the selection was dropped into a little white paper sack. Perhaps another kind would taste better? Or last longer? Mr. Wigden had a trick of scooping your selection into the sack, then pausing. Not a word was spoken, but every child understood that Mr. Wigden's raised eyebrows constituted a last-minute opportunity to make an exchange. Only after payment was laid upon the counter was the sack irrevocably twisted shut and the moment of indecision ended.

Our house was two blocks from the streetcar line, and you had to pass the shop going to and from the cars. Mother had taken me into town on some forgotten errand, and as we walked home from the trolley Mother turned into Mr. Wigden's.

"Let's see if we can find something good," she said, leading me up to the long glass case as the old man approached from behind a curtained aperture. My mother stood talking with him for a few minutes as I gazed rapturously at the display before my eyes. Finally Mother picked out something for me and paid Mr. Wigden.

"Isn't it enough?" I asked him anxiously.

Mother went into town once or twice a week, and, since in those days babysitters were almost unheard-of, I usually accompanied her. It became a regular routine for her to take me into the candy shop for some special treat, and after that first visit I was always allowed to make my own choice.

I knew nothing of money at that time. I would watch my mother hand something to people, who would then hand her a package or a bag, and slowly the idea of exchange percolated into my mind. Sometime about then I reached a decision. I would journey the interminable two blocks to Mr. Wigden's all alone. I remember the tinkle of the bell as I managed, after some considerable effort, to push open the big door. Enthralled, I worked my way slowly down the display counter.

Here were spearmint leaves with a fresh minty fragrance. There, gumdrops—the great big ones, so tender to bite into, all crusty with crystals of sugar. In the next tray were fudgy chocolate babies. The box behind them held enormous jawbreakers which made a satisfying bulge in your cheek. The hard, shiny, dark-brown-covered peanuts Mr. Wigden dished out with a little wooden scoop—two scoops for a cent. And, of course, there were the licorice whips. These lasted a long time if you let the bites dissolve instead of chewing them.

When I had picked out a promising assortment, Mr. Wigden leaned over and asked, "You have the money to pay for all these?"

"Oh, yes," I replied, "I have lots of money." I reached out my fist, and into Mr. Wigden's open hand I dumped a half-dozen cherry seeds carefully wrapped in shiny tinfoil.

Mr. Wigden stood gazing at the palm of his hand; then he looked searchingly at me for a long moment.

"Isn't it enough?" I asked him anxiously.

He sighed gently. "I think it is a bit too much," he answered. "You have some change coming." He walked over to his old-fashioned cash register and cranked open the drawer. Returning to the counter, he leaned over and dropped two pennies into my outstretched hand.

My mother scolded me about taking the trip alone when she found me out. I don't think it ever occurred to her to ask about the financial arrangement. I was simply cautioned not to go again unless I asked first. I must have obeyed and, evidently, when permission was granted for me to make the trip, a cent or two was given me for my purchases, since I don't remember using cherry seeds a second time. In fact, the whole affair, insignificant to me then, was soon forgotten in the busy occupation of growing up.

When I was 6 or 7 years old my family moved east, where I grew up, eventually married and established my own family. My wife and I opened a shop where we bred and sold exotic fish. The aquarium trade was then still in its infancy, and most of the fish were imported directly from Asia, Africa and South America. Few species sold for less than $5 a pair.

One sunny afternoon a little girl came in accompanied by her brother. They were perhaps 5 and 6 years old. I was busy cleaning the tanks. The two children stood with wide, round eyes, staring at the jeweled beauties swimming in the crystal clear water. "Gosh," exclaimed the boy, "can we buy some?"

"Yes," I replied. "If you can pay for them."

"Oh, we have lots of money," the little girl said confidently.

Something in the way she spoke gave me an odd feeling of familiarity. After watching the fish for some time, they asked me for pairs of several different kinds, pointing them out as they walked down the row of tanks. I netted their choices into a traveling container and slipped it into an insulated bag for transport, handing it to the boy. "Carry it carefully," I cautioned.

He nodded and turned to his sister. "You pay him," he said. I held out my hand, and as her clenched fist approached me I suddenly knew exactly what was going to happen, even what the little girl was going to say. Her fist opened, and into my outstretched palm she dumped two nickels and a dime.

At that instant I sensed the full impact of the legacy Mr. Wigden had given me so many years before. Only now did I recognize the challenge I had presented the old man, and realize how wonderfully he had met it.

I seemed to be standing again in the little candy shop as I looked at the coins in my own hand. I understood the innocence of the two children and the power to preserve or destroy that innocence, as Mr. Wigden had understood those long years ago. I was so filled up with the remembering that my throat ached. The little girl was standing expectantly before me. "Isn't it enough?" she asked in a small voice.

"It's a little too much," I managed to say, somehow, over the lump in my throat. "You have some change coming." I rummaged around in the cash drawer, dropped two pennies into her open hand, then stood in the doorway watching the children go down the walk carefully carrying their treasure.

When I turned back into the shop, my wife was standing on a stool with her arms submerged to the elbows in a tank where she was rearranging the plants. "Mind telling me what that was all about?" she asked. "Do you know how many fish you gave them?"

"About 30 dollars' worth," I answered, the lump still in my throat. "But I couldn't have done anything else."

When I'd finished telling her about old Mr. Wigden, her eyes were wet, and she stepped off the stool and gave me a gentle kiss on the cheek.

"I still smell the gumdrops," I sighed, and I'm certain I heard old Mr. Wigden chuckle over my shoulder as I swabbed down the last tank.

Originally published in the June 1965 issue of *Reader's Digest* magazine.

Humor Hall of Fame

© John Atkinson, Wrong Hands • wronghands1.com

Before Instagram

I'd like to teach y'all a southern phrase that will help you get off a phone/Zoom/Facetime call you don't want to be on but don't have an excuse to leave. Allow me to introduce you to the power of "Well, let me let you go."

—@_SARACANNON

I wake up to Alexa every morning before my wife is up. But one morning, I must have been in a deep sleep because my wife had to chime in to get Alexa to stop. "I wonder why Alexa didn't stop when I told her to," I mused. "Because you didn't tell Alexa to 'stop,'" my wife said. "You told her to 'shut up.'"

—PHILLIP SIENNA

WHERE, OH WHERE?

Tulip Farm

Looking at this lush landscape, you wouldn't guess that back in the summer of 2018, just as farmers here were preparing to harvest their best wheat crop in decades, a series of terrible fires scorched these fields black. Resilient farmers then spent the fall and winter planting cover crops to salvage the more than 200,000 acres of soil that burned that fire season—the worst in the area's history. This photo was taken the following spring, showing the verdant result of all their hard work. But where is it?

A. Dufur, Oregon

B. Hardin, Montana

C. Williston, North Dakota

D. Colby, Kansas

Answer on page 281. Photograph by Darrell Wyatt/Getty Images

Grizzly on the Nature Trail!

by John and Frankie O'Rear

A beauty-filled hike on a well-traveled park trail turned into a morning of terror and a never-to-be-forgotten struggle for survival

Outdoor enthusiasts Al and Nancy Auseklis, former competitors on the national ski-racing circuit, decided to take a break last September. With their two children, Alex and Anna, ages 3½ and 2½, they headed up to Jasper National Park for a hiking holiday.

On arrival in Jasper, Al and Nancy consulted a park map and chose a short, not-too-steep nature trail well-suited for the children. Alex forged ahead, with his sister skipping along behind, her blond ponytail flying. After about an hour of hiking, the children tired and asked to ride in their parents' backpacks. This may have saved their lives, for no sooner were they happily under way again, Alex in Al's pack and Anna in Nancy's, than a paralyzing roar knifed through the silence of the dark pines around them.

Nancy saw the grizzly bear first. Her heart all but stopped as she instantly recognized the dark, silver-tipped coat, the unmistakable hump between the shoulder blades, the sheer bulk of the awesome beast. Al and Alex were just ahead, out of Nancy's sight over a slight rise, and the grizzly was charging in their direction. From the corner of her eye, Nancy also saw a bear cub, running away in the opposite direction.

One horror-filled moment after the grizzly disappeared from sight, Nancy heard a "shattering roar and what sounded like a pack of angry dogs fighting." But "above that terrifying clatter"—and worst of all, she remembers—"came the ear-piercing screams of my son, Alex."

"It was then that an instinctive rage coursed through me," she says now. "I had to do something. I had to try to save all that was dear to me in life." Fighting off feelings of helplessness, she hunted for weapons—a tree branch, rocks, anything.

* * *

Warned by the grizzly's roars, Al had wheeled about just in time to see the bear "charging at us like a freight train." He tried frantically to pull up a young lodgepole pine, but the roots refused to let go. At the last instant, he jumped to one side, and the grizzly charged past. It turned immediately, however, and charged again—this time from behind Al, heading straight for his back, where Alex was strapped in the pack. Al pivoted fast, to protect the screaming child. This time the bear plowed headlong into Al, knocking him to the ground and pinning Alex beneath him.

Like a knight of old, she jousted with the panting grizzly.

Snarling with rage, the grizzly pounced on the fallen father and son. Al could feel his flesh tearing as the bear shook his left leg in its jaws. In desperation, Al kicked the bear on its sensitive nose with his free foot. The grizzly suddenly let go and headed toward Nancy. But when Al managed to struggle up onto his good leg, the grizzly charged back at him. Knocking Al to the ground again, it started chewing and tearing his right leg. Cursing the pain, Al kicked the bear's face with his injured leg. Once more the mother grizzly let go and charged toward Nancy.

* * *

Meanwhile, Nancy had scavenged a long pine pole and anchored it under her arm. Now she came running down the trail toward Al. When she caught sight of the onrushing bear, she ducked into a clump of pine saplings and backed up to a tree to protect Anna. Then, like a knight of old, she jousted with the panting grizzly —driving the pole into its shoulder each time it lunged. Not a sound came from little Anna: the child was frozen in shock.

Suddenly, unaccountably, the frenzied mother grizzly turned away and lumbered off down the trail that the Auseklis family had been following so happily only minutes earlier. In the eerie silence, Nancy felt a new flood of terror. Not daring to think about what she would find, she ran toward Al. He was struggling to get up and "swearing in anger that this could have happened. Somehow his cursing was a tremendous relief to me." Alex was trembling and crying in Al's backpack but, miraculously, was unharmed.

Both of Al's legs were brutally mangled, with gaping holes where chunks of flesh had been torn away. As Nancy ripped up her windbreaker to make pressure bandages, questions raced through her mind: *Should I leave Al and go for help? Could I find him again? Will he bleed to death? What if the bear comes back?* A whimper from Alex interrupted her jumbled thoughts. "Are we going to die, Mama?" he asked. "Is Daddy going to die?"

*   *   *

That was enough for Al. "Let's get out of here!" he said, struggling up with Nancy's help. In terrible pain, fighting shock, Al dragged himself along on crutches that they jury-rigged from tree branches." Nancy carried Alex in her backpack and cradled Anna in her arms—65 pounds in all.

"It was essential, at this point," says Nancy, "to appear lighthearted and unafraid, for there is nothing more terrifying for a child than to realize that his parents are hurt and unsure of what to do. Anna still had not said one word, and I was really beginning to worry about her."

Since the grizzly had headed down the trail in the direction they had been following, Al and Nancy bushwhacked through the thick brush in another direction that they hoped would lead them out. They came upon what they thought was another trail but after an hour it gave out. Arguing over which direction to take, Al and Nancy came to a clearing. From there they could see, at the base of a long slope, the Athabasca River. They headed toward the river, trusting it to lead them back to civilization.

A steep cliff blocked their way, but they found a trail zigzagging down through a wooded ravine—the only passable route. Nancy remembers that she was "near collapse from the weight of the children and my constant fear that Al would pass out." She persuaded Alex to get out and hike on his own.

To this day she's not sure how Al made it down the ravine. Al says simply that he knew he had to have medical attention, fast, so he literally crawled down on his belly, using the stick crutches when he could and sliding his legs behind him.

At the bottom they came upon railroad tracks and, with overwhelming relief, heard the throb of machinery from a nearby oil-pumping station. Knowing that help was near, Al gave in to a state of semiconsciousness. The children stayed with him while Nancy ran to the station and flung open the door. She shouted for help above the noise of the pumps. No answer. She finally found and pushed open a door marked Employees Only. Five men were seated inside, eating lunch. "Thank God!" she said to herself, and then, "Please help! My husband has been attacked by a grizzly!"

It took about two hours for a team of doctors to sew up Al's wounds. He had been lucky on three counts: Although both legs were horribly torn, all the vital tendons were intact; nerves and muscles were damaged, but not irreparably; and, most importantly, no main artery had been severed.

After two months of slow, painful convalescence, Al was up on his feet, eager to get back into training. By midwinter he was skiing as usual, with nothing to show for his ordeal but some scars and a bit of numbness in one leg. The children, too, have bounced back. "They still ask questions about the attack," says Nancy. "But we have tried to make them understand that the grizzly wasn't simply vicious. We had walked into her house, and got too close to her baby, and in that sense the attack was our fault."

Speaking of the ordeal, Nancy says, "In our family we love animals, and we want to keep it that way. Even now, we feel no real malice toward that grizzly. It was a mother's instinct that provoked her attack and a mother's instinct that drove me to courage I never knew I had. She was protecting her cubs; I was protecting mine."

Originally published in the July 1973 issue of *Reader's Digest* magazine.

I Married a Pack Rat

by Mary Roach

One man's trash is another man's treasure—
and the bane of his wife's existence

For the past decade, my husband's excuse for not going through his old LPs was that he'd do it when we move. We're moving on Saturday. The replacement excuse is that he doesn't have time because he has too much packing to do. One could make the point that there'd be less packing to do if he'd toss some of his stuff.

Bracing for high seas, one does. "So you're calling this junk?" Ed is holding aloft a Tony Bennett album. I am skating on thin ice here. Possibly I'm already down in the pond water, thrashing about with my skates. "Not specifically."

Ed says that many of his LPs are irreplaceable. I recognize this argument. I used it in explaining why I did not throw away, among other priceless items, a Pan Am airsickness bag, some rocks from the Arctic Circle with orange lichen on them, and a 1987 USDA press release entitled "Milestones in Dairy History." In those instances, it was my argument, so it made sense.

I press on. "But if you never listen to any of these albums, why would you want to replace them?"

Attempting to apply common sense in these scenarios is useless. I know this. Earlier in the week, I tried to discard a box of expired Super-8 movie film for which Ed has no camera. He vetoed the move, stating that he might one day find a Super-8 camera in a Goodwill store. Also vetoed was the throwing away of two shelves of college paperbacks. The pages were yellowed, and there was mildew on the covers. If you listened carefully you could hear them reaching out and making friends with my lichen. "Some of these books have meaning to me," said Ed, and then he paused. "I just don't know what the meaning is."

I recently read an article about hoarding in the animal kingdom. The male black wheatear bird, the article said, collects piles of heavy stones before the mating season. "Those with the largest piles are more likely to mate," the story explained and at the same time didn't really explain. If I should die suddenly, Ed should consider expanding his dating pool to include female wheatear birds. I'll make a note of it in my will.

> *"Some of these books have meaning to me," Ed said. "I just don't know what the meaning is."*

Ed tries to explain why he would want to keep a pile of records he never listens to. "It's just knowing that they're there. That I could listen to them if I wanted to." I remind him that his turntable doesn't work.

"So, actually you can't listen to them." Which reminds me. I pick up the turntable and put it on the designated throwaway pile, which I had envisioned at the beginning of this undertaking as a towering, teetering mound engulfing most of our front entryway and portions of the sidewalk, but is in reality closer in size to the little mounds of toenail parings Ed occasionally stacks up on the bedside table. These are, happily, replaceable, and I encounter only token resistance when I throw them away.

"You can't throw the turntable out. It belongs to Andrea." Andrea is his ex-wife.

"So let's return it to her."

Ed looks genuinely puzzled. "It's broken. Why would she want it?"

In the end, we compromised. He kept some, and he sold some. He forgave me for the anguish I'd caused him, because he was able to get $240 for his LPs at the new and used music store. This he used to buy 31 used CDs, which take up not quite but almost the same square footage as the LPs, and will impress the heck out of the next female wheatear who comes to town.

Originally published in the January 2005 issue of *Reader's Digest* magazine.

Rescue at Mogadishu

by Malcolm McConnell

A helicopter evacuation would be dangerous. But it was the only hope for Americans trapped in Somalia's war-torn capital.

Mogadishu, Somalia, Dec. 31, 1990. American embassy officials, gathered on the roof of the K-7 apartment building to greet the new year suddenly heard rocket-propelled grenades and machine-gun fire.

"That sounded close," Karen Aguilar, the embassy's public-affairs officer, told her husband, John Fox, also a diplomat. They could see the 160-acre U.S. embassy compound across Afgoy Road. Its 10-foot-high outer walls were thick concrete.

Three months earlier, Aguilar had arrived in this sprawling capital on the Horn of Africa. A career foreign service officer with seven years' African experience, she had witnessed military coups and tribal strife. But she had not expected Somalia's smoldering civil war to erupt so suddenly into massive urban combat. Ragtag rebel bands fighting dictator Mohammed Siad Barre, as well as renegade soldiers loyal only to their own clans, were roaming the streets, looting and robbing.

On Dec. 30, army troops raided a downtown neighborhood searching for weapons. The city center exploded, with armed civilians ambushing government forces. The army responded with artillery and mortar barrages. Looters sacked stores, warehouses and diplomatic residences.

That New Year's Eve, moments after automatic fire clattered below K-7, Aguilar and the others heard the voice of U.S. Ambassador James K. Bishop on the radio: "Everybody get off that roof. We'll try to get you into the compound after daylight."

*   *   *

January 1, 1991. Trucks carrying rebels and renegade troops careered past the embassy, their occupants blasting wildly with machine guns. By mid-morning, the firing had tapered off. Robert Noble, who led the embassy's contract security force, sat in an armored van inside the steel gates of the main entrance.

"Now!" he shouted, and his driver gunned the vehicle diagonally across the road to the gates of K-7. Aguilar and Fox scrambled into the van with a dozen other Americans. When the next lull in firing came, the vehicle sped back into the compound.

Bishop cabled Washington with a request for a contingency evacuation plan. It was only a matter of time before the embassy became a target of the looters, who were carrying weapons with which they could blast through the embassy's steel gates. But Washington's attention was focused on Operation Desert Shield, 1,600 miles to the northeast.

*   *   *

January 2. By morning the situation had become too dangerous for military transport planes to land at Mogadishu's airport. Bishop again contacted Washington to apprise them of the deteriorating situation.

At 5 p.m. the helicopter carrier USS *Guam* and the amphibious support ship USS *Trenton*, anchored off the coast of Oman, were ordered to steam toward Somalia. They would arrive offshore on Jan. 6.

*   *   *

January 3. Terrified foreign diplomats were braving snipers to seek refuge in the U.S. embassy. Hundreds of the embassy's Somalian employees and their families were also given sanctuary. Using the limited kitchen facilities, Aguilar and her colleagues began boiling huge pots of rice and pasta from emergency stocks to feed the throng. By nightfall, more than 500 people were in the compound, with more arriving every few minutes.

That evening, after another desperate message from Bishop, commanders on the *Guam* realized they could not wait. Fortunately, aboard the *Trenton* were two CH-53E Super Stallion helicopters; each could carry up to 50 passengers. The fastest and nimblest heavy choppers in the world, they were capable of high-speed, low-altitude "penetration flights" into hostile territory. Still, a long flight over the Indian Ocean would require several midair refuelings, a tricky, hazardous procedure, especially at night.

January 4. For Aguilar and her colleagues, this was the worst day of the siege. Machine-gun fire ripped through the compound, blowing chunks off buildings. Americans moving out of doors were fired on by snipers.

Inside the compound's administrative building, Aguilar found medical officer Karen McGuire Rugh cradling a tiny Somali baby who had been brought to the embassy. Caring for her had become a means of relieving the deadly tension of mortar barrages and machine-gun fire. The baby's dark, flashing eyes brought smiles to the embassy's exhausted officers.

The *Guam* sped through the night, but Mogadishu was still almost 500 miles ahead. Having flown over from the *Trenton*, the two Super Stallions sat on the *Guam*'s flight deck. Maj. Dan Schultz, one of the Marines' most experienced Super Stallion pilots, had the command pilot's seat in the lead helicopter, Haley One Zero. To his left was co-pilot Capt. Jeff Bowden. Capt Brian Phillips and his co-pilot, Capt. Kevin Moon, sat in the second chopper. Each of the Super Stallions' cargo compartments held 30 Marines commanded by Lt. Col. Willard Oates, including nine Navy SEALs under Cmdr. Steve Luoma.

The flight plan was for a one-way inbound leg of 486 miles, with a return flight almost as long. This would require an unprecedented three midair refuelings over the ocean, two in total darkness. The choppers would penetrate the Somali coast exactly at dawn, 7:10 a.m. The equatorial sun rising behind them would blind both machine-gunners and heat-seeking warheads of anti-aircraft missiles.

"Pulling power," Schultz said into his helmet microphone. The tips of Haley One Zero's huge rotors strained for flight. Then the chopper broke free and rumbled into the night. In Haley Zero Niner, Phillips followed.

Minutes later, co-pilot Bowden told Schultz, "Sir, we're in trouble." The Omega navigation system that was to guide the pilots to the tanker aircraft began blinking a warning light. They had lost the signals of the ground radio stations needed to maintain accurate navigation. The most prudent action would be an immediate abort.

A lot of people are depending on us in Mogadishu, Schultz thought. "We're pressing on," he announced. They were forced to fly on "dead reckoning," navigating with only a gyrocompass and stopwatch.

About 90 minutes later, the two helicopters reached the predetermined refueling site. Schultz spotted the dim white cone of the tanker's refueling "basket," extended the refueling probe from his chopper's nose and eased his aircraft ahead. A green light blinked on the instrument panel, signifying a solid connection.

Then the voice of the crew chief sounded in his earphones. "Emergency breakaway! We've got a leak." Jet fuel gushed from the passenger compartment panel, drenching several Marines. While Schultz broke the chopper free of the hose, crewmen repaired the fuel line, and he "plugged" again.

Haley One Zero took on 5 tons of precious fuel. Zero Niner took on a full load as well.

Before dawn, two embassy officers armed with submachine guns marked landing zones for the helicopters. Through gaps in the wall, they saw shadowy figures skulking toward the compound's southern wall, dragging awkward objects. "They've got ladders!" one staffer whispered.

After the two helicopters had refueled again, dawn was flooding the eastern horizon, and they began their descent. Bowden recited the penetration checklist while the crewmen test-fired their guns and pulled on their body armor. Schultz eased the nose down toward the ocean. He was flying at 150 knots, and the altimeter read 70 feet.

Then the radar warning set flashed—they had been "painted" by missile radar. "We've been acquired!" Bowden shouted.

"Dropping," Schultz answered. He increased power and pitched the

A CH-53E Super Stallion helicopter

nose down to the left to break the radar lock. Phillips followed. When they swung back on course, the two helicopters were only 35 feet above the water and moving at 170 knots.

The city of Mogadishu spread before them, a confusing whitewashed sprawl. Finding the embassy on their outdated map would not be easy. Schultz banked left to use a line of low hills as a shield between them and the airport missile sites. They were flying at rooftop level now and had to keep a sharp watch for power lines. At this height and speed, the choppers' rotor wash blasted the ground with the force of a 100-knot hurricane.

Suddenly, Bowden spotted the embassy's distinctive mushroom-shaped water tower. As they sailed toward the compound's southern perimeter, men with rifles and rocket-propelled grenades were climbing ladders set against the outside walls. Schultz hauled back on his controls to rear the big chopper just above the wall. The rotor wash blew away the looters and their ladders as if they were made of paper. Then Schultz eased the chopper forward to land inside the compound.

Climbing out, Luoma and Oates and their teams ran toward the embassy chancery. A thin, distinguished man in shirtsleeves was staring at them through tired eyes. "Good morning, Mr. Ambassador," Luoma said. "I'm Navy SEAL Commander Steve Luoma, and I'm here to get you out."

An hour after landing, the two Super Stallions departed with the first 61 evacuees, including all the foreign diplomats and private U.S. citizens in the compound. After a survey of the situation, it was decided that no more helicopters would land until around midnight. By then, the *Guam* would be in position to launch its smaller CH-46 choppers to assist in evacuation.

Soviet Ambassador Vladimir Korneev radioed Bishop. Several of the embassy's vehicles had been stolen, and he feared bringing his 38 Soviet nationals to the American compound for evacuation without an escort. Bob Noble convinced a Somali police friend, Major Sayed, to do the job for a fee. By late that afternoon, Sayed had earned several thousand dollars shepherding foreign diplomats to the embassy.

As night descended, over 200 evacuees were still sheltered in the compound, waiting for flights to the *Guam*.

* * *

January 6. The first five CH-46s landed right on schedule. They were being loaded when Noble radioed Bishop from the front gate that Sayed had

A year after the dramatic rescue described in this story, U.S. Marines entered the main gate of the embassy compound as part of a U.N. peacekeeping mission.

suddenly reappeared. "He's got a radio in one hand," Noble reported, "and a grenade in the other."

Sayed threatened to call in mortar and artillery fire if the helicopters tried to take off. He was outraged that the Americans had not "asked permission" from his government for the evacuation.

Bishop knew he had to stall for time. He arranged to meet with Sayed. When the wild-eyed officer appeared, Bishop suspected that Sayed was high on khat, a local plant whose leaves Somalis chew for their stimulating effect. Somehow the ambassador persuaded Sayed to put down his radio. Then he managed to keep Sayed's attention diverted while the first two relays of helicopters clattered away into the darkness.

Finally, with the last of the evacuees safely on their way, Oates and his Marines began boarding the choppers. Luoma, who had been covering Sayed from the shadows, signaled Bishop that it was time to leave. Then Bishop turned to Sayed and pointed out several shiny embassy sedans parked nearby. "Which car would you like to have, Major?" he asked, giving the confused Somali officer a set of car keys.

Leaving Sayed fumbling with the keys, Bishop walked down the embassy steps and climbed aboard the last of the helicopters. As it lifted into the darkness, armed men swarmed over the embassy walls.

January 10. The *Guam*'s 281 evacuee guests included 12 heads of diplomatic missions and men, women and children from 31 countries. As Aguilar walked among them, she came upon a group of Marines clustered around the tiny Somali baby that had been brought to the compound. One by one, these tough young men—now headed back to the Gulf for combat duty— took the infant in their arms to hold for one warm, fleeting moment.

To Karen Aguilar, this fragile human life plucked from the caldron of war was a happy reminder that even in the most desperate situations, salvation may be on hand. She felt a surge of gratitude for the bravery of the rescue team as she, too, took the infant in her arms.

Originally published in the July 1992 issue of *Reader's Digest* magazine.

Making Waves

Factory workers wearing traditional leaf hats mend fishing nets in the coastal city of Bac Liêu, Vietnam. The workers knit speedily, says photographer Ly Hoang Long, and employ tiny needles to weave nets tight enough to catch the various species of shrimp, fish and crabs that keep the local economy afloat. As they work, heaps of netting mound behind them, like the waves in which they'll soon be deployed.

Photograph by Ly Hoang Long

Changes of Heart

by Cathy Free

When a troubled teen cares for an unwanted dog, the healing begins for both

Spiker is only a year old, but he's already done time on death row. Abandoned by his owners, he landed in an animal shelter with a policy of destroying dogs that were passed over for adoption. Now, though, he's gotten a reprieve. "Come on, Spiker. You can do it," his trainer urges. "Shake, boy, shake!"

Spiker, a mix of German shorthaired pointer and Labrador retriever, gazes at the young woman, perplexed. Then he remembers: Last time he obeyed Marcy, a biscuit magically appeared. Slowly he raises his right paw. "Good boy," Marcy says, ruffling the dog's spotted coat and offering a treat.

Spiker is changing Marcy's life as surely as Marcy is changing his. The 18-year-old has lived at Echo Glen Children's Center, a state-operated juvenile correctional facility in Snoqualmie, Washington, for nine months. While she's there, she's participating in Canine Connections, a program that brings unwanted dogs and incarcerated kids together.

"I've never been attached to a dog before, because things always move away from me," Marcy says. "It's like with my family. They die or they leave me." Marcy never knew her father; her mother died of a drug overdose when Marcy was 8. After that, she began shuttling from one foster home to another—more than 50 in all. Unable to get along with any of her host families, she ended up on the streets selling crack. She was a regular in juvenile

Kyle, 14, runs with Brody, the year-old chocolate Lab he's trained for two months. "Brody makes me want to be more positive," he says.

71

Marcy, a juvenile offender at Echo Glen detention center in Washington state, spends a quiet moment with Spiker, the abandoned dog she trains as part of the Canine Connections program. "His story's pretty much the same as mine," she says.

court until a judge ordered her to spend a year at Echo Glen.

"I was real angry that I got sent up," Marcy says. "I didn't want to cooperate with anybody." But a few days after she arrived, she saw a group of other teenagers walking dogs outside her dorm. She learned that if her behavior improved, she could join the program. "Those dogs were in trouble like I was," says Marcy. "I knew I could give one a second chance."

*　　*　　*

Ringed by tall pines, Echo Glen resembles a summer camp, with cottages, fields and an indoor swimming pool. But the 160 kids who live there—some wearing orange jumpsuits indicating they're a security or flight risk—have staff members with them wherever they go. The residents (boys ages 10 to 16; girls, 10 to 21) have committed serious, often violent, crimes, including robbery and murder. Most have a history of drug abuse, and 70% have been diagnosed with depression or other mental illnesses. Canine Connections takes on some of the toughest cases.

"These kids come in with the same kind of issues as the dogs do—abandonment, neglect, abuse," says Jo Simpson, 56, a longtime supervisor at Echo Glen and a veteran dog trainer and 4-H leader who modeled Canine Connections on a similar program in Oregon.

Her eight-week course, which provides intensive training in dog handling and grooming, takes 10 students at a time. The kids acquire skills they can use in the outside world. They also learn how to care. "Working with the dogs teaches the kids responsibility," Simpson says. "And for many of them, it's the first time they feel empathy for another living thing."

The program is as economical as it is effective. Simpson's annual budget is $12,000, funded by private donors. An informal follow-up by Echo Glen found that only 10% of Canine Connections graduates were arrested again—less than one-fifth the average rate for juvenile offenders. The statistics, however, tell only part of the story. "By making a difference to the dogs," says Neil Kirkpatrick, PhD, a psychologist with the state's Department of Social and Health Services, "the kids see that they can make positive changes in their own lives."

As Spiker romps through the grass with Marcy after his lesson, it's obvious that the two have bonded. "I was afraid to get close at first," Marcy admits. "But once I got to know him, I just couldn't give up on him."

When Simpson assigns a dog to a student, she also hands over the animal's case file. The kids learn about each dog's background and personality; in class, they discuss their dogs' challenges and how to overcome them. "They have to analyze the dog's behavior: Why is he doing that?" says Simpson. "And they also have to do that to themselves: What in my past is causing me to act this way?"

So far, most of the pairings have worked. Only a couple of dogs have been sent back to shelters for being aggressive, and only a few kids have been expelled from the program.

But eventually the dogs do leave. After two months, they've learned basic commands, corrected the worst of their behavior problems, and are ready for adoption. Each year, about 100 dogs come through the program and are advertised on websites like petfinder.org and dogfriendly.com. Simpson has no trouble placing the animals, which are ideal for people who want to adopt a rescued dog but lack the time or expertise to train one.

* * *

"Let's get a move on, Mulley," says Teal, gently tugging her Australian-German shepherd into the gym. Mulley was beaten by her former owner, leaving her easily intimidated and hungry for affection. "I have to be real slow and patient with her because of her background," says Teal, 15.

As the other handlers line up with their leashed dogs for a drill, loud barks bounce off the walls. "That is not appropriate behavior—tell them to stop," shouts Simpson.

"Stop!" the kids command.

Teal, 15, delivers dinner to the dogs. "Be kind and gentle," she says, "and they'll love you for the rest of your life."

Program director Jo Simpson teaches a class in animal care.

There is immediate silence, broken by a few whimpers. "Good. Let's go," says Simpson. "Heel!" The handlers trek across the gym as Simpson calls out other commands, which the teens pass along to their dogs. "About-turn, halt!" "Forward, left turn!" "Forward, right turn!" "Sit!" "Shake!"

"Good girl, Mulley!" Teal says after the session, noting that the dog's improved attitude reflects her own. "She's stubborn like me. I want to do my own thing, but now I've learned to slow down a little."

Patience, persistence, praise and practice are the watchwords of Simpson's program. But they can't protect her students from the pain of separation. The kids will soon turn the animals over to their new owners. For some, the sorrow can be overwhelming.

Justin, a slender 14-year-old with blond hair and a shy smile, is worried about giving his dog, Cherry, to a new family. "I wonder if they'll treat her as well as I did," says the boy, who's been in and out of trouble since age 12, when his father went to prison. "I was pretty freaked-out when they brought me here," he recalls. "But now I've mellowed a lot. Cherry helped me. I can tell her anything."

Spiker's training complete, Marcy turns him over to his new owners, Kerry Kellogg and Sean Eller. "Don't worry," Kellogg tells Marcy. "We'll take good care of him."

When Justin was first introduced to the 2-year-old Shar-Pei-Lab mix, she wouldn't make eye contact. So he sat in the dog's kennel holding a treat until Cherry inched her way over. Within minutes, the two were friends. "I'll be sad when she leaves," Justin says, the dog in his lap. "I wish I could take her with me when I get out."

To ease the transition, adoptive families take the dogs home on weekends at first. Later, the kids conduct exit interviews with the new owners, discussing the pet's care and training, history and health, likes and dislikes. Says Simpson, "They take a lot of pride in knowing they've molded these dogs into good pets."

Marcy still has a few months to go before she's released. But it's time for her to say goodbye to Spiker. On graduation day, she leads him through several commands in front of a crowd of kids, instructors and prospective owners. When the applause dies down, she puts on a brave face and gives her dog one last biscuit before crouching down and hugging him. Spiker's new owners, Kerry Kellogg and Sean Eller, are here to take the dog home to Kellogg's 7-year-old daughter.

Marcy watches as the couple lead Spiker out of the kennel, her sadness lightened by the knowledge that she'll soon begin training another dog: a 5-month-old German shepherd named Spunky.

"When I get out of here, I'm going to work with dogs, maybe become a groomer," she says. "Then I can have them around me all the time."

Originally published in the January 2009 issue of *Reader's Digest* magazine.

The Canine Connections program is still going strong at Echo Glen Children's Center and now offers Reading with Rover and Pet Therapy when the kids need it.

On the practice field, students lead their dogs through commands and drills. At the start of the program, the animals are unruly and wary. By the end, the trainers and dogs are tightknit teams. "The kids say, 'Wow, my dog's behavior turned around because of me,'" says Simpson. "They feel good about what they've done."

COVID PETALS

My friend was dealing with some vision issues. During the coronavirus pandemic, she asked her husband, "Why do they keep showing those red and gray flowers?" He said, "What flowers?" He used the rewind feature until she excitedly cried out, "Those!" "Those are not flowers," he said, "It's what the virus looks like under a microscope." She's not alone—her mom thought they were raspberries.

—Marian Redick, *Hopwood, PA*

TREATS, NOT CHORES

I was babysitting for my 4-year-old grandson when he asked me for fruit snacks. I told him they were in the basement. When I went to the basement I began folding a blanket that was in the dryer. Since my grandson thought I was taking too long, he came down and with his hands on his hips said, "Grandma, I didn't send you down here to do laundry."

—Ligia Sardanopoli, *Emerson, NJ*

The Inanity Defense

by Andy Simmons

Every year we track down the dumbest criminals in the world. Thinking of joining their ranks? You will if ...

... You believe flattery will get you anywhere. Adan Juarez Ramirez had it all figured out—he could be a cop without having to take the boring test. But he was arrested in Grapevine, Texas, after pulling over a driver in his pickup truck, which was outfitted with flashing lights. He even had an ID badge, which he'd made by blacking out a restaurant gift card and etching in the word *POLICE*. However, he'd kept the restaurant's logo, a jalapeno pepper surrounded by the words *Chipotle Mexican Grill*.

... You leave IOUs. Graham Price of South Wales ripped off the bank where he worked, but he wasn't completely duplicitous. He left a note in the safe: "Borrowed, seven million pounds"—signed "Graham Price."

... You vastly overrate your powers of persuasion. Marlon Moore of Miami filed a fraudulent tax return, and the IRS promptly sent him a $10,000 refund. So figuring, *Why not try my luck again?*, he sent in three more tax returns. But even the IRS raised an eyebrow at cutting him a check for the total amount of the refunds: more than $14 trillion. Moore pleaded guilty to cashing the $10,000 check.

... You think presidents need a promotion. James Rhyne of Memphis was charged with forgery after he handed a waitress a $100 bill. The waitress knew something was funny with the money: Instead of the portly visage of Ben Franklin, it was the star of the $5 bill, Abe Lincoln, who was staring back at her.

... You leave a paper trail. Hickory, North Carolina, cops were able to solve in record time the mystery of the two cash registers purloined from the Captain's Galley restaurant. Their big break came when they discovered a trail of white register tape. They followed it 50 yards to an apartment, where, they say, Donny Guy was cracking the registers open.

... You love too much. Maybe Stephfon Bennett should try online dating. After he and two accomplices allegedly mugged a couple in Columbus, Ohio, police say he found the woman's ID in her purse, then showed up at her door with a simple proposal: How about a date? Since a girl likes to play hard to get, she called the cops, who arrested Bennett outside her home.

... You skimp on travel expenses. Twelve Middle Eastern immigrants forgot the first rule of sneaking into a country: Don't call attention to yourself. En route to England from Germany, they sneaked a ride in the back of a man's truck. They stayed mum throughout their trip, even as they crossed the Channel into England. But once they hit Dover, they celebrated their arrival with songs and whoops. Not for long, though. The startled driver headed to a police station, where the 12 were apprehended.

... You're not picky about your office location. Christopher Oxley of Everett, Washington, was arrested for conducting a drug deal over the phone—in the bathroom of the Everett Police Department.

... You text and rob. Nicholas Greenly dropped his cellphone near where an 84-year-old woman had her purse snatched in Mount Lebanon, Pennsylvania. Cops suspected that he might be involved in the crime when they read the phone's last outgoing text message: "I am ready to grab some old lady's purse."

... You take the holidays too seriously. Robert E. Dendy of upstate New York presented the local police station with a Christmas wreath. Since the officers were well acquainted with Dendy, they did some snooping and arrested him for stealing the wreath from a store down the block.

... You're convinced the laws of physics don't apply to you. Clive Halford thinks big! The British career criminal stole a truck and loaded it with 18 pallets of stolen nickel and copper worth around 150,000 pounds (about $250,000). Yes, the haul was huge—too huge. Cops arrested Halford after the truck's suspension collapsed under the weight. Earlier, Halford had stolen a car, overloaded it, and broken its suspension too.

... You play both roles in a game of cops and robbers. Being a key suspect in a robbery wasn't going to stop Romeo Montillano from realizing his dream of becoming a Chula Vista, California, police officer. Unfortunately for Montillano, his would-be colleagues put the kibosh on his plans, arresting him when he showed up to take the entrance exam. As he was led away, Montillano had one question: Could he take the test later? His request was denied.

... You make every day Take Your Child to Work Day. Callie Rough of Middletown, Ohio, was picked up for shoplifting from a Dollar General store with her two young children in tow. Among the booty was a book, *101 Ways to Be a Great Mom*.

... You let your supply of antismoking patches run out. An Indiana state trooper stopped a car for a traffic violation. When a passenger, Honesty Knight, asked if she could smoke, the officer said yes. She proceeded, police say, to light up a joint.

... You air your neighbor's dirty laundry. As she walked around her neighbor's yard sale in Severn, Maryland, a woman couldn't help admiring the items. The Oriental rug, the luggage, the shoes—they were exactly her style. And why not? They were hers, as was everything else on display. David Perticone says somebody sold him the stuff. But cops think Perticone did the deed himself.

... You don't know when to write off a loss. John Opperman-Green robbed a Kissimmee, Florida, 7-Eleven, then called the cops to complain when he tried to hitch a ride with strangers, who, in turn, robbed him.

… You can't let go of your friends. Two New Zealand prisoners had the brilliant idea of fleeing the courthouse while tethered together by handcuffs. They might have escaped had a light pole not gotten between them. Like a pair of click-clacks, they slammed into each other and were arrested trying to get back to their feet.

… You neglect to look up local hotels on your GPS. Mitchell Deslatte walked into a Baton Rouge, Louisiana, hotel and asked the clerk for a room. Only, the clerk wasn't a clerk—he was a state trooper. And the hotel was actually a state trooper station. That's when Deslatte was arrested and charged with driving while intoxicated.

… You depend on the kindness of strangers. Christopher Wilson of Spokane left his name and phone number with clerks at a home-improvement store should anyone find something of his that he'd dropped, according to police. They did find something, and Wilson was arrested for possession of methamphetamines.

... You harbor grudges. Joseph Goetz's alleged attempt to rob a York, Pennsylvania, bank met with some snags. Cops say the first teller he tried to rob fainted and the next two insisted they had no cash in their drawers. Fed up, Goetz stormed out, threatening to write an angry letter to the bank.

... You leave a far-too-indelible impression. Victims of a home robbery in Riverview, Florida, easily picked out Sean Roberts from police photos. Turns out, there aren't too many other people with a map of Florida tattooed on their face. Still, Roberts pleaded not guilty.

... Even your wardrobe turns against you. When pleading guilty to a DUI charge, let your lawyer do the talking. New Zealander Keisha Lee Kubala ignored that sensible advice and instead showed up in court wearing a T-shirt that said it all: "Miss Wasted."

Originally published in the November 2009 issue of *Reader's Digest* magazine.

When Amy Met Duane Online

by Doug Shadel and David Dudley, from *AARP The Magazine*

She gave him her heart— and he took $300,000 from her

She wrote him first, on a Thursday evening in December 2013. "You were listed as a 100% Match! I am not sure what a 100% match means… First, would you be interested in me? Check my profile."

Later, when Amy* puzzled over their relationship, she'd remember this. She had contacted him, not the other way around. That had been a fateful move; it had made everything easier for him. But she didn't know that yet.

It had been over two years since Amy had experienced the death of her husband of 20 years, four since she had lost her mother—two sharp blows in her 50s. Her marriage had been troubled—her husband was abusive— but cancer took him before she could process what was happening. Now she was alone in a house in Virginia.

In the fall of 2013, she signed up for a six-month subscription to a popular online dating site. She considered herself pretty tech savvy. She had a website for her business, was on Facebook, and carried a smartphone. In her profile, she was honest about her age (57) and finances ("self-sufficient"), and her pitch was straightforward: "looking for a life partner …

Names have been changed.

85

successful, spiritually minded, intelligent, good sense of humor, enjoys dancing and traveling. No games!"

She exchanged messages and had a few phone calls with men; she even met some for coffee or lunch. But either they weren't her type or they weren't who they'd said they were in their profiles. She resolved to contact only men who were close matches according to the site's algorithm.

Then she saw this guy with a mysterious profile name: darkandsugarclue. The photo showed a trim, silver-haired man with a salt-and-pepper beard. He was 61, liked bluegrass music, and lived an hour away. And he was a "100% match," so she wrote to him.

More than a week later, she got this message: "Thank you so much for the email and I am really sorry for the delay in reply, I don't come on here often ... I really like your profile and I like what I have gotten to know about you so far. I would love to get to know you as you sound like a very interesting person plus you are beautiful. Tell me more about you. It would be my pleasure if you wrote me at my email as I hardly come on here often."

He gave her a Yahoo email address and a name, Duane. When she went back to the dating site to look at his profile, it had disappeared.

She wrote: "Your profile is no longer there—did you pull it? As I am recalling the information you shared intrigued me. I would like to know more about you. Please email me with information about yourself and pictures so I can get to know you better."

Duane sent a long message that sketched a peripatetic life. He was a "computer systems analyst" from California who had grown up in Manchester, England, and had lived in Virginia for five months. Much of his note consisted of flirty jokes ("If I could be bottled I would be called 'eau de enigma'") and an imaginary description of their first meeting: "It's 11 a.m. when we arrive at the restaurant for brunch. The restaurant is a white painted weatherboard, simple but well-kept, set on the edge of a lake ..."

Duane was nothing like the men Amy had met so far. "You certainly have a great sense of humor and a way with words," she wrote. She mentioned the deception she'd encountered on dates: "It is amazing what people will do without conscience. I think it is always best to be whom we are and not mislead others."

Within two weeks, they'd exchanged eight more emails. Duane suggested they fill out questionnaires listing their favorite foods, hobbies, quirks and financial status. He also sent a link to a song, Marc Anthony's "I Need You."

"It holds a message," he told her, "that delivers the exact way I feel for you."

Amy clicked on the link to the ballad, which ends with the singer begging his lover to marry him. Then she listened to it again.

*   *   *

It's an ancient con. An impostor poses as a suitor, woos the victim, then loots his or her finances. In pre-digital times, scammers found prey in the personal ads of magazines. Today, technology has streamlined communication, given scammers new tools and opened up a vast pool of victims. Fifteen percent of adults in the United States said they've used a dating website or app. In 2015, the FBI received 12,509 complaints related to online-dating fraud, with losses of $203.3 million. That figure may be low because many victims never report the crime or tell their loved ones. Their silence stems from shame, fear of ridicule and denial.

When Amy talks about how she fell in love, she always mentions Duane's voice. It was musical, clipped, flecked with endearing British-isms. Soon after they connected online, they began talking for hours every day in addition to emailing and texting. His years in England explained the accent, but there was also a wisp of something

She saw this guy with a mysterious profile name: darkandsugarclue.

else in his voice. Still, this did nothing to deter her interest. In their conversations, Amy opened up to Duane about her marriage, her job and her conviction that things happened for a reason. She had never met a man who was so curious about her.

She was just as fascinated by Duane. Or was it Dwayne? The spelling switched from his earlier emails. There were other curiosities. She'd be fixing breakfast, and he'd be talking about going out for the evening. He traveled for work, he explained. He was calling from Malaysia, where he was finishing a computer job.

Since Amy loved to travel, the fact that Dwayne was living overseas added to his "eau de enigma." He sent her a link to an old John Denver song, "Shanghai Breezes," about two lovers separated by distance.

She wrote: "Wow ... It feels like the universe is manifesting my perfect partner right before my very eyes. Prayers answered and yes it does seem like we have known each other a long time."

Amy sent that note a week after her first message from Dwayne. In emails and calls, they shared the day-to-day minutiae about their lives—her upcoming trip to Sarasota, Florida, with a friend; his visit to a textiles museum in Kuala Lumpur. Mixed in were his ardent declarations of affection: "Last night, in my dreams, I saw you on the pier. The wind was blowing through your hair, and your eyes held the fading sunlight."

Those florid words cast a powerful spell on Amy. "You are filling my days and nights with wonder," she confessed to Dwayne on Christmas. "Are you real? Will you appear someday ... hold me in your arms, kiss my lips and caress me gently. Or are you just a beautiful, exotic dream ... if you are ... I don't want to wake up!"

When she returned from her trip to Florida, Amy found a bouquet of flowers, with a note: "My life will never be the same since I met you. Happy New Year. Love, Dwayne."

Enitan* lives in a small village in Nigeria. (Most dating fraud originates in Nigeria and Ghana, as well as in Malaysia and England, two countries with large West African communities.) In 2004, when he was 18, he fell in with a group of young Nigerian men known as Yahoo Boys, named for their use of free Yahoo.com email accounts. "Ignorance and desperation," he says, drove him to crime.

Enitan is not Dwayne; his fraud career ended five years before Amy contacted her suitor. Based on his account, the playbook he followed has not changed. He estimates that over four years, he took more than $800,000 from about 20 victims, both men and women. He'd change his voice to sound feminine when speaking on the phone to his male victims, he said; only once did he get caught.

He describes a three-stage strategy. Using stolen credit card numbers, he would flood dating sites with fake profiles. Photos were pirated from social media. To snare women, he'd pose as older, financially secure men. For male victims, he just needed a picture of an alluring woman. All his victims, he says, were divorced or widowed: "The lonely heart is a vulnerable heart."

Ideally, Enitan let the victims make the first move. "It's always better if they respond to your ad first because that means they already like something about you," he says. "If you respond first, you have a lot of convincing to do." After learning everything about his target, he'd launch a campaign of love notes and gifts. "This is where you need lots of patience," he says. "This is where the real game is."

In the 2008 book *Truth, Lies and Trust on the Internet*, Monica Whitty, a psychologist at the University of Leicester in the United Kingdom, wrote about how online romances can be "hyperpersonal—more strong and intimate than physical relationships." Because the parties are spared the distractions of face-to-face interaction, they can create idealized avatars that command more trust and closeness than their true selves might.

Not only are older victims more likely to lose larger sums of money, but there's evidence that the ability to detect deception declines with age. When Whitty surveyed scam victims, she found that people who were romantics and risk takers, believers in fate and destiny, were particularly vulnerable. Many, like Amy, were survivors of abusive relationships. Women were slightly less likely to be scammed than men, but were far more likely to report it.

One term that Amy later learned was love bombing, a phrase referring to the smothering displays of affection that victims receive from suitors. A person's defenses are broken down by exhaustion, social isolation and an overwhelming amount of attention. Amy described the feeling as akin to being brainwashed. Enitan calls it "taking the brain," where the goal is to get the victims to transfer allegiance to the scammer. "You want them thinking, *My dreams are your dreams, my goals are your goals and my financial interests are your financial interests*," he says. "You can't ask for money until you have achieved this."

* * *

Slightly less than a month since his first contact with Amy, Dwayne brought up his money troubles. He'd planned to fly back to Virginia in January after he finished a big project, but some components were stuck in customs. Dwayne had a U.K. trust fund and would retire after this job, he said. But he couldn't use the fund to cover the customs fees. And he couldn't come back to the States until he completed the job. If Amy could help him, he'd pay her back when he returned.

Amy had money, and Dwayne knew it. She owned her home and two other properties, and she had inheritances from her mother and husband. He also knew she was in love with him. Amy wired $8,000 to the fiance of a friend of Dwayne's in Alabama, who'd get the funds to Dwayne.

Then he asked her for $10,000 to bribe officials because of an expired visa. Finally, he set a day for his flight home—Jan. 25—and emailed her his itinerary. Amy bought tickets for their first date, a Latin dance concert that night, and she told her brothers and friends they'd finally meet her mysterious boyfriend.

Then a problem came up: Dwayne had to pay his workers. While he'd received $2.5 million for the project—he even emailed her an image of the check—he couldn't open a bank account in Malaysia to access it. She sent more money. Jan. 25 came and went without Dwayne. He apologized profusely and sent more flowers.

Soon he needed more help. She wired another $15,000. This is a familiar pattern in love cons: The scammer promises a payoff—a face-to-face meeting—that forever recedes as crises and barriers intervene. As February wore on, Amy told friends that Dwayne was coming soon. But she never mentioned the loans. She knew the situation would be hard to understand, especially now that she had given more than $100,000.

"How do I know you're not a Nigerian scammer?" she asked playfully.

Dwayne would pay her back, of course. When doubt crept in, Amy would look at his pictures or read his messages. Still, little things were odd. At times, he'd send a series of rapid messages that felt almost as if she were getting them from someone else. Another time, she asked what he'd had for dinner. He said stir-fried chicken.

But I thought you hated chicken, she replied.

He laughed. "Oh, Amy. You know me better than that."

One night she commanded Dwayne, "Send me a selfie, right now." She got a photo moments later. There he was, sitting on a bench in the sun.

"How do I know you're not a Nigerian scammer?" she asked playfully.

He laughed. "Oh, Amy. You know me better than that."

Psychologists call this confirmation bias—if you love someone, you look for reasons he or she is telling the truth, and Amy was looking, desperately, for reasons to trust Dwayne. Besides, he'd be there on Feb. 28. He sent a text from the Kuala Lumpur airport: "I'll be home soon my love."

Then he went silent, and Amy tried to tamp down the panic. He texted her three days later—something about being held up by immigration in Malaysia and needing money to bribe the officials. This was the third time he'd failed to show. Still, she wired him the funds, putting the total amount she'd sent him over $300,000.

Amy's sister-in-law figured it out. "You need to see this," she told Amy, sending her a link to an episode of Dr. Phil that featured two women who had been unknowingly engaged to imaginary men they'd met online. Amy watched in horror.

A few days later, Malaysia Airlines Flight MH370 disappeared. This was the same route that Dwayne had planned to be on. Amy couldn't help worrying that he'd been on board. Finally, he phoned. They spoke for only a few moments before the call broke up. She was relieved but also disturbed. Something was different.

That week, the daily siege of calls, emails, and texts from Dwayne ended, and Amy wondered: How much did she know him? She fed the photos he'd sent into Google's image search. Eventually, up popped the LinkedIn page of a man with an unfamiliar name. She Googled the phrase "romance scam" and started reading. Yet even as she learned the truth, part of her hoped that her case was somehow different, that she was the lucky one.

*　　*　　*

At romancescams.org, a resource center and support group for dating fraud, you'll find scores of similar stories. In a decade, the site has collected about

60,000 reports, from men and women, young and old. "People think that victims are all lonely old women who can't get a date, but I've seen doctors, lawyers, police officers [get conned]," says Barbara Sluppick, who founded the site in 2005.

Some of the most aggressive anti-scam efforts have come from Australia. Brian Hay, the head of a fraud unit in Brisbane, has orchestrated stings that have led to the arrest of criminals in Malaysia and Nigeria. But so dim are the chances of finding offenders that he rarely tells victims about these cases. "The strongest drug in the world is love," Hay says. "These bastards know that. And they're brilliant at it." He notes that face-to-face support groups can be helpful for victims.

When Amy went to her regional FBI office, she says, an agent took her report—and told her that a woman in the next town had lost $800,000. The psychological trauma suffered by victims is twofold. First, they must cope with the end of a serious relationship. "It's like finding out someone you loved has died, and you'll never see them again," Sluppick says. To compound the damage, victims blame themselves—and their loved ones often do too. "People think, *Why did I let this happen to me?*" she says. "But you're a victim of a crime."

Some victims try the risky practice of scam baiting, attempting to turn the tables on fraudsters. Months after she discovered the con, Amy continued talking to Dwayne, promising him $50,000 if he sent various documents. She wanted to lure him into giving up something incriminating.

Eventually, Amy had to accept that Dwayne would never show his true face or give her the confession she yearned to hear. On New Year's Eve 2014, a year after he'd sent that first bouquet of flowers, she emailed him telling him not to contact her again.

A few minutes later, he texted. He promised not to call. "I know you're innocent," he wrote. "And so am I."

Originally published in the June 2016 issue of *Reader's Digest* magazine.

"Not in Our Town!"

How could they protect victims of hatred during the season of love and light?

As Tammie Schnitzer came to the intersection near the synagogue in Billings, Montana, she noticed something on the stop sign. She got out of her car to look closer, and a shiver shot down her spine. A sticker showed a swastika over a Star of David and the words "Want more oil? Nuke Israel."

Suddenly Tammie recalled a conversation with her husband, Brian, when they began dating years earlier. "There's something I have to tell you," he had said gravely. "I'm Jewish." Tammie was amused that he would make such a fuss over a difference that could never impede their relationship. Before marrying Brian, a physician who had come to Montana to work with the Indian Health Service, Tammie, a Billings native, converted to Judaism. Now on that morning in May 1992 she saw how life as a Jew could be very unpleasant.

The display of raw hate unnerved Tammie. She felt vulnerable and worried about their 3-year-old son, Isaac, and 8-month-old daughter, Rachel. Then the 33-year-old homemaker came up with an idea. She called Wayne Schile, publisher of the *Billings Gazette*, to talk about the problem of hate groups in their community. "What problem?" Schile replied.

A few days later Tammie visited Schile. "This problem," she said, handing over hate literature which had been circulated in Billings.

Schile was stunned.

In the months that followed, Tammie returned often to Schile's office with the latest hate literature. Finally, in October, the *Gazette* ran a front-page story on local skinheads, detailing their attitudes toward minorities and their links to the Ku Klux Klan.

*   *   *

For most of the 85,000 residents of Billings, the story was a revelation of organized hate in their midst. But Wayne Inman, chief of the Billings Police Department, knew through informants that a group of angry young men and their hangers-on, most of them poorly educated and underemployed, were followers of the KKK, and he worried about what might come next.

On Jan. 18, 1993, leaflets were placed on cars during an interfaith Martin Luther King Jr. Day observance at the First United Methodist Church. The fliers insulted a number of minorities, including the town's small community of about 120 Jews.

Inman called a press conference. "I can't do anything about this filth," he said, "because no crime has been committed. But the community can, and should, before it's too late."

Then Inman told a story. Before coming to Billings, he had been the assistant police chief in Portland, Oregon, where leafleting had escalated to vicious crimes: Minorities were assaulted, their property was vandalized. Finally, three skinheads beat an Ethiopian man to death with baseball bats. "Only then," Inman said, "did the people of Portland acknowledge the problem."

"Silence is acceptance," Inman continued. "These people are testing us. And if we do nothing, there's going to be more trouble. Billings should stand up and say, 'Harass one of us and you harass us all.'"

In response, leafleting increased. One September morning, Brian Schnitzer discovered that most of the headstones in the Jewish cemetery were tilted or laid face down. Someone had vandalized the small burial ground.

"This is not a prank," Inman later told reporters. "This is a hate crime."

*   *   *

On the evening of Dec. 2, a stranger stole into the Schnitzers' yard after Brian and Tammie had each driven away. Looking in a window, the stranger could not have failed to notice Isaac's toys and child-size bed. Nor could there have been doubt about the Schnitzers' religion. Resting on the chest of drawers was a menorah, the candelabrum Jews display during Hanukkah. The banner on the window proclaimed "Happy Hanukkah."

The intruder heaved a cinder block through the window. Glass exploded as the concrete bounced across the bed and landed on the floor. Luckily, Isaac was in the rec room playing with Rachel and their sitter.

When Tammie returned, Brian led her into Isaac's room. Her legs went weak and she began to cry. "I'm scared, Brian, " Tammie said. "Whoever did this waited until we left. They were watching us."

They discussed restricting the children's activities. Gradually Tammie's worry turned to anger. *Why should my children have to live in fear?* Only one force could protect Isaac and Rachel, she realized—the community.

The next day Tammie called Schile. "You're setting yourself up for more trouble," Schile warned.

"I don't care," Tammie said. "This is a quality of life issue, not a Jewish issue." That evening, the Schnitzers observed the beginning of the Sabbath. In a corner of the kitchen, far from windows, they lit the ceremonial candles.

* * *

The following morning, Margie MacDonald read about the Schnitzers in the *Gazette*. As executive director of the Montana Association of Churches, she educated religious leaders about the dangers of allowing bigotry to go unchallenged.

One passage caught her eye. The night of the attack, a police officer had suggested that Brian and Tammie take down their Hanukkah decorations. "How do I explain that to my children?" Tammie had asked. "I shouldn't have to do that."

MacDonald remembered the story of King Christian of Denmark. When the Nazis informed him that all Jews would be forced to display the yellow Star of David on their coats, the king responded that he would be first to wear it, and all Danes would follow his lead. The Nazis withdrew the order.

Now MacDonald reasoned, *What if, instead of the Jews removing menorahs from their windows, Christians placed menorahs in theirs?* She contacted the Rev. Keith Torney, pastor of the First Congregational Church. "Margie, that's a great idea," he said.

That Saturday afternoon, Torney called the pastors of several other churches, asking if they would distribute paper menorahs. The response was enthusiastic.

Torney gave out 300 paper menorahs at his church. In his sermon that Sunday he said: "We dare not remain silent as our Jewish sisters and brothers are threatened. I will put a menorah in my window and in my heart, for what happens to Jews also happens to me."

On Wednesday, Dec. 8, the *Billings Gazette* ran an editorial under the headline "Show the Vandals That Hatred Has No Place in This Season of Love and Light," urging readers to place menorahs in their windows.

A 68-year-old member of Torney's congregation placed a menorah on a window where it would be seen from the street. A neighbor begged her to take it down. "Don't you know what's going on?" the neighbor said.

"Yes," the woman replied. "That's exactly why I'm putting it up."

*   *   *

Rick Smith, manager of Universal Athletics, placed a message on the reader board outside his store: "Not in our town! No hate, no violence. Peace on earth." Ron Nistler, principal of Billings Central Catholic High School, proclaimed on the school's electronic sign: "Happy Hanukkah to our Jewish friends."

Reaction among Jews to the sudden outpouring of support was mixed. Many feared the Schnitzers' efforts to draw attention to antisemitism in Billings would only further incite bigots. Thus, it was a divided congregation that greeted Samuel Cohon, Beth Aaron Synagogue's new student rabbi, as he planned a vigil to precede Sabbath services on Dec. 10, the third night of Hanukkah.

At 6:30 p.m. on that chilly Friday, about 200 people, mostly Christians, gathered across the street from the synagogue. Cohon lit a menorah and blessed it, saying that it symbolized the human spirit. "You cannot stifle it."

Then Tammie stepped forward. She said that the block that smashed her son's window was aimed at everyone who is a victim of prejudice. Just then a few skinheads arrived, glowering at the crowd. Staring at one of the young men, Tammie declared, "Leave our babies alone!"

Rabbi Cohon quoted British statesman Edmund Burke: "The only thing necessary for the triumph of evil is for good men to do nothing." Then he led his congregants into the synagogue. The skinheads wandered off.

The next morning's *Gazette* featured a front-page story about the vigil, a full-page reproduction of a menorah and a statement urging readers to display it.

But the following day the paper carried unsettling news: Bullets had shattered windows at Central Catholic High School, near the sign that extended greetings to Jews. The incident was a first in a weeklong spree of hate crimes.

Late Sunday, two families received anonymous phone calls: "Go look at your car, Jew lover." The homeowners found their cars' roofs stomped on and windshields shattered. Four other residents discovered their cars similarly damaged. None of the victims was Jewish but all had exhibited paper menorahs.

Two nights later, vandals broke windows that displayed menorahs at First United Methodist. The glass doors at the Evangelical United Methodist Church were shattered.

"The hate groups are trying to silence us through scare tactics," Chief Inman declared. "We can't allow it. For every act of vandalism, I hope 100 people will put menorahs in their windows."

Tammie Schnitzer said: "This is not a Jewish issue. It's a human issue."

This time the entire town was aroused. Soon the symbol could be seen everywhere—on office windows, in homes and apartments, on cars and trucks, in restaurants and stores, schools and other public buildings—thousands in all.

One night before Christmas, Tammie Schnitzer took Isaac and Rachel for a drive around Billings. She wanted them to see that they lived in a community that stood by its children. Tammie pointed out the menorahs that hung in windows ringed by bright colored lights.

"Gosh," Isaac said, "are all these people Jewish?"

"No, Isaac," Tammie replied, "they're your friends."

Originally published in the November 1994 issue of *Reader's Digest* magazine.

Humor Hall of Fame

I was singing a lullaby to my 3-year-old and he told me he hated it. "That's a shame," I said. "I used to sing it to you before you were born, when you were still in my tummy." "I hated it then, too," he replied.

—@ALICETAYLORM

My 6-year-old, to her crying brother: It's OK to be sad. Sometimes we just need to let our feelings out. Just let yourself be sad.

Me: Oh darling, that's so lovely. Well done. Why is he crying anyway?

My 6-year-old: I hit him.

—@ELSPELLS13

"Yaaawn! My imaginary friend kept me up late last night."

"How many times do I have to tell you to slouch?"

It was the first time my 5-year-old had been to church, and she was very excited. After what must have felt like an eternity to her, waiting for the service to begin, she whispered in my ear, "When does God come on?"

—CONNIE PINELLA

"Mummy has no idea how to raise children," said a child to his father.

"How can you say such a thing?" replied the father.

"Well, Mummy always sends me to bed at night when I'm not sleepy, and wakes me up in the morning when I am."

—SANDOR SZABO

Hot. Thirsty. Lost.

by Kenneth Miller

Three women took a drive to Death Valley for a day of exploring. Three days and 300 miles later, they were out of gas—and hope.

Death Valley, the 3,000-square-mile sprawl of sand dunes and arid mountains along California's southeastern border, is the hottest, driest place in North America. Temperatures soar into the triple digits from June through September. Annual rainfall averages 2.5 inches; most months, there's none at all. Though nearly a million tourists visit each year, few venture into the valley during the summer, when the sun is most brutal.

Like most of her neighbors in Pahrump, Nevada—a dusty town of 36,000, just 60 miles from the entrance to Death Valley National Park—Donna Cooper had driven through the valley many times. But one Thursday morning in July 2010, the 62-year-old retiree decided to explore a corner of the park she'd never visited: Scotty's Castle, a Spanish-style mansion built in the 1920s. Her daughter Gina, 17, and Donna's friend and houseguest from Hong Kong, Jenny Leung, 19, joined her.

The trio arrived at the mansion around 1 p.m. and spent two hours touring the place. As they left the parking lot on the way home, they saw a sign for the Racetrack—a dry lake bed, where shifting boulders have left skid marks in the cracked mud. "I've always wanted to check that out," Donna said.

The other two women went along with the idea. Gina, who was driving, pointed their Hyundai west on Route 267, then turned south on a dirt road. The temperature outside the tiny car was over 125 degrees. After about an hour, they reached an intersection, but the sign indicating the way to the Racetrack was unclear. Gina turned left. After 10 more miles, she realized she'd made a wrong turn. She tried to reverse course, but they were soon climbing into the high country.

After 10 more miles, Gina realized they'd taken a wrong turn.

Donna consulted the road atlas, but its map of Death Valley showed only the park's main roads. "Let's ask Nell how to get back to Scotty's Castle," she said, referring to the GPS device she'd named after her mother.

Donna took the wheel and followed the machine's instructions. "Drive 550 feet, then turn right on unnamed road," Nell commanded in a voice brimming with digital certainty. "Turn left, then drive 1 mile. Turn right. Turn left. Recalculating. Drive 5 miles, then make a U-turn."

* * *

Travelers have been losing their way in Death Valley—often fatally—since 1849, when pioneers began using it as a shortcut to California's gold fields. Recently, growing numbers have been led astray by GPS devices, whose databases for remote areas such as Death Valley may include maps that haven't been updated for decades. As Donna drove in loops and zigzags on unmarked roads that grew ever narrower and rockier, Gina's head throbbed; nausea set in.

"I want to go home," Gina moaned.

"Stop being so immature," Donna snapped.

In the front seat, Jenny struggled not to cry. Since arriving in the United States in May, she'd enjoyed traveling with Donna to Florida, the Grand Canyon, San Francisco and Los Angeles. This, however, was more adventure than she wanted. Though the car was air-conditioned, her lips had become painfully dry. But three of the four 16-ounce bottles of water they'd brought along were already empty, and she couldn't bring herself to touch the last one. When Donna handed her the bottle, Jenny pretended to take a swig.

Hot. Thirsty. Lost.

"Cut that out," Donna said sternly. "You've got to drink your share."

Jenny took a sip and swished it in her mouth for a long time before she swallowed.

As they drove on, the shadows lengthened, but the heat barely diminished. Outside the car, sand, scrub and rubble stretched for miles around. At intervals, all three women tried calling 911 on their cellphones. No reception. Donna took inventory: Besides the remaining water, they had two apples, what was left of a bag of chips, and some cookies. The hatchback's cargo hold contained blankets, sweaters, extra shoes, a toolkit and a first-aid kit. There was still more than a quarter tank of gas.

Donna inhaled deeply, then exhaled the fear that had been building inside her. She'd survived worse fixes than this—including a serious accident in her 20s that had left her hospitalized for weeks and a near-fatal intestinal illness in Haiti earlier that year. She and her husband had raised eight children. Now, she knew, two young lives were depending on her to get them out of the desert alive.

The women survived their first 24 hours in the desert on 64 ounces of water.

Outdated GPS software often leads travelers astray in Death Valley, which is too remote for many systems to map accurately.

Around 8 p.m., Nell's robotic voice led them into a rock-rimmed dead end. Gina spotted a faint trail leading into the brush, and they followed it downhill to a smoother dirt road. As they rounded a bend, past a mostly dried-up salt lake shimmering in the sunset, they noticed a sign of civilization—a mailbox. Inside, Donna found a crinkled, handwritten note: "Sorry we missed you," it read. Farther along was a wire fence, a padlocked gate and an isolated stand of trees.

"Let's see if anybody's back there," Gina said.

"We can't waste time," Donna replied. "We're on a good road now. We're going to find our way out."

Following Nell's instructions, Donna kept to the road as it rose into the barren mountains. As they gained altitude, Gina glanced back at where they'd come from. Behind the trees, she thought she saw some kind of habitation. But night was falling, and they'd gone too far to turn around.

At home in Pahrump, Charlene Dean, an old friend of Donna's and a reporter for a local newspaper, wasn't worried when Donna and the girls didn't show up for dinner. Dean, 51, was boarding with the Coopers in exchange for house-sitting when they were out of town. She'd known Donna long enough to assume that her friend had changed her plans.

Donna's husband, Rodger, 62, was in North Port, Florida, visiting their daughter Sky. He, too, was used to Donna's independent ways. But Sky, a 21-year-old nursing home aide, had undergone gallbladder surgery that afternoon, and she couldn't believe that her mother wouldn't get in touch. "Something's wrong," she kept saying.

*   *   *

Donna drove until the gas gauge read empty, then pulled over. It was 10 p.m., and the odometer indicated they'd covered more than 200 miles since leaving Scotty's Castle. Huge boulders loomed beside the car. The black sky blazed with stars.

"Looks like we'll be camping," Donna said.

"Are there wild animals here?" asked Jenny, her voice quavering.

"Mountain lions. Bears," Donna replied. "Roll up the windows."

The girls did as they were told. Donna passed around the last of the food, and they took a swallow apiece of their nearly depleted water. Then, with blankets they dug out of the back, they tried to sleep. Gina dropped off quickly, but Jenny was worried about wildlife, and Donna fretted about a boulder flattening the car. Both agonized about the next day. "Don't be scared," Donna said, as she and Jenny sat staring into the darkness. "We just need a plan." A long silence followed.

"We're on a good road now," said Donna. "We're going to find our way out."

At 6 a.m. Friday, the rising sun revealed that they were parked high above the valley, in a sparse grove of pines. Beside the road was a drop of several hundred feet. Donna tried starting the car, but the engine wouldn't turn over.

"We have to get someone to see us," Gina said. Donna and Jenny used stones to write HELP on a patch of flat ground. Gina built a fire pit, piling it full of branches and pamphlets from Scotty's Castle. But when she pressed the car's cigarette lighter to the kindling, it just smoldered.

In the distance, the women saw an airplane. Gina grabbed a CD and used it as a signal mirror, while Jenny waved a yellow emergency blanket. That plane—and several more after it—flew on. Around 11 a.m., after they'd finished off the bottle of water, Gina hiked up the winding road for 2 miles, past a cluster of long-abandoned campsites, to where the trees thinned out. She gazed out over the landscape: nothing but desert.

They gathered some pine needles to chew, for moisture and nutrients.

Back at the car, Donna was peeling cacti with her jackknife. She'd read that one variety contained drinkable liquid—but as she and Jenny extracted the sticky pulp, they realized this one wasn't it. Next, they gathered pine needles to chew; Donna knew they contained moisture and some nutrients. The two were digging for cactus roots as Gina returned.

"We've got to go back to that place where we stopped yesterday," she said.

"How are we going to do that?" Donna asked. "The car won't start."

"Let's try it again," Gina suggested.

Donna said a silent prayer, then turned the key. The engine roared to life, startling them all, and they took off down the mountainside. Donna stomped on the accelerator at each dip in the road, so that they'd have enough momentum to make it up the next rise; if they stalled, she knew, it'd be over for them. Five, 10, 20, 30 miles—they were in the flats now and turning left onto the road by the salt lake. The locked gate finally came into view, and the women burst into excited screams: Here, at least, was a chance at shelter.

They left the car and ducked under the wire fence, the ground burning through their sneaker soles as they walked up the long driveway. As they emerged from the trees, they saw three trailers clustered around a free-standing wooden porch. They called out, but no one answered. The trailers were all locked. But behind the largest one, Donna found something incredible—a garden hose attached to a spigot. The water was hot, but the trio gulped it greedily. Then they lay down for a nap on the porch.

When they awoke, Gina fetched the toolkit from the car. She unscrewed the hinges on the big trailer but couldn't get the door open. Using a crowbar, she pried a padlock off one of the smaller trailers. Inside, they found a few cans of chili and beans, some packets of instant ramen and cranberry oatmeal, half a box of spaghetti. There were also eight half-cases of beer. The food would last only a couple of days, Donna figured, but the beer could sustain them for two weeks—assuming they survived the heat.

The air inside the trailer was furnace-like, so they pulled the mattresses from the two bunks and laid them on the porch, where it was slightly cooler. Donna opened the beans and chili, and everyone sat down to eat. Then they found a collection of jars and bottles in a trash bin and began filling them with water in case the hose ran dry.

In Florida, after arriving home from the hospital that morning, Sky tried calling Donna's phone, only to be routed to voicemail. She checked her mother's Facebook page: no updates. Then she checked Donna's credit card account. The last charges were on Thursday at 1 p.m., when Donna bought three tickets to Scotty's Castle. Sky called Charlene Dean, who said she hadn't heard from Donna either. That evening, she called the supermarket where Gina worked as a courtesy clerk. Gina's shift had started at 4 p.m. Nevada time. "She hasn't punched in," Sky was told. Her father grimaced as Sky hung up the phone. "Now I'm worried," Rodger said.

Sky phoned Charlene again, and the two called the sheriff's departments in several counties, the California Highway Patrol and the ranger station at Death Valley National Park. But authorities said it was too late in the day to mount a full search.

At nightfall, Gina lit a signal fire, using matches from the trailer kitchen and logs she found stacked in the yard. Then the women bedded down on the porch. The heat on the valley floor was so intense that they had to get up every 15 minutes to douse themselves with water.

As morning approached, Donna and Jenny walked out to the road and made a cross in the dirt with tree branches. They wrote, HELP, CALL POLICE in the dust coating the car.

The women then broke into the big trailer, finding little of use. Next, Gina pried open a window on the smallest trailer, and Jenny crawled inside. There, on a table, was a CB radio. But after hauling it out, along with the antenna, and hooking it up to the car battery, there was only static when Jenny twirled the dial. After 10 minutes, the static died out too.

Gina was ready to weep. But her mother had a better idea: "Let's get cleaned up."

Jenny and Donna took baths first, filling the tub in the first trailer with water from outside. Around 5 p.m., it was Gina's turn. Donna washed Gina's hair, her hands firm on her daughter's scalp.

Gina thought she heard screaming. It was Jenny. "Come out!" she was yelling. "Come out!"

Donna ran outside, and Gina—pulling on her clothes without drying off—followed. Jenny was waving the yellow emergency blanket madly.

A deafening racket came from the sky. A helicopter marked California Highway Patrol was slowly circling. They'd been found!

After landing, the pilots, who were also EMTs, checked the women's vital signs and gave them as much fresh water as they could guzzle. "We were about to give you up for dead and fly back to base," one of the men said. The women appeared healthy, so the pilots offered them two options: to board the helicopter, one by one, and be flown to Lone Pine, the nearest town, or to wait for a backcountry campground operator to bring a can of gas and give them directions to the highway. They chose the latter.

After the park official showed up, they filled their tank, thanked their rescuers and drove away into the night. This time, they knew where they were going.

You could say that getting lost gave Gina and Jenny some direction. Inspired by a conversation with one of the helicopter rescuers, Gina decided to enroll in nursing school. Jenny went back to Hong Kong shortly after the ordeal but returned to the United States to live with the Coopers and attend a local college. And Donna remains undaunted by that wide swath of desert in her backyard. "Never for a second," she says, "did I doubt that we would make it out of there."

Originally published in the September 2012 issue of *Reader's Digest* magazine.

INSPIRED SHOPPING

While shopping one day at Publix, I made a pit stop at the women's restroom. Upon entering, I saw an African American cleaning lady. She was singing to herself as she mopped. I recognized the song ("How Great Is Our God") and couldn't hold back—I joined in! Then we hugged, tears in our eyes. We were so thankful for each other. Now I look—and listen—for her every time I go shopping.

—Dorothy Morse, *Lake Placid, FL*

TEACHING MOMENT

One day last December, a young lady ringing up my purchases greeted me with an enthusiastic "Merry Christmas!" I was not offended, but I am a Muslim, and at the time I was wearing a beautiful scarf draped around my head in a manner identifying my spiritual convictions. I smiled and responded, "Happy Birthday!" At first she was taken aback, but then she nodded and laughed good-naturedly, acknowledging my point. I smiled back at her and said, "Merry Christmas to you."

—Mahasin Shamsiddeen, *Prince George, VA*

Giving Creatures Comfort

by Juliana LaBianca

Farmer Jenny Brown gives abandoned animals new life

Shortly after doctors diagnosed 10-year-old Jenny Brown with bone cancer, they had to amputate her right leg below the knee to save her life. Facing a year of chemotherapy after the surgery, Jenny begged her mother for a kitten. The orange calico Jenny named Boogie rarely left her side, licking tears from her cheeks after hospital visits and curling up in her lap as she adjusted to life with a prosthetic leg.

"My relationship with Boogie showed me that animals think, feel and suffer as much as we do," says Jenny, now 44.

In 1994, Jenny graduated from Columbia College Chicago with a concentration in film and video, and began a career in television and documentary production. On the side, she volunteered as a videographer for animal rights groups, and in 2002, she shot undercover footage of gruesome animal mistreatment at several Texas farm animal stockyards. "After seeing that, I knew I needed to help animals," says Jenny.

A year later, she gave up her film career to work as an animal caregiver at Farm Sanctuary in Watkins Glen, New York.

"Farm animals are typically very timid," says Jenny. "But in a loving environment, you begin to see their personalities."

Jenny learned the ropes of farm life and, with her fiance, Doug Abel, a film editor, opened the Woodstock Farm Sanctuary, a nonprofit organization dedicated to rescuing and rehabilitating farm animals, on a 22-acre property they bought in the rolling hills of Woodstock, New York, the next year.

Her earliest tenants were six hens rescued from an Ohio egg factory. The sanctuary's first goat, Olivia, had been abandoned after her owner's house burned down. When Jenny rescued a calf named Dylan, Olivia became his care-taker. "The animals form bonds with the creatures around them," says Jenny.

In August 2007, she received a call from Animal Care and Control of NYC about a small goat it had found hobbling around Prospect Park. Jenny guessed it had run away from one of the city's slaughterhouses. The goat's legs were severely injured, probably from being bound together with wire, and its mouth was covered in sores.

Jenny and her team brought the goat, which they named Albie, to the sanctuary, but they soon realized that Albie's left front leg was injured beyond repair. After a veterinarian amputated the leg, Jenny asked Erik Tomkins, the doctor who makes Jenny's prostheses, to fashion a leg for Albie. To date, seven of the sanctuary's animals have received prosthetic limbs or braces. "On most farms, animals with these ailments would be immediately killed," says Jenny.

"In a loving environment, you begin to see the animals' personalities," says Jenny.

Last September, Jenny and Doug moved the sanctuary to a 150-acre farm in High Falls, New York, which has a commercially equipped kitchen and a dining hall in addition to several lodges, a barn and other buildings. The new space has allowed their team of 17, including five full-time animal caretakers and a shelter director, to host vegan cooking classes and a camp for kids.

"People love spending time with the animals. It's therapy for them," says Jenny. "We have a 2,000-pound steer who loves to cuddle. There's a magic that happens here."

Originally published in the May 2016 issue of *Reader's Digest* magazine.

Attacked by Pirates

by Donovan Webster

Their six-year voyage around the world was a dream come true until one horrific day

They attacked out of the sun.

As the two yachts approached, sailing westward through the Gulf of Aden between Somalia and Yemen, Carol Martini—on the 47-foot sloop *Gandalf*—scanned the horizon, still oblivious to the danger 500 yards off her bow.

Then, flickering in the distance, she glimpsed something: two low shapes, silhouetted inside the sun's reflected brilliance on the water. Picking up the radio handset, she hailed the nearby sloop *Mahdi* and its captain, Rod Nowlin. "Uh, Rod," she said. "I think I see something."

Martini called belowdecks, waking her partner, Jay Barry. He was topside in an instant. "I'll take the wheel," he said. "You roll up the jib. Let's get running."

Seconds later, the boats in the distance fired their engines, sending plumes of thick black exhaust into the air. Then things began exploding around Barry as rounds from AK-47s ripped apart the decking. "Gunfire," says Barry, "sounds quite different when you're standing in front of a gun instead of behind it."

The unthinkable was happening. Despite weeks of planning to avoid precisely this fate, *Gandalf* and *Mahdi* were under siege by modern-day pirates.

*   *   *

Carol Martini is slight and sun-blond, a Harvard-trained MD and former instructor at Harvard's School of Medicine. As she sits in the cockpit of *Gandalf*—sipping a mug of tea in the Mediterranean harbor at Finike, Turkey—she seems less an East Coast elitist than somebody's friendly, cool-headed sister.

In the burly Jay Barry, 53, she has found her ideal counterpart. Disarmingly funny, Barry, who's more at home in a pub than a country club, financed this expedition by selling his north-of-Boston auto-restoration business.

Sailing around the globe had been a mutual goal since their second date. As a boy, Barry stared at a map of the world on his bedroom wall, and had always had an itch to travel far and wide. As for Martini, she fell in love with the guy and, subsequently, his dreams of adventure.

It took Barry a year to find the right vessel. But when he brought Martini to the boatyard to see it, she thought it was a joke. "The thing looked like a flying Dumpster," she says.

The sloop, built in 1960, was a charred wreck. Despite its 5 mm-thick plate-steel hull and 61-foot mast of Sitka spruce, a fire in the boatyard had singed the paint off the vessel's port side. Its original canvas sails and rigging were still aboard—and moldy. Garbage overflowed its decks.

Over the next year, working nights and weekends, the two rebuilt the sloop, discovering a fantastic design. "Beyond the hull's steel," says Barry, "the thing is reinforced with angle iron riveted to the hull every 2 inches. It's incredibly solid—though with all those rivets, it's really a boat made of a thousand holes."

In 1992, they launched their re-created vessel, *Gandalf*. It was named for J.R.R. Tolkien's *Lord of the Rings* wizard who recognizes all forms of humanity. In November 1999, they set off from Gloucester, Massachusetts, to fulfill their dream—a trip around the world. Their extended vacation would take them to the most beautiful parts of the Earth, as well as the most treacherous: stretches of ocean known to harbor pirates.

Carol Martini and Jay Barry, aboard Gandalf, *survived storms and long stretches of isolation. Those would be the least of their problems.*

By March 2000, Carol Martini and Jay Barry had sailed down the U.S. Atlantic coast, cruised the Caribbean and entered the Panama Canal. By November, they'd visited the Galapagos, the Marquesas, Fiji and much of Polynesia, before stopping in Bundaberg, Australia, for their first winter. "We did 14,500 miles under sail in a year—that's not recommended. It was hard," Barry says.

"Yeah," Martini adds, "but we were having a wonderful time."

Gandalf continued north, through Indonesia, stopping to see the Komodo dragons before going on to Bali. They explored Sumatra and Kalimantan; then they pressed on for Singapore. So far, their trip had surpassed Barry's childhood dreams.

After weeks of screwing tight their courage, they left Singapore and sailed into the Strait of Malacca, an area known for pirates brazen enough to attack freighters. "So there we were, all prepared for the infamous Malacca Strait pirates, and nothin' happened except a bad storm," says Martini. As they sailed on, they hoped the worst was behind them.

*   *   *

By late December 2004, *Gandalf* was moored in Nai Harn Bay, Thailand. By then, Martini and Barry had befriended another pair of round-the-world sailors, Rod and Becky Nowlin, of Whidbey Island, Washington. The Nowlins were sailing their 45-foot yacht, *Mahdi*—a word that means "savior" or "peaceful one" in Arabic.

Rod Nowlin, 62, is a solid, athletic man. Retired from the U.S. Navy, he enjoys slow-paced exotic travel and a love of good cigars. His wife, Becky, aside from being a legendary cook, is said to be a hoot.

Because of the piracy threat in the Red Sea, the two crews planned to leave Thailand together. "I wanted someone who could get through the area quickly. I didn't want to carry anyone," Barry explains.

The two captains were well aware that any seagoing vessel, from a yacht to an ocean liner, is a potential target. Using sophisticated technology like radar and radio scanners, as well as lethally modern weapons, pirates thrive in areas with limited naval presence and numerous places to hide. One favorite spot is the narrow neck of the Gulf of Aden, where the Indian Ocean separates the government-less nation of Somalia and the impoverished country of Yemen. It's a zone known to sailors as Pirate Alley. And on Jan. 20, 2005, it was where *Gandalf* and *Mahdi* set sail for, pausing a few days in Salalah, Oman.

*   *   *

"Salalah is where we got stuck with an idiot," Barry says.

By this time, *Gandalf* and *Mahdi* had helped another sailor—a Californian and his wife in a smaller, less-hardy vessel—repair their boat at a number of anchorages since departing Thailand. "This guy had no business being on the water," says Barry. And in Salalah, the smaller boat turned up again, insinuating itself into the other boats' plans.

Barry and Rod Nowlin both knew that this third vessel, a 37-foot sloop, couldn't keep pace with their larger boats. They hooked up with another craft, a well-captained 37-foot Catalina, and on March 7, 2005, all four left on the

Worse still, the two boats would have to cross Pirate Alley in broad daylight.

treacherous, 600-mile trek through the Gulf of Aden. Their plan was to run all day, making good time; then, under cover of darkness—with radios and lights turned off—they would transit Pirate Alley, ending at the harbor in Aden, Yemen.

At least, that was the plan. The Californian's boat quickly broke down, and he started using the radio for repair advice. "All night long we were on the radio, trying to diagnose his problems," says Barry.

Finally, at dawn on March 8, the two smaller vessels stayed behind to regroup, leaving *Mahdi* and *Gandalf* to continue on by themselves.

They were headed into Pirate Alley with 14 hours of advance radio emergency calls alerting everyone within range. Worse still, they would have to cross it in broad daylight.

*   *   *

At 9 a.m. that day, roughly 30 miles off the coast of Al Mukalla, Yemen, two long, narrow powerboats—pushed full-bore by large outboard motors—approached *Mahdi* and *Gandalf* from behind, then passed them.

Undeterred, *Mahdi* and *Gandalf* kept sailing. Fifteen miles later, the boats returned, this time coming at the sailboats across their bows. "That's when I knew they were fixing our course," Barry says. "We all realized then, we were in trouble."

As quickly as they arrived, the motorboats were gone. Eight hours later, after sailing on deserted seas, Martini spotted something in the distance.

Two new, different boats—larger vessels with inboard motors—hiding in the slick glare of the sun.

"These two boats came at us, shooting," says Martini. "One came down our starboard side; the other came down *Mahdi*'s port side. They had these 6-foot-tall spars rising from their gunwales. Wrapped around the spars was this orange tarp, so we couldn't see how many people were inside each boat. They'd pop up and shoot; then they'd duck back down behind the tarp."

As bullets ripped through *Gandalf*'s Plexiglas windows, shattered metal rail stanchions and passed clean through its 12-inch-thick Sitka spruce mast, Martini ducked belowdecks, while Barry dove behind the wheel, putting as much steel hull as possible between himself and the pirates. He wasn't going to make it easy for them to kill him.

Glancing over to *Mahdi*, Barry saw that Becky Nowlin was driving—Rod was strangely missing—and as the second pirate boat roared closer, they were firing at Becky, who was also hiding for her life behind the wheel.

Then, carrying the 12-gauge shotgun he kept for emergencies, Rod Nowlin appeared in the companionway on *Mahdi*—just in time for a bullet to whiz past his head. Wheeling around, he saw a hand reaching over the orange tarp of the second boat firing an AK-47 at him. Bullets shattered the *Mahdi*'s self-steering mechanism, raining hot shards of stainless steel on Rod and Becky, burning their legs.

> *"Hold on to something. I'm going to ram them!" Barry yelled.*

Rod Nowlin lifted his weapon to fire back, but found himself face-to-face with another pirate. This one was no more than 17 years old.

"He was a young kid, on a boat filled with men," Nowlin says. "And I was looking at him, right in the eye, and I couldn't shoot him." Nowlin motioned with the shotgun for him to get down. The kid ducked and Nowlin fired into the boat, responding to the spray of AK-47 rounds.

On *Gandalf*, the pirate boat that had attacked them was finally past—but it wasn't leaving. Instead, it made a U-turn, preparing a second assault. For the first time, Martini and Barry understood that the tall staves rising from the boat's gunwales were rudimentary supports, handholds meant to steady the pirates for one reason.

"They planned to board us," says Barry. "They were coming back and shooting." The sound of a bullet barely missing him confirmed something Barry already knew. He and Martini were going to die unless he did something. But there was nowhere to go. They couldn't hide, and they certainly couldn't outrun the pirate speedboats. Barry was left with one option. "I yelled down to Carol, 'Find something to hold on to. I'm gonna ram the bastards.'"

With the mainsail up and the propeller going full-throttle, Barry whipped the wheel, turning *Gandalf* on a dime. He headed straight for the pirates, slowing only after ramming them square amidships.

That's when the couple got their first good look at their attackers. "As we hit, I saw four pirates aboard, and their eyes got really big—just huge. They weren't used to boats doing business this way," Barry says. "When our bow hit them, their boat rolled toward us; the side closest to us went under our bow, so their decks rolled up exposed. They were rolling over."

The sailboat kept driving forward, into the pirate boat's interior decking. Barry jammed the engine in reverse to free himself. But he wasn't going anywhere. The pirate boat was stuck on *Gandalf's* bow.

* * *

As Barry tried to knock the first pirate boat off, the second pirate boat—now repelled from *Mahdi* by Rod Nowlin's shotgun blasts—had also swung around to attack Barry and Martini, sneaking up on the distracted and impaired *Gandalf* from astern. The second vessel drew upon the unsuspecting Barry—with a pair of armed pirates standing on its bow ready to board.

"I was belowdecks, using the radio [to call for help]," Martini says. "And all of a sudden, behind Jay, I saw these two heads."

There was one final crack of gunfire—and they were gone. Rod Nowlin had shot back at them. "The only pirate I didn't shoot, it turns out, was the kid I saw first," says Nowlin. "I don't know what happened to him."

Within seconds, both pirate vessels were disappearing astern as the two sailboats beat a hasty route northwest. "I think the sea finally shook the first pirate boat off our bow," says Barry.

When it was over, Rod Nowlin had fired six times. Both pirate boats were dead in the water, severely damaged.

A day later, *Gandalf* and *Mahdi* both limped into the harbor at Aden, Yemen. On *Gandalf*, bullets had pierced the boat in 14 places, and the ramming had scraped a large hole from the smooth green paint of the boat's bow. "Those pirates tore up old *Gandalf* pretty good," Barry says.

Martini and Barry hope that local governments will learn from their experience and take concrete actions.

"We've tried to get authorities in the area to give recreational sailors more security," says Barry. "Maybe they could escort sailboats through the area. But, so far, they've stayed deaf to us." Here's one more reason to do something: Some believe that certain pirates are actually members of al-Qaida, trolling for hostages.

And what of the two smaller boats, especially the one with all the mechanical problems, that *Gandalf* and *Mahdi* left behind?

Carol Martini laughs. "They got through Pirate Alley without incident," she says. "Go figure!"

Originally published in the April 2006 issue of *Reader's Digest* magazine.

Jay Barry and Carol Martini completed their round-the-world trip in 2007 and returned home to Beverly, Massachusetts, where Martini resumed her medical practice and Barry started a business selling luxury cars. They retired in 2019 and moved to Hawaii. They still sail on Gandalf. *Before Rod and Becky Nowlin could return home,* Mahdi *was rammed by a German ferry and irreparably damaged. The couple then purchased* R-N-R, *a 41-foot trawler. They live on* R-N-R, *which is based in Anchorage. Both couples keep in touch.*

How Sweet It Is

by Andy Simmons, from the book *Now That's Funny*

Humor editor at Reader's Digest *recalls his father's petty thievery—and the way they always had each other's backs*

"What are you doing?"

"I'm reading the menu."

"No, with your hand," I said.

"I'm holding the menu," my father said defensively.

"With the other hand."

We were seated at a booth in a diner. Dad was hiding something in that paw, which he stealthily slid across the tabletop before stuffing it into his pocket.

"You're stealing Sweet 'N Low, aren't you?"

"It's not stealing; they want you to take it. That's why they leave it out here."

"They leave it out here for you to put in the coffee that they serve you."

"How else am I expected to get Sweet 'N Low for my coffee at home?"

"Dad, I know you don't get around as much anymore. But let me clue you in to something: They have these things called supermarkets. And inside these stores are aisles. And in the aisles are shelves. Lots of shelves filled with goods. And next to the sugar ..."

"Everybody does it."

"I don't."

"And you never have Sweet 'N Low in your house. Next time I come over I'd appreciate it if you stopped by a coffee shop and picked up a few packets."

"If it's not stealing, then why are you sneaking them? Why not go from table to table stuffing all the Sweet 'N Low packets into your pockets?"

"Because those customers wouldn't have any to take home with them."

Dad was a remarkably ethical criminal. I'd recently read an article about a thief who, after robbing a home, cleaned the house and even did the dishes. If Dad took to breaking and entering, I'd like to think he'd do the same.

"He saw me," he said. Dad's fingers were in the sweetener bowl when he noticed the manager eyeballing him. "Quick, take the Sweet 'N Low." He shoved seven packets of pink gold my way.

"Why don't you just put the Sweet 'N Low back?"

"And admit I'm wrong?"

"You are wrong!"

"Can I help you, gentlemen?" asked the manager. I ripped open the seven packets of Sweet 'N Low and dumped the contents into my half-empty coffee cup and took a sip. All that was missing was some perfume dripped into my eyes and I would have had the full lab-rat experience.

"Yeah, two more cups," said Dad, cool as a cucumber. The manager spotted the empty sweetener bowl. Dad smiled. The man smiled back, then took a full bowl from another table and placed it on ours before leaving. Dad quickly emptied the contents into his pockets.

All that was missing was some perfume dripped into my eyes and I would have had the full lab-rat experience.

I'm not sure why he steals Sweet 'N Low. I think it's because Dad comes from a long line of petty thieves who looked upon restaurants and supermarkets as bargain-basement dollar stores. On those rare occasions his mother dined out, it was to stock up on provisions. She'd bring along a handbag large enough to store bread, pats of butter, salt and pepper shakers, any silverware she might be short on at the time, and the occasional salad plate. One of his aunts thought nothing of strolling around the supermarket snacking on grapes and cherries before settling down for lunch at the olive bar.

Dad rifled through the bowl again, making sure he hadn't missed anything worth filching. He won't take the yellow or blue. He's loyal to his brand.

It's funny, other than his long-time love for Sweet 'N Low, there isn't one specific thing that I really remember about my father growing up. He had a good sense of humor. He was always around. He never spanked me. Hell, I can't recall him ever really yelling at me, except maybe when I deserved it. And even then it was drudgery for him. But that one thing?

Friends of mine have fond memories of an incredible trip to the Grand Canyon that their fathers took them on, or the ski trip to Vail. We never did any of that. Dad was a true son of Brooklyn, before the hipsters took over. And as tough as he was, the Grand Canyon had snakes and soil, and he wanted no part of any of that. As for skiing, why be cold when you could stay inside a nice, warm apartment in New York? Our vacations, when we took them, were usually spent near a racetrack or up at the Holiday Inn in Tarrytown, about 40 minutes from home. It had a pool and it had ... a pool. What else did we need? Plus there was a basketball hoop and a field big enough to toss a ball.

We were a formidable two-on-two basketball team, Dad and I. I'd feed him the ball, and he'd take it to the hoop. In football, it was reversed. He was the quarterback, a southpaw whose delivery confounded everyone. I was the fleet-footed receiver who longed to be on the other end of one of his perfect passes.

We were complementary teammates, and teammates we would remain, even when I got older.

Once when I was visiting home from college, my dog had gotten sick all over the white living-room rug—my mother's pride and joy. I was furiously cleaning it up when Dad happened by. "What are you doing?" he said, blissfully unaware of the horror to come.

"Phineas crapped all over the rug!" I whispered anxiously.

His smile disappeared, and his mouth formed a large oval shape as he placed both hands on his cheeks. Depending on your reference point, he was either *The Scream* or Macaulay Culkin in *Home Alone*. He then looked furtively around. "I'll distract your mother," he said, before running off into the other room.

Dad had my back, always. That I do remember. No matter what I said, or what idiocy I engaged in, I was protected.

* * *

"Here you are, gentlemen." The manager placed two new cups of coffee in front of us and turned to leave.

"Excuse me," I said, freezing him. I held up the bowl of sweeteners. "There are no Sweet 'N Lows. Mind getting us some?"

Originally published in *Now That's Funny* by Andy Simmons, published in 2012 by the *Reader's Digest* Association

Humor Hall of Fame

"You're just the kind of person we're looking for to test our airline seats."

The line at our local post office was out the door, and, seeing that only one postal worker was on duty, the customers were getting testy. To help hurry things along, a customer called out, "How can I help you go faster?" The postal worker yelled back, "Go home!"

—SCARLETT BUZEK

I was supervising some prospective employees at our construction company as they filled out their application forms. Everyone was busily writing away except for one guy, who appeared stumped. He turned to his friend and whispered, "Hey George, what's my maiden name?"

—RICHARD L. HORTON

Tide Pools

In an area known for its natural tide pools, this man-made example is as mysterious as it is beautiful. It's believed to have been built in the 1920s for former state Sen. William E. Brown, because he had another striking structure built on the same beach—a 60-foot tower that connected his summer home to the shore. A retired naval officer bought the site in the 1940s and hosted treasure hunts for local children in and around the tower. Where is this?

    A. Hanalei Bay, Hawaii

    B. Kiawah Island, South Carolina

    C. Key West, Florida

    D. Laguna Beach, California

Answer on page 281. Photograph by Pete Ark/Getty Images

Mission Impossible

by Tim Hulse

Far underground, in Germany's deepest cave, a man lies seriously injured. Can he be saved? The challenge for rescuers is immense.

Roberto Antonini is walking in the woods near his house in the mountains above Trieste when he gets the call. It's early on a Sunday evening in June 2014 and the voice on the other end of the line belongs to Roberto Corti, the head of Italy's national cave rescue service. Antonini is the leader of the service's Friuli-Venezia Giulia region, so he knows Corti well, but there's something about Corti's tone that tells him this is serious.

Corti explains that the German rescue services are saying there's been an accident more than 1,000 meters (3,200 feet) down in a cave in the Bavarian mountains. Three men were exploring and one of them was struck on the head by a rock. One of the cavers climbed out to raise the alarm and says it's serious. The authorities in Munich are saying they may need help.

A thousand meters. That really is deep, thinks Antonini. Straightaway his mind goes back a quarter of a century to the hardest rescue he's ever been involved in. It was in the network of caves beneath Mount Canin, high in the Julian Alps between Italy and Slovenia. That was deep, too: around 1,100 meters (3,600 feet). A caver had been injured and was trapped by falling rocks. It took seven days and a team of more than 100 to get him out. One of the rescuers died, a caver whom Antonini knew well.

Antonini has been caving since he was a boy and has been with the rescue service since he was 18. He was 27 at the time of the Mount Canin rescue, and he's 51 now. In the intervening years he's done countless rescues, but nothing like Canin. Its unique challenge was its deep, vertical descents. Now this new incident sounds eerily similar.

* * *

Corti has been ringing round the heads of the different Alpine region rescue services, and Antonini's is the first number he's dialed. He knows his team has the best skills for going deep into a mountain. There's been no official invitation from the Germans, so for now they must wait. He asks Antonini to tell his men to pack their bags and be ready for the call.

The next day, more detail emerges about the cave. Its name is Riesending-Schachthöhle. It was discovered in 1996 and is Germany's deepest cave, known as "the Everest of the deep."

The mouth is a deceptively small fissure on an isolated mountaintop 2,000 meters (1.2 miles) up in the Bavarian Alps, close to the border with Austria. Its network of tunnels and shafts stretches below for more than 19 kilometers (almost 12 miles), starting with big vertical drops to about 900 meters (3,000 feet), then branching out horizontally. Somewhere around 3 kilometers (1.9 miles) along this horizontal passage lies the injured man, Johann Westhauser.

Westhauser, a 52-year-old physicist and experienced caver, was one of the first to explore the Riesending network. At the time of his injury, he was carrying out a further exploration of the system with two colleagues.

The network of tunnels and shafts stretches for almost 12 miles, and somewhere there lies the injured man.

Antonini and Corti are aware of the huge challenges Westhauser's rescue will involve: a dangerous cave system with confined spaces and falling rocks—and a huge amount of ground to cover just to get a stretcher to the injured man. But how much ground exactly? It's unclear. There's still a lot of uncertainty. They hear there's a doctor on the scene who's communicating from the cave. Or is there? They hear that Westhauser is well enough to walk. Can that possibly be true? The flow of information is chaotic.

On Monday evening the call finally comes. Although there's been no formal permission from the Interior Ministry for the Italians to be involved, around 16 of them, including Corti and Antonini, get in their rescue vans and head for Berchtesgaden, the closest town to the cave.

Like the other rescuers, Corti and Antonini have left their day jobs behind to take part. The 52-year-old Corti works in logistics for a chemicals company, while Antonini has a shop that sells mountaineering gear.

When the Italians arrive, they're given a place to bed down in a local military barracks, and the following morning, after just three hours' sleep, they head for the rescue headquarters, which has been set up in a local fire station. They're raring to go, but they're told to wait. For now a Swiss team has been put in charge of the rescue effort.

Later in the day, the Italians are strengthened by the arrival of Rino Bregani, a specialist doctor. The 50-year-old Bregani works in the emergency ward of a Milan hospital and has been a volunteer with the Italian cave rescue service for 25 years. He was on holiday at the seaside with his children when he got a call asking if he was willing to help. So he drove his kids home, left them with his wife and headed straight to the mountains.

Swiss cavers have apparently reached the injured man, and a German doctor has made an attempt to go down into the cave but couldn't get beyond 400 meters (1,300 feet) deep. And now a second Swiss team has been sent in, together with an Austrian doctor.

Bregani's initial thoughts are that Westhauser has no chance of survival. Surely it will be impossible to get him out with that sort of injury? They're talking about a serious brain trauma, coma, seizures ... and he's already been down there for three days.

That night a message comes: The Swiss are stuck at 700 meters (2,300 feet) down. It's finally time for the Italians to go in.

*　*　*

At 5 a.m. on Wednesday a helicopter takes off from the barracks carrying a team of seven Italian rescuers to the mouth of the Riesending cave.

Rescuers en route: (from left to right) Bregani, Antonini and Göksu at 700 meters (2,300 feet)

Antonini is leading them, and Bregani is also on board.

Antonini is glad that he's finally on his way. But he's also on his mettle. He knows that it will require all his skill and experience to get down to where Westhauser is lying injured. It may take as long as 12 hours to reach him.

Bregani is scared. The Germans have told them it's a very, very difficult cave. They asked him if he was sure he could make it. He'd said sure, no problem. But really he's worried. He's not sure he can get down to that depth and still be useful. But there's no one else. The Austrian doctor has stopped at 700 meters and can't continue. He tells himself that maybe he's one of the few doctors who can do it.

The Italians skillfully negotiate the opening descents, and three hours after entering the cave, they reach the Swiss rescuers at 700 meters. Antonini can see that they're cold and exhausted and in no state to continue, so he sends them back to the top. But he asks the Austrian doctor, Martin Göksu, if he will continue down with them.

Göksu needs some persuading. Antonini tells Göksu it will be helpful to have a second doctor with them and that they'll carry all his supplies. He agrees to go with them.

Once they reach the horizontal section of the cave, the Italians discover it's similar to other systems they've explored, especially the caves below Mount Canin. But that's not to underestimate the difficulty. There are narrow sections they have to crawl through and giant rocks to clamber over—this saps energy, and there's the ever-present danger of slipping off the top.

Dangerous as they are, these barely explored depths are also undeniably beautiful. Giant stalagmites and stalactites, cascading underground waterfalls, giant, cathedral-like caverns … Bregani is particularly struck by some sections of gleaming white marble.

Back at HQ, Corti is waiting for news of his team. Earlier he had a call telling him they'd reached the Austrian doctor in just three hours. That seemed very quick—was there some kind of error in the transmission of the message? But now, four hours later, he receives another message, saying they've reached Westhauser. They've done it in just seven hours—five hours less than they projected.

*　　*　　*

When Antonini's team reaches Westhauser, they are greeted by the three Swiss cavers who were first on the scene. Westhauser is lying unconscious in a large chamber about 20 meters (66 feet) across. Above is a large chimney where he'd been climbing when the accident happened. His face is bloodied, but it's unclear exactly how he was injured. There's no scratch on his helmet as evidence of a falling rock. Could he have been hit by a large chunk of mud dislodged by one of his colleagues climbing above him?

Westhauser is covered in sleeping bags and foil to try to keep him warm. Inside the cave, the temperature is about 3 degrees Celsius (37.4 degrees Fahrenheit), with almost 100% humidity. They can't tell Bregani much about Westhauser's condition but they say he's been slipping further into unconsciousness, and had been having regular seizures.

Bregani is scared. He's not sure he can get to that depth and still be useful. But there's no one else.

Bregani touches Westhauser's shoulder and manages to bring him round. He asks him questions, which Göksu translates into German. Westhauser responds, but it's clear he doesn't know where he is or what has happened to him. Bregani asks him how he is. "I'm fine. How are you?" he replies. He doesn't ask who the Italians are or why they're here.

Nonetheless, Bregani is encouraged; he expected to find Westhauser in a worse condition. The fact that he's still speaking after three days is a good sign. *OK*, Bregani tells himself, *we're here and we'll try to do our best. We have medication and fluids, and strong cavers from Italy. Let's make a start.*

Westhauser is severely dehydrated, so Bregani's first job is to attach an IV line to get fluid into him. Then he can undertake a physical examination.

He finds that Westhauser is suffering partial paralysis in his left arm, signs of facial fractures and two black eyes (so-called "panda eyes"). The pupils of his eyes are unequal sizes, which can be a sign of increased pressure inside the skull. This could mean he has a skull fracture or brain hemorrhage. He gives Westhauser antibiotics and medication to prevent seizures.

Both Bregani and Antonini know that they have to act quickly. They need a stretcher, as clearly Westhauser is in no fit state to walk, and they need to get more people down into the cave to help get Westhauser out.

The only way to communicate with the surface is by using a radio transmission system that can send short text messages over a very low frequency. But it isn't working well at this depth. When they send a message, it can take 10 minutes before they get a response, and usually it is a request for them to repeat the message.

After a few hours, the Swiss team decides to go back up. They've already been in the cave for a few days. They tell Antonini that he's in charge now, and that once they get back to the surface, they'll send more people down.

The Italians must sit and wait.

Bregani busies himself with monitoring Westhauser's vital signs on a regular basis. The rest of the time, the team rest and try unsuccessfully to speak with the outside world, to find out what's happening. They wait and wait. And as the hours pass, they become more and more worried.

Eventually Antonini decides to go back to the surface. He thinks maybe the authorities have decided not to send down any more men, and he wants to try to convince them; his experience at Canin has taught him that for an operation like this to succeed you need to have as many rescuers on the scene as possible. It takes him seven hours to get back up to the mouth of the cave—and on the way he's relieved to meet other men coming down.

It's Thursday afternoon when Antonini exits the cave and he heads straight to rescue HQ. He tells them far more men are needed. He provides medical feedback on Westhauser and requests from the two doctors at the scene for medicine, and he asks for a stretcher to be taken down.

He has some video of Westhauser, so everyone can see exactly what the situation is. Antonini and Corti ask for a larger team to be brought in from Italy. As it stands, there are simply not enough people to bring up a seriously injured man from such a depth. As night falls, a Swiss team enters the cave with a stretcher.

＊   ＊   ＊

It's 5:38 p.m. the following day when the stretcher, now containing Westhauser, begins its ascent from the cave. Enough Italian, Swiss and Austrian cavers have arrived in the underground chamber to begin the evacuation, and Bregani, as the doctor on site, is in charge.

He's feeling more positive, because Westhauser's condition has been improving; the medication and food seem to be helping him. His body is strapped tightly into the stretcher, with Styrofoam added as insulation. His head and neck are in a brace, and a Perspex visor covers his face.

At the start, the 100-kilogram (220-pound) stretcher needs to be hauled up a couple of tricky shafts of 70 and 30 meters (230 and 98 feet). They're full of mud and moving stones, and it's perilous. But once this section is completed, progress is quicker.

Around 10 to 15 rescuers surround the stretcher as they move it forward. Ahead of them, another five or 10 prepare the way. Sometimes it's possible to carry the stretcher by hand; at other times it must be slowly eased through narrow crevices or suspended by ropes as it's inched forward.

There are passages that cavers call "meanders"—deep, narrow crevices carved into the stone by water over the millennia, often bottomless. In order to pass through them, the rescuers use a series of pulleys, using their bodies as counterweights, to hold the stretcher and slowly move it forward along the vertical wall of the meander. It's slow, painstaking work. Each pulley needs to be secured into the rock, meaning

Rescue workers bring Westhauser to the surface on a stretcher.

three holes have to be drilled to anchor each one. A single pulley can take half an hour to fix in place.

There's no concept of night and day down here, so the operation continues unceasingly, and the stretcher stops only occasionally to allow Westhauser's vital signs to be checked and medication to be administered. There's no time for sleep. If a rescuer is too tired to continue, he is replaced by someone else. A series of five bivouacs have been set up through the cave system to allow the rescuers to grab vital rest on their journey out.

They reach the foot of the vertical ascent— above them stretches a height equivalent to three Eiffel towers.

Soon it's time for Bregani himself to be replaced. He hands over to a German doctor and heads for the surface with Göksu. By the time Bregani reaches the surface, he's spent a total of 87 hours below ground. His part in the rescue is over.

It's now a truly multinational operation. More and more rescuers have been arriving, and Italian, German, Swiss and Austrian cavers are working together. Shortly, they'll be joined by a team from Croatia, who will play a decisive role of their own.

*   *   *

Dinko Novosel, the co-founder of the caving section of Croatia's mountain rescue service, was at a family barbecue when he heard about the accident, and he's been following the progress of the rescue operation from his home in Karlovac. He's got a team of 20 rescuers ready to go, but there's a lot of red tape to take care of before they'll be allowed to work in Germany.

As the days have gone by, he's become convinced that his team won't be needed. The Italians are doing a good job. In his opinion they're first-rate cave rescuers. Tough people.

And it's true that the rescue is progressing well, as the multinational team moves Westhauser ever forward. By Sunday evening, two days after they first began transporting the stretcher out of the cave, they have reached the foot of the vertical ascent, and above them stretches a height equivalent to three Eiffel Towers. Up at ground level, a cable communication system has been installed and a shipping container has been placed at the mouth of the cave.

Despite occasionally stormy weather, the six helicopters have continued to make dozens of daily flights ferrying rescuers and materials from the barracks. It's the only means of getting to the cave, although dozens of soldiers and a team of mules were put on standby when the weather was particularly bad.

So convinced is the 41-year-old Novosel that he won't be needed that he's just set off on holiday with his wife and small son. Then, 10 minutes down the road, he gets a call asking him to come to Bavaria. He turns the car around, drops his family back home, picks up his gear and heads off.

Novosel, a veterinarian pathologist in his everyday life, arrives in Berchtesgaden on Sunday evening; the following afternoon he's joined by a team of 36 Croatian rescuers. They're still not really expecting to be involved, but they're prepared for any task.

Like the Italians, they're experts when it comes to deep caves, and they're highly skilled in working on long vertical shafts. They're told they're just there as backup. Ten of the team are taken by helicopter to a mountain hut near the mouth of the cave, and the rest stay in the barracks on standby.

On Tuesday evening, they finally get the call. The stretcher has reached a particularly difficult section 400 meters (1,300 feet) from the surface, and the rescue has stalled. The team that's with it is exhausted—some of them have been in the cave for more than 50 hours. The 10 Croatians stationed in the mountain hut head straight to the cave entrance, while 10 more are airlifted up. Novosel remains at HQ, coordinating with the other teams.

* * *

The problem the Croatians face is a pair of extremely narrow "meanders," one of 400 meters (1,300 feet) and the other of 200 meters (650 feet), at a horizontal section of the ascent, sloping slightly uphill. They are dressed in caving gear—waterproof caving suits, rubber boots, helmets with powerful LED lamps on the front—and are carrying the kind of equipment more normally associated with mountaineers: ropes, harnesses and carabiners.

Working in the narrow confines, they use the pulley and counterweight system to inch the stretcher along. It's painfully slow work, yet they're

Westhauser is carried to a helicopter to be taken to a hospital.

making progress. But here's the real problem: At one point, the meander is too narrow for the stretcher to pass.

One option is to wait a day or two while the crevice is blasted to make it wider. The other option is to raise Westhauser into a vertical position. This is risky. It will mean a change in his blood pressure and could lead to complications. But his condition has been improving and he's conscious and talking, so the doctor makes the decision to raise him to a vertical position. It pays off, and they're able to continue.

After 30 hours, the Croatians have succeeded in negotiating the most difficult part of the ascent and they hand over to another team. The final 300 meters (980 feet) will be undertaken by a joint team of German and Austrian cavers. And at 11:44 a.m. on Thursday, Westhauser is raised from the mouth of the cave, more than 11 days after he was injured.

Dozens of cavers are at the scene. They form a guard of honor and applaud as the stretcher is carried by a team of 10 men, two from each of the countries who have collaborated to bring it up safely. They take it to a waiting helicopter to whisk Westhauser to a hospital.

More than 200 cavers have taken part in the operation underground, with more than 700 people helping above ground. Westhauser will spend six days in intensive care before being transferred to a general ward.

Four months later, delegates at the annual meeting of the European Cave Rescue Association in Trieste welcome a surprise guest: Johann Westhauser. He has come to express his thanks in person to his rescuers. Conti, Antonini and Novosel are all there. Westhauser is happy and laughing. He shakes the hand of every person in the room.

Originally published in the January 2017 *Reader's Digest* international editions.

"I Turned In My Son"

by Charles Hurt

Sometimes an FBI agent's work takes him too close to home

Retired FBI agent John Cook sat expectantly in the visitor's room at the state penitentiary in Jackson, Georgia, one day last summer. Waiting here was a routine he'd grown used to in the past two and a half years. A door opened and even now, after many visits, Cook was brought up short. Standing there was a younger version of himself.

"Hi, Dad."

The two men sat across from each other and all Cook could wonder—all it seemed that he ever pondered these days—was how fate had led them both there.

It was a crime that shocked Monroe County, Georgia. College students Michele Cartagena, 19, and Grant Hendrickson, 22, had driven to Lake Juliette, a park frequented by picnickers by day and young lovers by moonlight. Shortly after midnight another car pulled in behind them. The driver leveled an AR-15 assault rifle and fired into the couple's Honda Civic. In the numbed silence after the barrage, the killer walked to the car and fired five more shots from a handgun. Then he dragged Cartagena from the passenger seat, spat on her body and drove away.

The evidence left for the Monroe County sheriff and Georgia Bureau of Investigation (GBI) was difficult to trace: two brutalized bodies,

139

19 bullet casings from two different guns and a single speck of saliva from the unknown killer.

* * *

Like everyone in the area, John Cook, a 27-year veteran of the FBI, followed the Lake Juliette case in the news. As the father of four children, he couldn't fathom the despair of losing a child in such a violent manner.

And he was sickened that such a brutal crime had come to this peaceful corner of rural Georgia.

He recalled mornings when his kids were young that he'd jovially tell them, "I'm off to make the streets safe for little children, pretty women and old dogs." But for all the hard work he'd done, violence had still touched the community.

So while 22 state and local investigators were working on the murders, Cook, a relief supervisor in the Macon FBI office, directed his agents to assist local law enforcement in cracking the case. But superior manpower could not replace solid evidence. With leads that were seemingly going nowhere, the team of 22 dwindled to two, and by fall 1996 the killer's trail had grown cold.

* * *

On the evening of Dec. 4, 1996, John Cook picked up the phone at home. It was Randy Upton, one of the agents with the GBI who was still on the Lake Juliette case. He'd recently spoken to Cook's son Andy about those murders and had some follow-up questions. But he was having difficulty getting hold of him. Cook promised he'd get in touch with his son.

Cook gripped the phone. He could only hope Andy was a witness, nothing more.

Andy, 22, bad been born on the Fourth of July, 1974. The youngest of four children, he was a shy, solitary child most of the time. Yet on some level, John and Andy connected: The boy chose to live with his father after his parents divorced.

Cook could recall the moment when his son emerged from his shell. Andy was 12 and on a camping trip with a church group. In the outdoors, fishing and hunting, the boy was suddenly in his element. Since that time, outdoor activities had kept father and son connected.

It was around 11 p.m. when Andy returned his father's pages. "The GBI is looking for you concerning the Lake Juliette homicide. Do you know anything about it?" Cook asked his son.

Andy had once owned an AR-15 rifle, the type used to kill the two students. Upton had asked about it, and Andy had told the agent that he'd pawned the weapon and didn't know anything more about it.

But to Cook it sounded as if his son knew something.

"Daddy, I can't tell you," Andy told his father. "You're one of them; you're a cop."

"Well, Andy," Cook countered, "I'm your father first." He felt the familiar gut instinct that took hold during interrogations. He pressed further, starting with the basics. Did Andy know something about the murders?

"Yes," Andy said.

"Were you there?"

Again, Andy answered, "Yes." Cook gripped the phone. He could only hope that Andy was a witness, nothing more. He needed to ask the last, crucial question.

"Did you shoot them?" The silence on the other end of the telephone stretched for a long, tense moment.

"Yes," came Andy's reply, and his father's world spun out of focus. His own son had committed a merciless act. For the rest of the night, Cook sat alone in his living room, wondering how Andy's life—his own life—had taken such a horrendous turn.

He'd lived by the FBI's motto: "Fidelity, Bravery, Integrity." Now these same words gave him no options. As a man of the law, he knew what he had to do—yet as a father it was something he dreaded. He pondered how he had failed his son and the two victims. Later that morning he visited his minister, but answers to his questions, relief from his doubts did not come.

It seemed there was only one action left that would unburden him. Cook went to the sheriff and recounted his son's confession. As it turned out, Andy had been arrested that morning on illegal hunting charges. Ending a whirlwind 24 hours, GBI agent Upton had linked the young man

John and Andrew Cook

to the Lake Juliette murders, but not closely enough to make an arrest.

"Can I talk to him?" Cook asked. The sheriff escorted Andy into an office, then left the two men alone. "Andy, we have to do the right thing," Cook said. "What really happened?"

"It wasn't me, Daddy. It wasn't me." Andy paused, trembling. "Somebody or someone or something just took over me."

Later that day Andy was charged with the murders of Michele Cartagena and Grant Hendrickson. He never discussed the crime again. A conviction would rest on the ballistics and DNA tests. But the most direct and devastating evidence, John Cook realized, was in his possession: his son's own words.

Cook recalled the first time he'd heard about the murders, how he could not comprehend the pain a parent felt on losing a child. He was feeling that pain now.

* * *

It would be more than a year before Andy's trial began, but it moved quickly once it started. On March 19, 1998, John Cook sat in the court-room listening as the prosecution methodically built a case against his son. Cook had fought this moment for weeks, had tried to bargain for a plea agreement for Andy: life without the possibility of parole, not death. But there was no deal to be made. Finally District Attorney Tommy Floyd called his final witness: John Cook. All eyes were on him as he approached the wood-paneled witness box. His gait was that of a condemned man's final walk, and in many ways it was. Given the circumstances of the murders—two lives taken in one brutal act—Andy was facing the death penalty.

Cook raised his right hand as he had so many times before as an FBI agent. "Do you solemnly swear the evidence and testimony that you are about to give ... shall be the truth, the whole truth and nothing but the truth, so help you God?"

Without pausing he replied, "I do."

Floyd began his questioning. "How do you know the defendant?" Cook glanced over at the defense table, where Andy was sitting, staring down.

"He is my son," Cook said, his hands shifting nervously. When asked about his talk with Andy in the sheriff's office, Cook held the attention of the courtroom as he recounted Andy's confessions to killing Michele Cartagena and Grant Hendrickson.

He glanced at the jury listening to his words, the words of a man who had tried to teach his son right from wrong, who had talked of sparing the world of violence.

In a soft but firm voice, Cook answered the questions put to him. In less than an hour he was done. As he exited the courtroom, he summoned enough courage to look into the eyes of the Cartagena and Hendrickson families and mouth the words, "I'm sorry."

The jury went into deliberations, but not for long. They needed little more than an hour to find Andy Cook guilty of four counts of first degree murder.

After hearing his son's verdict—one he felt largely responsible for—John Cook returned home to a ringing phone. He glanced at the Caller ID box and saw that it was coming from the Monroe County jail. He answered it.

"Daddy, are you OK?" The voice was Andy's, the voice he'd known for years as his hunting and fishing partner, as his baby boy. It was warm and filled with concern.

"It wasn't me, Daddy." Andy paused. "Somebody or something just took over me."

"Andy, I'm so sorry that I've had to do that," Cook replied.

"Don't worry, Daddy," Andy said. "It'll be OK. I love you."

The jury had seen no redeeming value in his child, and had found him to be a merciless killer. But that phone call gave Cook one moment to draw on when he returned to court during the sentencing phase to plead for his son's life.

"I would ask, since you are the servants of Lady Justice, that you close your eyes for a moment and put yourself in the shoes of the Hendricksons and the Cartagenas," Cook told the jury. "Most of you probably are parents, and you can taste our bitterness for them. Then I want you to close your eyes and think where I am today. We never think our children are going to do anything despicable."

"[Andy] lives in disgrace and dishonor, in shame and blame, and I live there, too, and the rest of his family lives there also." Cook said Andy's crime was "done with a malignant heart, but I don't believe his heart is totally malignant. I believe there is a kernel of value somewhere in him ..."

But the jury did not see it John Cook's way. They sentenced Andrew Cook to the electric chair.

Originally published in the December 2000 issue of *Reader's Digest* magazine.

Andrew Cook was executed by lethal injection on Feb. 21, 2013. As he was strapped to the gurney before his execution, he apologized to the families of his victims and to his own family. John Cook is retired from the FBI.

Failing in his life's mission will likely haunt Cook forever. "Of all the people in the world I should have been able to protect, I should have been able to protect my own son from evil," he says. "But I didn't do that. I was busy looking out the front door for evil, and it somehow came in the back door and consumed my son."

IN FRONT OF OUR EYES

My wife and I like to take walks down the quiet roads in our small town. One day, we noticed a key and hung it on a fence where a deflated balloon had settled. We hoped that eventually someone would spot their missing key. A week later, we realized our shed key was missing. We searched and searched, but it was nowhere. Then a lightbulb went on. Luckily the remnants of that colorful balloon helped us spot it. We took it home for a test. Sure enough, we had lost and found our own key!

—Ron Edgington, *Snowflake, AZ*

LIFESAVING ANNOYANCE

While sitting in the waiting room to donate blood, another patient was called out of turn. As I sat there irritated, I overheard a young couple. The wife's iron count was too low to donate for her baby who was having surgery the next day. I got up and went over to the mom. I said, "I'll donate for your baby." I knew I could as I have type O-negative blood. If I had been called in turn I would have never heard the story. My irritation turned to joy for this family.

—Linda Tipon, *San Diego, CA*

The Boxer and the Boys

by Meera Jagannathan

A Pittsburgh cop saves two brothers from abuse

Jack Mook, a Gulf War veteran and Pittsburgh police detective, met Josh and Jessee Lyle at Steel City Boxing Association, a nonprofit gym that pairs coaching mentors with inner-city kids, in April 2007. As he coached the brothers, Jack, 45, learned some disturbing details about their traumatic home life. Their parents were drug addicts, and the family lived in an area where drug trafficking, prostitution and violence were everyday realities.

The gym became a refuge for Josh and Jessee. Josh, in particular, worked out tirelessly nearly every day. For five years, "it was an escape from home," Josh says.

By late summer 2012, though, the boys had stopped going to the gym. Jack went to track them down and found Josh, then 13, after school about a week before Christmas.

He looked terrible, with bags under his eyes and sunken cheeks. His hair was missing in patches, and he had a rash on his neck. Josh told Jack that social services had removed the boys from their neglectful parents and placed them in foster care with an aunt and uncle.

"The best thing I've ever done," says Jack Mook, of adopting Josh, pictured, and Jessee.

147

But the new house was infested with rats, roaches and fleas, Josh said, and their guardians peddled drugs, and hit and screamed at the boys. Suspicious of their nephews' association with a police officer, their guardians kept them away from the gym. "I wanted to sleep my life away," Josh says.

Jack went home thinking, *I've got a house to myself. What am I doing?*

He contacted a caseworker from the Office of Children, Youth and Families about taking over custody of the boys, but she claimed that by the agency's standards, they were "fine."

Two weeks later, the police arrested the boys' uncle for heroin possession. Jack alerted a high-ranking official in the Pittsburgh court system, who put him in touch with the boys' family-court lawyer. After conducting the required background checks on Jack, the court placed Josh and Jessee in foster care with him on Feb. 5, 2013. "That was the most relieved I've ever felt," Josh says.

Under Jack's care, Jessee, now 11, became a straight-A student, and Josh aspires to attend a military academy and someday join the special forces. Both were 2014 champions in their respective weight classes in the Pennsylvania Western District Golden Gloves, a prestigious national boxing tournament, probably aided by their daily meals of meat and vegetables.

"Josh's record was 1-8 before … now it's 7-2," says Jack. "I think I just put some food in the boy."

With the boys thriving, Jack officially adopted them in September 2014. On the car ride to the courthouse, Josh was afraid his aunt and uncle would interrupt the proceedings and prevent the adoption from going through. But when the judge declared Jack the boys' adoptive father, "the biggest smile" spread across Josh's face. "I knew this was permanent and [that] my brother and I will live a happy life," Josh says.

Jack finds fatherhood rewarding and humbling. "They're my best friends," he says. "There's no way I'm going to let anyone harm them again."

Originally published in the June 2015 issue of *Reader's Digest* magazine.

The Woman Who Wrestled a Cougar

by Mary Murray

When a wild animal attacks the children under her care, a woman musters all her strength and courage to protect them

Nudged awake by the morning sun, the young cougar opened its jaws in a teeth-baring yawn and stretched its muscular forelegs. Then it started down the mountainside, crossed a narrow highway and loped toward the wide, rushing river. For days, the cougar had been edging closer to the small village of Lillooet on the Fraser River, at the edge of the mountains of southern British Columbia, Canada. Now, after drinking the river's cold water, the cougar bedded down again in the nest of tall grass.

On July 3, 1991, the five children in Larrane Leech's day-care group were outdoors early, painting bright tempera landscapes under the penetrating sun. By 10 a.m., it was time to find shade, so Larrane decided they would walk down to the river. "We're going to pick berries now," she announced.

At 44 years old, she had made one of her dreams come true when she turned her home into a day-care center. It had taken hard work and determination to get her certification. After completing her coursework in early childhood education, she had worked as a volunteer in a day-care center while holding down a job at the local lumber mill and raising three teen sons alone.

So far, the center was operating smoothly. But it was too soon to tell whether the families she worked for would be happy with it. And she worried about being able to care for enough children to make the business pay off.

Larrane had known all five children in her care since they were infants. Three were siblings: playful Mikey, age 2; Jessica, 5, the exuberant leader; and 3½-year-old Alleshia Allen, the tough little athlete. Four-year-old Natani Leech, who had long hair, was actually their aunt, and Larrane in turn was her aunt. Only the bubbly toddler Lisa O'Laney, a few months shy of 2, was unrelated to them. All were Indigenous people living near Lillooet, more than 160 kilometers (99 miles) northeast of Vancouver.

The children had fallen easily into Larrane's daily routine. A nature lover, she insisted they spend as much time as possible outdoors. Everyone loved circle time, when they passed around a black-and-white eagle feather; the child who held it could then talk about whatever they wanted.

After clearing away the painting supplies and handing each child an empty jar, Larrane called for Pal, her 1-year-old part-German shepherd. Giggling with anticipation, Jessica and Natani paired off in front. Larrane linked Mikey's hand with Alleshia's, took little Lisa's in her own and said, "Let's go."

Larrane's house stood on a wooded slope not far up from the mighty Fraser River. The group made its way over the dusty gravel road and then onto a dirt trail through the trees. The two oldest girls broke into a run through the tall brown grass at the trail's edge, Natani's waist-length hair swaying back and forth. Larrane and the little ones hurried to keep up.

Stopping the children at the first berry bush, Larrane pointed to the long branches bearing clusters of plump, sweet navy-blue fruit. "Look, the berries are all over," she said. She helped Lisa find some. Mikey watched, then tentatively bit into a berry. "Mmm, good," he said, and got busy plucking more.

* * *

The cougar cocked an ear toward the birdlike chatter and reflexively sniffed the air. Cougars rarely attack people or show themselves, but as towns expanded into mountainous countryside, there had been more and more sightings, especially in southern British Columbia. At the time, the province was home to some 3,000 of them.

The cougar was instinctively versed in hunting strategies: step silently and downwind through the brush to avoid being heard, scented or seen; choose the weakest prey and attack from behind, clamping powerful jaws on the vital nerves and blood vessels of the prey's neck.

*　*　*

Larrane and the children moved slowly from bush to bush. Pal stopped frequently in the shade, panting. In 20 minutes, the children filled their jars and were almost to the river. Here, the ground fell steeply to a cool, shady strip of sand about 4 meters (13 feet) wide.

"OK," Larrane commanded after the group clambered down to the sandbank, "let's get in our circle." She could not risk letting a child wander off. Suddenly Alleshia jumped up and scooted toward the trees. "Come back, Alleshia," Larrane called. Running after her, she caught up with the child and leaned over to help her back to the sandbank.

*　*　*

Now the young cougar could see the funny little creatures that had been making all the noise. Automatically, its predatory machinery kicked in. These were perfect prey: small, wiggly and oblivious to any possible attack.

151

Stepping over the thick carpet of pine needles, the cat slunk toward the children, never so much as rustling a leaf or snapping a twig. Then it did something remarkable, something only a young, inexperienced cat would do. It walked onto the bank and merely nudged one of the children, the young boy, Mikey, backward onto the sand. The rules of hunting required that the cougar grab the boy's head in its mouth and carry him away. But the young cat paused, and to remove any hair before attacking and feeding, it began to lick the boy's smooth skin with its rough tongue.

* * *

Larrane sensed the children suddenly go quiet. She looked up to see the back end of a cat the size of Pal standing over Mikey. The cat's head was down, out of sight behind its peaked shoulder blades, and its plumped, black-tipped tail swiped back and forth like a whip.

Larrane was momentarily frozen by the sight. Now Natani was giggling nervously. "Stop licking Mikey's face," she said playfully, as though talking to a house cat.

Larrane couldn't tell whether Mikey had been bitten; he was silent and hidden beneath the beast. Her mind racing wildly, she sprang impulsively toward the cougar. Blindly intending to grab its tail, she shifted aim at the last minute and seized the cat by the scruff of the neck. Tugging once, she shook it from side to side.

Instantly, the cougar unsheathed its claws and wheeled toward Larrane, swiping Mikey's face and Lisa's, too. Growling and hissing, it stretched up high and brought its paws down upon the head of the 5-foot-1-inch woman. As she stumbled backward, one paw slipped onto her right shoulder, the claws grazing her ear.

Larrane grabbed the big cat by the scruff of its neck and shook it from side to side.

This animal was capable of killing her. Although still in its youth, it had all the teeth and muscle a cougar needs to pull down a victim three times its size.

Aware now of the danger, four of the children shrieked and ran behind Larrane. Mikey lay still on the ground.

"Stay behind me," Larrane screamed as she faced the beast. Acting before she could think, she grabbed the animal's forelegs and pulled them off her. The cougar's thrashing forced her back into a crouch. Her soft sandals shifted and slipped in the sand, making it difficult to keep a secure stance. Summoning all her strength, Larrane forced herself back upright, still grasping the cat's thick legs. Then she thrust her arms forward and locked them straight out in front of her. At the same time, she used her thumbs to push the animal's paws inward to protect herself from being cut.

> *"Just go away and leave us alone!" Larrane yelled into the animal's face.*

Locked in a deadly dance with the cougar, Larrane felt as though she were watching herself in slow motion. She stared at the animal's pink tongue and long ivory fangs. Stepping back and forth on its hind legs, the cat let out a menacing growl as it tried to tug its paws with their sharp claws away from her.

"Pal, do something!" Larrane yelled at the dog cowering on the sand not 3 meters (10 feet) away. She felt the muscles in her arms, legs and back weakening. *What in the world am I going to do?* she thought. *No one will ever find us here, and if the cat gets away from me, he'll surely kill the children.* "Just go away and leave us alone!" she yelled into the animal's face. "Leave us alone, and we'll leave you alone."

The cougar was now trying a new tactic to break Larrane's grip. It began thrashing its upper body from side to side, and Larrane could sense its imminent escape. Again acting without any conscious plan, she arched her back to gather momentum, then shoved forward with all her might, thrusting the cat directly at the dog and shouting, "Pal, do something!"

The cougar fell backward but rolled instantly onto its feet and darted past Pal through the brush farther along the sandbank.

Without knowing it, Larrane had responded perfectly. She had distracted the cougar from Mikey only a fraction of a second before it had a chance to crush the boy's skull in its mighty jaws. Then her aggressive movements and loud shouting probably scared the animal. Cougar experts say the cats often lose their appetite for killing when angrily confronted.

Watching the cat retreat, Pal gave chase, barking madly. In one bound, the cougar leaped halfway up a pine tree, then climbed to the top, wrapped

Larrane Leech on the day she received the Star of Courage award

its paws around a branch and hung there, looking down at the dog.

Larrane rushed to Mikey, who lay quietly on the sand. The left side of his face and neck was bathed in blood. But he was breathing, and his eyes were open so wide they seemed to bulge from his face.

He's alive, Larrane thought, gasping in relief. But he was eerily still. *He must be in shock.* She pulled him into her arms.

Then her eyes fell on Lisa, wailing at her side. The girl's face was also covered with blood.

Shifting Mikey to her right side and scooping Lisa up in her left arm, Larrane called to the other children. "We have to run home now." She saw their terror as they looked at her. She touched her face and felt blood dripping. *It's scaring them just to look at me*, she realized. "Let's go," she ordered, "as fast as we can!"

They scrambled up the hill, Lisa still crying, Mikey remaining silent. Larrane soon found the two children too heavy to carry and eased Mikey down. He suddenly jolted from his stupor. "Owie, owie, owie!" he screamed, tears coursing down his face.

Larrane pulled him along toward the house. Pal lingered behind, watching the cougar, before finally following the others. "Everything will be all right," Larrane called out to the kids. But deep down, she was not so certain. The cougar could be anywhere. She considered what it had already done— to Lisa, to Mikey and to the dream she had worked so long to realize. Would any parents trust her with their children after this?

In five minutes, they were all inside the front door. Suddenly Larrane was aware of her own pain. Her thighs were bruised, and the scratches on her arm, forehead and ear burned. Her hands shook as she telephoned the hospital and the parents of Lisa and Mikey.

At the Lillooet Hospital, Mikey needed 40 stitches to close the lacerations on his chin and neck, but all his wounds were shallow. Lisa had been lucky too. The cat had clawed within an inch of her right eye. The doctors used 20 stitches to repair the cuts on her face and gave both children tetanus shots.

Larrane's scratch needed only to be cleaned and left to heal. But the muscles in her arms, back and legs were so sore that she had difficulty walking.

The next morning she felt profound relief when she opened the front door to four of her day-care children—including Mikey. Only Lisa did not return.

For several days, as they sat in a circle passing the eagle feather, the children remained quiet. The pictures they painted at art time were showered with splatters of red.

Finally, a week later, Mikey took the eagle feather in his hand and said, "I had a dream last night."

"And what did you see in your dream?" Larrane asked gently.

"I saw an eagle. And he was sitting on my bed. Then he flew over me."

Larrane smiled. In Lillooet folklore, the eagle is a sign of strength, sent by ancestors as an assurance that the person who sees it will be kept safe. She knew the child was beginning to feel secure again.

Larrane felt secure too. She had met the greatest challenge of her life head on. Her friends and neighbors applauded her strength. And now, she felt, she could accomplish anything.

Originally published in the May 1993 issue of *Reader's Digest* magazine.

In December 1992, the Governor General of Canada awarded Larrane the Star of Courage. And the village of Lillooet gave her a commendation for "outstanding bravery."

Larrane continued running a day care out of her home for several more years. She passed away on Sept. 14, 2020, at age 73.

Swirl Pool

Why isn't the diver (below) swimming as fast as he can from this terrifying—though beautiful—swarm of fish? Because these bigeye trevallies in Mexico's Cabo Pulmo National Marine Park are looking to make love, not war. The "fish tornado," as researchers sometimes call it, is part of a courtship ritual, a sort of mass underwater hunt for the perfect mate. One reason this school is especially large is that fishing for the bigeye trevally was banned in this park in 1995. The population there increased by 463% in 10 years. "What used to be an almost lifeless place now has a complete life chain," says photographer Anuar Patjane Floriuk. "It's an example that by leaving the ocean alone, it will recover by itself."

Photograph by Anuar Patjane Floriuk

Man in the Crowd

by Joni Rodgers

*Joni Rodgers meets her match as she passes
through Montana with a traveling show*

In 1983, I was traveling with a tiny theater company doing vaudeville-type shows in community centers and bars—anywhere we could earn $25 each plus enough gas money to get to the next small town in our ramshackle yellow bus.

As we passed through Bozeman, Montana, in early February, a heavy snow slowed us down. The radio crackled warnings about black ice and poor visibility, so we opted to impose on friends who were doing a production of *Fiddler on the Roof* at Montana State University. See a show, hit a few bars, sleep on a sofa: This is as close to prudence as it gets when you're an itinerant 20-something troubadour.

After the show, well-wishers and stagehands milled behind the curtain. I hugged my coat around me, humming that "If I Were a Rich Man" riff from the show, aching for sunrise and sunset, missing my sisters. What a wonderful show that was—and is.

A heavy metal door swung open, allowing in a blast of frigid air, and clanged shut behind two men who stomped snow from their boots. One was big and bearlike in an Irish wool sweater and gaiters; the other was as tall and skinny as a chimney sweep in a peacoat.

"… but I'm just saying, it would be nice to see some serious theater,"

Still loving the journey: Joni and Gary Rodgers at their 1983 wedding (above) and today, in Spring Lakes, Texas

one of them said. "Chekhov, Ibsen, anything but this musical comedy shtick."

"Excuse me?" I huffed, hackles raised. "Anyone who doesn't think comedy is an art form certainly hasn't read much Shakespeare, have they?"

I informed them that I was a "professional shticktress" and went on to deliver a tart, pedantic lecture on the French neoclassics, the cultural impact of Punch and Judy as an *I Love Lucy* prototype, and the importance of *Fiddler on the Roof* as both artistic and oral history. The shrill diatribe left a puff of frozen breath in the air. I felt my snootiness showing like a stray bra strap as the sweep in the peacoat rolled his eyes and walked away.

The bear stood there for a moment, an easy smile in his brown eyes. Then he put his arms around me and whispered in my ear, "I love you."

I took in a deep, startled breath—winter, Irish wool, coffee and fresh-baked bread—and then pushed away with a jittery half-joke. Something like, "Watch it. I have pepper spray."

"OK," he said with a broad baritone laugh. "Come for a walk, then. It'll be nice."

I shook my head. Alarm and skepticism warred with spreading, unsteady warmth behind my collarbone. "Walking around in the freezing dark with a total stranger is not nice," I said. I tipped a glance to the well-worn gaiters. "Planning to do some cross-country skiing?"

"Riding my bike," he said, and then added without apology, "I'm between vehicles."

He held the heavy door open expectantly. I moved the pepper spray from my purse to my coat pocket and followed my heart out under the clear, cold stars.

"What are you reading?" I asked, because that question always opens doors of its own. I was in the habit of asking the nuns at the bus stop, a barber who paid me to scrub his floor once a week, elderly ladies and children at the park. To this day, I ask people who sit beside me on airplanes, baristas at Starbucks, exchange students standing in line with me. Over the years, "What are you reading?" has introduced me to many of my favorite books and favorite people.

The bear had a good answer: "*Chesapeake*. Have you read it?"

"No, but I love James Michener," I said. "When I was 12, I fell in love with *Hawaii* and vowed that if I ever had a daughter, I'd name her Jerusha after the heroine."

"Big book for a 12-year-old."

"We didn't have a TV. And I was a dork."

He laughed that broad baritone laugh again. "Literature: last refuge of the tragically uncool."

"Same could be said of bicycling in your ski gaiters."

The conversation ranged organically from books and theater to politics and our personal histories.

Having embraced the life of an artsy party girl, I was the black sheep of my conservative midwestern family, thoroughly enjoying my freedom and a steady diet of wild oats. He'd spent a dysfunctional childhood on the East Coast. A troubled path of drug and alcohol abuse had brought him to one of those legendary moments of clarity at which he made a hard right turn to an almost monkish existence in a tiny mountain cabin. He'd built an ascetic life that was solitary but substantive, baking bread at a local restaurant, splitting wood for his heating stove, staying out of trouble.

"That probably sounds pretty dull to you," he said.

"Agonizingly dull, but don't worry," I said, and then patted his arm. "Maybe someday you'll remember how to have fun."

He shrugged. "Maybe someday you'll forget."

We talked about the things people tend to avoid when they're trying to make a good impression: hopes subverted by mistakes, relationships sabotaged by shortcomings. My bus was leaving in the morning, and we would never see each other again, so there was no need to posture.

Fingers and chins numb with cold, we found refuge in a Four B's Restaurant and sat across from each other in a red vinyl booth. We had enough money between us for a short stack of buckwheat pancakes. A few morning papers were delivered to the front door, and we worked our way through the crossword puzzle, coffee cups between our hands.

The sun came up, and we emerged from Four B's to discover a warm chinook blowing in. Already the eaves were weeping, icicles thinning on trees and telephone wires. This is what Montana does in midwinter: clears off and gets bitter cold, and then suddenly it's as warm and exhilarating as Easter morning. Don't believe it for a minute, you tell yourself as the streets turn into trout streams, but the sheer pleasure of the feeling makes a fool of you. You forget your scarf and mittens on a hook behind the door. You know it's still winter, but that's just what you know; the chinook is what you believe in.

The bear held my hand inside his coat pocket as we walked in silence back to the parking lot to meet my company's bus. Before he kissed me, he asked me if I was ready. Ready for what I have no idea, but ready is how I felt. I was stricken with readiness. Humbled by it.

"I hope you have a wonderful life," I told him.

"You too," he replied before nodding stiffly and walking away.

The bus lumbered through the slush and labored over the mountains to a fading Highline town where we were booked to play a quaintly shabby old opera house. The guy at the box office immediately pegged me as a party girl who'd been up all night and invited me to go to the bar next door for a hair of the dog before the show, but I could not for the life of me remember why that used to sound like fun.

Later that evening, as I did my shtick out on the foot-lit stage, I heard the bear's distinctive baritone laughter from somewhere in the audience. After the show, he was waiting for me by the door. I didn't bother asking him how he'd gotten there. He didn't bother asking me where I wanted to go.

I can't endorse the idea of love at first sight, but maybe there are moments when God or fate or some cosmic sense of humor rolls its eyes at two stammering human hearts and says, "Oh, for crying out loud."

I married the bear a few months later in a meadow above his tiny cabin in the Bridger Mountains. We weren't exempted from any of the hard work a long marriage demands, but for better or worse, in sickness and in health, that moment of unguarded, chinook-blown folly has somehow lasted 30 years.

We laugh. We read. I do dishes; he bakes bread. Every morning, we work through the daily crossword puzzle. Our daughter, Jerusha, and son, Malachi Blackstone (named after his great-grandfather and an island in Chesapeake Bay), tell us we are agonizingly dull.

We listen to their 20-something diatribes and smile.

Originally published in the June 2013 issue of *Reader's Digest* magazine.

Swept off Mount McKinley!

by Peter Michelmore

A rogue wind hurled the tent and the three men in it off the mountain ledge toward a glacier 1,500 feet below

Winds gusted to gale force, creating a near whiteout on the upper reaches of the highest mountain in North America. Guide Dave Staeheli, 35, and his party of eight climbers bivouacked for the night of May 25, 1989. They made camp at 16,440 feet on a small icy shelf. The next day they would press on in their attempt to reach the 20,320-foot summit.

The men set their three dome-shaped nylon tents about a foot into the shelf's surface, then built a 2-foot wall around each with chunks of snow. Staeheli, who had climbed Mount McKinley 16 times, preferred higher walls, but the ice was like concrete. He compensated with metal stakes at all guy lines and anchor flukes driven hard through the floor loops—12 to a tent. *We're bombproof,* he thought as he zipped into his sleeping bag for the night.

By morning, the storm had not abated. So all that day—and the next—the group stayed put, listening to the nylon snap in the wind.

* * *

At about 9 p.m. that Saturday John Richard, 39, a Kentucky lawyer and an ardent mountaineer, checked the anchors one last time before entering his tent. His companions, experienced climbers Howard Tuthill, 31, and Jim Johnson, 41, were reading in the long Alaskan daylight.

Richard suddenly raised his head. Coming through the whistle of the wind was a roar, louder and louder. He felt a blast of it against the tent roof, then popping sounds as wind thundered down on all sides. "We're moving!" Tuthill shouted. The tent pivoted, heeled over, then began sliding. Richard dived for the zippered door but fell short, somersaulting as the tent spun over the side of the ridge. In the same instant, Johnson, slashing at the nylon wall with a knife, was slammed onto his back.

As the tent gathered speed down the slope, men and equipment tumbling inside, Richard's hands touched snow through the gap opened by the knife. Clawing, he tried to drag his body clear. A sound of ripping nylon and he was outside, on his face, skidding downhill.

When he came to rest, deep in snow, he was alone. The tent with Tuthill and Johnson inside had rocketed off into the milky gloom toward Peters Glacier, 1,500 feet below.

Up above, in the two remaining tents, Staeheli and the others were dozing, unaware of the catastrophe. Then a cry brought Staeheli to his feet. He unzipped the tent, and John Richard, wild-eyed and shaking, stumbled inside. "They're gone," he cried hoarsely. "The tent just went!"

Staeheli peered outside, dumbstruck at the empty tent site, anchors and stakes still in place. Dressing rapidly, he dashed to the edge of the ridge and stared. Two hundred feet below, sky and ground melted together in silvery light. *They're dead*, thought Staeheli. *They trusted me, and I let them down.*

Back at his tent, Staeheli quickly put together an emergency pack—sleeping pad and bag, stove, water bottles and shovel. Then he radioed a medical-research base at 14,000 feet so medics could mobilize a rescue team. "Mayday! Mayday!" The only response was static, but he went on, "This is Staeheli at 16,400, transmitting in the blind. Two people were blown off the ridge toward Peters Glacier. Situation unknown. I'm going after them."

*   *   *

Swept off Mount McKinley!

Plunging down the main climbing path, Staeheli headed for a camp occupied by five climbers at 16,100 feet. He roused the men in one tent and used their radio to try to reach the medical base. Again, static.

The climbers offered to help. "Just keep trying the radio," said Staeheli.

He left the ridge and cut around the mountain, searching for signs of the tent's passage. The snow became softer. His crampons sank more than a foot into the crust. Underfoot, beneath the soft layer, he felt shifting, granular snow. He was on a loaded slope. His weight could set it into a murderous avalanche.

Then his eye caught a scrape mark in the snow. The tent had bounced against the slope. Down the fall line he went, heedless of the danger. Tuthill had two children, Johnson had five. "Give me a break, mountain," Staeheli begged.

About 1,200 feet below his camp, he stopped short at a brow. A few feet below, a flat ledge about 15 feet across ended in a sheer drop to the glacier. Coming closer, his heart almost flew from his body.

Under the lip, close to the mountain, were two ice-encrusted men.

"Jim! Howie!" Staeheli cried.

Jim Johnson lifted his head, saying nothing. Howard Tuthill turned slowly. "Who are you?" he murmured.

The flood of relief at seeing his friends alive drained out of Staeheli. Tuthill showed no expression. "I'm cold," he said. Both men had blood on their faces. Their hands were rigid white claws. Their languor and confusion indicated severe hypothermia in the minus-30-degree wind chill.

Gloveless and capless, Tuthill and Johnson had been exposed for at least an hour, maybe two. They were beyond shivering and therefore generating no internal heat. Soon they would sink into coma.

From his pack Staeheli yanked the foam sleeping pad and spread it as far back on the ledge as he could. He rolled Johnson onto the pad and dragged Tuthill over by his arms. Opening up his sleeping bag, he covered both men, then began hacking at the packed snow with a shovel to build a windbreak.

The sun, now a small orange ball, was setting; it was 11:15 p.m. The air temperature would drop a degree a minute for 20 minutes, and the wind chill would plunge to 60 degrees below zero.

Throwing aside the shovel, Staeheli pushed a sock and a mitten on Johnson's hands. The other mitten would not fit on Tuthill's hand, so Staeheli switched it with one of his own. He found another sock for Tuthill's left hand. He had slowed their heat loss, but to warm them he needed the stove.

Huddling under the covers with the two men, Staeheli assembled it. Presto! A flick of his lighter and an orange flame curled around the burner jets. A few seconds and the jets would hiss with hot blue flame. "C'mon," he urged.

The flame died in a skittering wind under the flap of the bag. Again and again, he flicked at the lighter. Not a spark. His wet hands had dampened the wick. Staeheli was close to panic. "Maintain yourself," he growled in rebuke.

Then he saw Johnson try to peel back his side of the sleeping bag. "Leave it on!" Staeheli yelled. "Get under there, Jim."

Johnson was approaching final-stage hypothermia, in which victims feel a warm flush and try to fling off their covers and clothes. Without heat, Staeheli knew there was no hope for these men. He piled snow on Johnson's legs to hold him in place. "I'm going for help," he said. "I'll be right back."

He heaved himself over the lip above, swung his ice ax into the slope and began the ascent to the five-man camp at 16,100.

*　　*　　*

Down at the medical camp, at 14,000 feet, Dr. Peter Hackett had caught one of Staeheli's mayday calls at 10:25 p.m. He established communication with the climbers at the 16,100-foot camp and alerted a rescue team—guides, park-service rangers, a physician. But winds were now gusting to 60 mph, and the five-hour climb up the headwall from base and along the ridge remained perilous. "We don't want anyone else to die," said Hackett. "We won't go until we hear from Dave that the men are alive."

"They're alive!" Staeheli screamed, motioning them on. The climbers took off, roped together in case of an avalanche.

Staeheli would normally take an hour to climb the 900 feet ahead. Not this night. Johnson and Tuthill didn't have that long. Leaning into the slope, ax flying and legs stomping, Staeheli doubled his pace. His breathing was rapid-fire, the cold air seared his throat. *Don't collapse*, he told himself.

Swept off Mount McKinley!

Halfway up, his arms and legs grew leaden, and he began wheezing and coughing. Still he raced on, not resting, through the Alaskan dusk. For 10 years he had climbed McKinley's slopes, but he had never been tested like this. In 15 minutes, he had made an astonishing 600 feet.

Two climbers were coming down from the 16,100-foot camp. "They're alive!" Staeheli screamed, motioning them on. "Straight down the fall line." The two climbers took off, roped together in case of an avalanche.

Up at the camp, another 300 feet, their companions had heard Staeheli's cry and quickly radioed the medical base. "OK," said Hackett, "we're on the way." It was now past midnight. When Staeheli got to the camp, two other climbers were dressed and ready to move. "They need a tent," he gasped.

The men struck one of their two tents and departed. Staeheli took cover in the other tent, coughing, shivering, unable to take another step.

The first pair down found Tuthill semiconscious, his hands frozen to the wrists. Johnson, struggling weakly under the snow pile, had snatched off his cap.

The rescuers were trying to get more covers on the men and were building the snow wall higher when the second pair arrived. It took them a nerve-racking half-hour to raise the tent. One wall was 2 feet from the cliff-fall to the glacier. Another wall backed up to a crevasse that swallowed one of the rescuers up to his armpits before he was pulled free.

After wrestling Tuthill and Johnson into the tent and sleeping bags, two of the men eased into the bags and nestled against bodies so cold that they themselves were set to shivering. Johnson protested, insisting that he had to take a shower and go to work. "The train's left," they told him. "You can sleep in."

It took two hours in the damp and cold before the men were able to get a stove operating. Finally, at daylight, Tuthill and Johnson sipped warm cider and nibbled on chocolate.

At about 6 a.m. two expert climbers from the medical group reached the 16,100-foot camp. Staeheli, distraught and exhausted, briefed them on the terrain. As they left, Dr. Mark Selland and two others arrived from the medical base and stayed with Staeheli. When the first two reached the ledge, Selland radioed, "Are they still alive?" The static hum seemed interminable before a voice crackled, "Yes, they're alive." Staeheli's eyes closed in thanks, and he let the tears roll down his checks.

Selland then descended and took over from the weary quartet that had spent the night with Tuthill and Johnson. Both were severely frost-bitten, and Johnson's back was injured. But Staeheli had made all the right moves to stop profound hypothermia, and both were warming up. Unwilling to submit them to further exposure, Selland called for an evacuation helicopter.

As the morning passed, clouds blew in to shroud the western slopes. Helicopter pilot Craig Dunn used all his fuel trying to thread through clouds to the ledge, went back for more, and kept trying.

In the early afternoon, at 15,000 feet, Dunn flew through a break in the clouds. Ahead of him, he saw people waving on the ledge. Circling, he wiggled the chopper in. The right skid touched the snow; half of the left skid stuck out over the precipice.

The men on the ledge heaved Tuthill and Johnson into the hovering chopper, and at the instant the clouds rolled back in, Dunn whirled away.

Alone at 16,100 feet, a bearded mountaineer watched the helicopter disappearing into the clouds on its way to Anchorage. *We made it*, Staecheli thought. *I made it.*

Johnson suffered six vertebral fractures, two broken ribs, a bruised kidney and frostbite. Three months later, all extremities intact, he was back at work. Tuthill's fingers blistered as hoped after repeated warm body baths. But the blood vessels and tissue failed to regenerate. On June 23, the tips of six of his fingers were amputated.

"I had two choices," says Tuthill, "feel sorry for myself or get on with life. Dave Staeheli gave me a second chance at life, and I decided I was not going to waste it on self-pity."

Staeheli had long been known among mountain men for his courage and stamina. Though he claims his actions that day were "no big deal, just doing what I had to do," fellow climbers say that Staeheli's performance was nothing less than superhuman.

Originally published in the May 1991 issue of *Reader's Digest* magazine.

Dave Staeheli retired as a climbing guide after a 2001 expedition on Mount McKinley turned deadly.

Humor Hall of Fame

A classmate was examining my driver's license. She seemed surprised when she noticed that it indicated that I was an organ donor. So much so that she asked, "Which organ did you donate?"

—@LEXADELGAY

My brother-in-law, a newly minted volunteer firefighter, was riding in the fire engine for the first time when he felt the need to offer the driver some advice. "I think you should pull over," he said. "Don't you hear the siren?" A more experienced colleague patiently explained, "That's us."

—ERNEST ECHELBARGER

Fox in the Kitchen

by Avril Johannes

A family rescues an Alaskan fox— or is it the other way around?

When my daughter, Jan, was 12, our family got devastating news. Jan had a malignant growth that would require a leg amputation. She would have to undergo surgery and long months of rehabilitation.

As any mother would, I worried about my young daughter's spirits. Then one night in the hospital, when sleep eluded her, Jan surprised me by asking, "Mom, remember Vicky?"

* * *

Our family lived on a farm along an old logging road near Fairbanks, Alaska. Wildlife abounded in the quiet countryside. One winter night while out walking, my husband, Joe, and I heard a distant cry.

A young fox, the color of autumn maples against the snow, was twisting in an illegal trap. Arching her back to spring into the air, she smashed back to the ground and collapsed.

"Look at that leg," Joe said. "It's destroyed."

Removing his jacket, he gently placed it over the animal. I released her torn leg from the trap, expecting her to lunge to bite me. But under Joe's coat she did not struggle. Her yellow eyes, bright with pain and fear, stared at us unflinchingly. On the way home we named the little vixen Vicky.

As a veterinary assistant with a background in animal husbandry, I was qualified to rehabilitate injured wildlife for the state of Alaska. When we brought Vicky into the kitchen, she was watched by two owls with frozen feet, hanging in slings inside their cages. A bald eagle with a broken wing clung to the back of the couch, staring. A caged mink we'd found almost frozen to death stuck its nose through the wire and hissed, while our family cat, hair on end, eyed the newcomer warily.

Joe sat at the table, gripping Vicky's head securely while I prepared to fix her leg. Our three children gathered around. "Try not to hurt her," whispered 7-year-old Jan, her blond head bent close to the delicate little fox.

Using cotton balls soaked with ether, Joe administered anesthetic. As soon as Vicky was out, I cleaned and disinfected her wound. With tweezers I removed splinters of bone, then scissored away the surrounding fur to expose the shattered bones.

There were four breaks in all. I matched the bones as closely as possible while Joe monitored Vicky's heartbeat. Finally, tying the bones in place with suture, I sewed the skin together, bandaged the entire leg, then strapped on a splint.

Hours after surgery Vicky's eyes fluttered open. She raised her head to look around, but made no move to stand. I draped a blanket over her cage for privacy and left her door ajar.

The next morning Vicky lay on her side breathing evenly. To my astonishment her head rested on a pink, fluffy rug she'd managed to pull into her cage from the living room sometime during the night.

Two mornings later, though, something was very wrong. During the night Vicky had tried to chew off the splint. Now she was trapped by a shaft of broken bone caught on a bar at the bottom of her cage. The tattered, infected limb was beyond repair. There was no choice—later that day I amputated Vicky's leg.

Long, anxious hours passed before the little fox stirred. I squeezed cold water from a washcloth into her mouth. Joe and I took turns staying close to her the remainder of that day and all through the night. Jan and her brothers, Mark and Scott, left her side only long enough to eat and run to the bathroom.

Within days, however, Vicky began to eat, lap water and be more alert. I noticed her staring into the living room. Finally it dawned on me what she wanted: the pink rug, which I'd removed from her cage to wash. When I moved it closer, Vicky stuck her face through the bars and pulled it in with her.

We decided to open the cage door again and give her the run of the house. Vicky stood, lost her balance, fell and tried again. "Oh, Mom," Jan whispered. "She's so brave, and she keeps trying." My own heart ached.

Late that night I heard soft pads cross our bedroom floor. A cool nose brushed my hand.

After a few more attempts Vicky managed to stand. From the safety of her cage, she gazed about the room but showed no desire to walk. But late that night I awoke to hear her soft pads cross our bedroom floor. A cool nose brushed against my hand. Then I heard her moving down the hall to the children's rooms.

Soon it seemed that the cage had become her den, the place she returned to for security. She groomed herself there and buried food under her pink rug. No doubt about it, she considered the rug hers. Sometimes she'd take it to sleep with behind the fireplace grate. All we would see was a glimpse of pink.

Vicky now moved about freely, scurrying away if we got too close. Stalking her favorite toy, an old glove, she'd pounce, throw it in the air and catch it. Then one night I watched fascinated as she padded to the door, stood with her nose to the crack and sniffed the outside air.

* * *

More than seven weeks had slipped by. With breeding season only months away, Vicky needed her freedom to find a new mate and a new den. But before she could be released back into the wild, Joe and I had to know if she could kill prey for herself.

One night Joe released a sacrificial chicken in the kitchen. Vicky didn't make a move. Disappointed, I went to bed. But in the morning Vicky lay in her cage, the partially eaten chicken forming a mound beneath her pink rug.

Almost daily now her restlessness increased. At night she paced the house and looked out the window. In the light of day, fox, ermine and hare tracks told us what she'd seen.

I had no more excuses. Hadn't I told our children that wild animals should never be considered pets? Though I wanted her to live the life she was born for, I hated the idea of giving her up.

Finally we decided Vicky should go. Dreading the moment, I slowly opened the door, fully expecting her to rush out and vanish. Instead, Vicky stood in the doorway, then went back to her cage and curled up on her rug. "See, Mom," said our son Scott. "She doesn't want to go."

The next evening I opened the door again. Vicky rushed to look. She smelled the night air, reading all it carried. Again she returned to her cage.

Five nights later our fox finally ventured out and disappeared into the trees. Torn by happiness and sadness, Joe and I carried her cage outside in case she returned during the night. Jan and her brothers followed with Vicky's pink rug, her favorite glove and bones, and some food scraps.

Eagerly the next morning we checked the cage. Some of the scraps had been eaten. The rest were buried under her rug. In the snow were Vicky's distinctive three paw prints.

For three weeks Vicky returned every night to eat an egg we'd left for her. One by one she took away the glove and bones. Then one day we found a freshly killed grouse buried in her cage. Jan turned to me and said, "She's going to make it, Mom."

The following night Vicky took away her pink rug. Though we knew she was nearby, this was the last time she would return to her cage.

In June we had to move. The day we left, Vicky sat on a berm watching us. She looked healthy but shaggy in her summer coat.

"Vicky," I said, stopping my car for a final goodbye, "look after yourself." She yapped twice, the only time I ever heard her bark, then scampered off to the life she was designed to live.

*   *   *

Jan and I talked about Vicky for a long time that night in the hospital. Her blue eyes floated in unspilled tears. "You know, Mom," she said, "I won't let anything stop me from doing the things I want to do in life."

My heart quivered. As Jan had once said of Vicky, I found myself thinking of my brave daughter: She's going to make it. And so she has. Today Jan is a wife and full-time mother of two small boys.

As for Vicky, I like to think she found a partner and raised young. Many times I've pictured her unique tracks in the snow. And many times I've wondered if her coming was meant to be, to show us about dealing with life's hardships and joys.

In my heart, I know the answer.

Originally published in the December 1998 issue of *Reader's Digest* magazine.

CAUGHT IN THE ACT

After a week of chatting online, we decided to meet in person. Our long stroll gave us an appetite, so we decided to stop at a restaurant and get dinner. In the parking lot, something overcame the both of us and we embraced. I had a sense someone was watching us. Sure enough, someone was. A policeman patrolling the area had stopped in front of us. With a grin, he asked if everything was OK. "Yes, officer," we replied. To this day, we tease each other about arousing police suspicions on our first date.

—Kelli Donigan, *Grand Rapids, MI*

MISTAKEN IDENTITY

As a letter carrier in the town where I lived, I would occasionally run into people from my mail route at local establishments. One Sunday, my wife and I were food shopping, and, of course, I was not wearing my postal uniform. A young, attractive woman who lived on my route approached us in the dairy aisle and said to me, "Hi, don't I know you from somewhere?" I smiled and said, "Yes, I'm your mailman, Frank." With a broad grin, she stated loudly, "Oh, that's how I know you! I just didn't recognize you with clothes on."

—Frank Mongiello, *Lakewood, NJ*

A Lobster Tale

by Julie Powell, from the book *Julie & Julia*

Famed chef Julia Child got one young writer into hot water

During the winter of 2002, at the exhortation of Julia Child, I went on a murderous rampage. I committed gruesome, atrocious acts, and for my intended victims, no murky corner of New York City was safe. If news of the carnage was not widely remarked upon in the local press, it was only because my victims were not human, but crustacean. I have blood on my hands, even if it is the clear blood of lobsters.

I had undertaken a project: to cook, in one year, in my crummy, tiny apartment kitchen, all 524 recipes in the classic *Mastering the Art of French Cooking, Volume 1*, by Julia Child, Louisette Bertholle and Simone Beck. On the day I got to the section about lobsters, I was awake by dawn, worrying. It was Sunday in Long Island City, in the borough of Queens. Forget killing a lobster—how would I even get one? How much would it cost? How would I get it home? I peppered my husband, Eric, with these questions, hoping that he would reply, "Oooh, you're right. Guess we'll have to save lobster for another day. Domino's? Bacon and jalapeno?"

Instead, he got out the Yellow Pages and made a phone call, and before long we were on our way home from the fish market with two live lobsters in a paper bag in the backseat of our car. My ears stayed pricked for the crinkle of a lobster claw venturing out of the bag—but the lobsters just sat there.

I had read up on all sorts of methods for humanely euthanizing lobsters—sticking them in the freezer, placing them in ice water, then bringing it up to a boil (which is supposed to fool them into not realizing they're boiling alive), slicing the spinal cord with a knife beforehand. But all these struck me as palliatives thought up more to save boilers from emotional anguish than boilees from physical distress. In the end, I just dumped them out of the paper bag into a pot with some boiling water and vermouth and vegetables.

And then I freaked out.

The pot wasn't big enough. Though the lobsters didn't shriek in horror the second I dropped them in, their initial stillness only drew out the excruciating moment. It was like that instant when your car begins to skid out of control and, before your eyes, you see the burning wreck that is your destiny. Any second, the pain would awaken the creatures from their comas, I knew it, and I couldn't get the lid down! It was just too horrible. My husband had to take things in hand, and managed to get those bugs subdued with a minimum of fuss.

People say lobsters make a terrible racket, trying—reasonably enough—to claw their way out of the pot. I wouldn't know. I spent the next 20 minutes watching a golf game on TV with the volume turned up to Metallica concert level.

When I ventured back into the kitchen, the lobsters were very red and not making any racket at all. Poor little beasties. I took them out of the pot and cooked down their liquid with juices from some mushrooms I'd stewed. I reduced and strained the liquid, then beat it into a light roux I'd made of butter and flour.

When Eric and I start our crime conglomerate, he can be in charge of death; I'll take care of dismemberment. The same no-nonsense guy who brusquely stripped two crustaceans of their mortal coils had to leave the kitchen when I read aloud that next I was to "split the lobsters in half lengthwise, keeping the shell halves intact." I used the shells to hold the finished mixture of lobster meat, egg yolks, cream, mustard, cayenne, the lobster broth/roux sauce and the stewed mushrooms. The final touch was to sprinkle them with Parmesan, dot them with butter and run them under the broiler.

They were, I must say, delicious.

I stalked my third victim in Chinatown. The second murder went much as the first—steamed in water spiked with vermouth and some celery, carrot and onion. The rosy-red dead lobster was bisected in just the same way and its shell stuffed with its sauteed meat, this time napped in a cream sauce made with the lobster's cooking juices. I confessed to Eric as we sat down to our *Homard aux Aromates* that cutting lobsters in half was beginning to prove eerily satisfying. "I just feel like I've got a knack for this stuff."

He looked at me, and I could see him wondering where was the finicky, soft-hearted young girl he had married. "By the end of this, you'll be comfortable filleting puppies."

That chilled me. I laid low after that for a good long while. The reason was the next recipe, *Homard à l'Américaine*, which involved cutting up the lobster while it was still alive. Even more frightening was the thought Eric had planted in my head: *What if I found that I liked it?*

My final victim was another Chinatown denizen, spryer than his predecessors, flailing around in his bag for the entire subway ride. I put him in the freezer for a while when I got home, to try to numb him, maybe make it go a little easier, but is there such a thing as an easy vivisection, really? After half an hour or so, while Eric retreated to the living room and cranked up the volume on the TV, I took the lobster out of the freezer and laid him on the cutting board. I stood over him, my largest knife poised at the juncture of chest and tail. I took a deep breath, let it out. "All right, all right. OK. One. Two. Three."

I pressed down, making an incision in the shell where Julia said I could quickly sever the spinal cord. The thing began to flail. "He doesn't seem to think this is particularly painless, Julia." Chop it in two. Quickly. Start at the head. I placed the tip of my knife between its eyes and, muttering "I'm sorry I'm sorry I'm sorry," plunged.

I had to leave the room for a bit. After that, things got easier. My final victim was fricasseed with carrots, onion, shallots and garlic, doused with cognac, lit on fire, then baked in an oven with vermouth, tomato, parsley and tarragon, and served atop rice. I arranged the rice into a ring on the plate, as Julia asked. I piled the lobster pieces in the middle and ladled the sauce over. "Dinner's served."

Eric dug in. "I suppose it's no worse to eat an animal you killed yourself instead of one they kill in the factory. Maybe it's better."

"It's true." I took a bite of lobster meat with rice. It was quite delicious.

Still, I was inordinately grateful that the main ingredient in the next recipe, *Bifteck Haché* (basically, hamburger), would not require execution. My life of crime was over, at least for the present.

Originally published in the October 2005 issue of *Reader's Digest* magazine.

Julie & Julia *was published in 2005. A film version was released in 2009. Julie Powell died in 2022 at the age of 49.*

The Psychic, the Novelist and the $17 Million Scam

by Robert Andrew Powell

*The fortuneteller's grandmotherly air
hid her true intentions*

Start the whole nightmare on a whim. Kind of as a joke, really.

Walk up Fifth Avenue in Manhattan with a little time on your hands. As you turn past the Plaza Hotel, spy a sandwich board on the sidewalk advertising fortunetelling and psychic insights. Notice how the sign points to a prewar building where the rents must be astronomical. The address alone signals that this operation—you're unsure what exactly psychics do, to be honest—is legit, that it isn't some carnival-barker-at-the-fair scam. Not that you're thinking about it so deeply. This isn't to be a big deal, a major financial mistake, an event in your life that you will later come to describe with the words disgust and shame. It's just a little entertainment. Harmless.

Be at your lowest point, emotionally. Really suffering. Susan Abraham, an Englishwoman in town with her husband, doesn't know whom to talk to about him. How he's always criticizing her. How she feels like a bird trapped in a cage. And how she wants out of the marriage so very badly.

Jennifer Hill, a marketing executive from Hawaii, has just ended a long relationship. The breakup leaves her without any prospects as she sees her last chance at childbearing fade away. Jude Deveraux, a romance novelist from New Mexico by way of Kentucky, feels stuck in a terrible marriage too. Unable to turn to her husband, Deveraux walks alone with her problems, like the others. She craves someone she can open up to.

Rose Marks will be that person. She's a grandmother in her 60s. Matronly in appearance, with silver hair, olive skin, designer eyeglasses. She's of Roma heritage, one of a long line of women brought up in the dark art of fortunetelling. Her mother was a psychic; her grandmother too. Marks has been in the business since being pulled out of school in the third grade.

> *"Take off your bracelet," the fortuneteller commands. That's a test. Do you trust?*

Her operation is a scam, prosecutors argue. But Marks regards herself as a life coach of sorts. In federal criminal court facing charges of fraud, money laundering and falsifying tax returns, Marks insists through her attorney that she was an independent contractor who was hired by clients for her keen ability to offer guidance. Not a grifter, she was a combination of psychologist, social worker, financial counselor, spiritual teacher and friend.

"I gave my life to these people," Marks says in an interview with Fort Lauderdale's *Sun-Sentinel* before the trial begins. "We're talking about clients of 20 years, 30 years, 40 years. We're not talking about someone I just met and took all their money and ran off."

* * *

Marks is not the only fortuneteller to find herself in a criminal courtroom in 2013. Another Manhattan psychic, working under the name Zena the Clairvoyant, was convicted of swindling $138,000 from her clients.

Marks, though, is the next level. No other clairvoyant has raked in anything close to her financial haul. That novelist she counseled, Jude Deveraux? Her bestselling books—*Scarlet Nights*, *Days of Gold* and others that if you haven't read, you've seen in airport bookstores—have sold some 60 million copies. Marks took from the writer more than $17 million of her profits, an eye-popping sum that the defense does not dispute. Again, Marks claims this money was simply payment for services rendered. Just like the several million dollars she was given by more than a dozen other alleged victims listed on the indictment, adding up to a grand total of $25 million.

"You're going to hear many references to 'the work," Assistant U.S. Attorney Larry Bardfeld tells prospective jurors when the trial opens in West Palm Beach, Florida. As witnesses testify over the course of the following month, what the work entails will become clear—and how easy it is to fall for it.

Inside the storefront, you'll be ushered into a room—closet-size, windowless, so tiny there's space only for two chairs and a small round table. A menu, just like at a restaurant, lists the services. You want to see your future in tarot cards? Anyone can do tarot cards, you're told. Choose something else. A palm reading? Again, no, too common. "Take off your bracelet and let me see it," the fortuneteller instructed Hill, the Hawaiian executive who, prior to this, says she'd always considered herself street-smart. That's your first test: handing over something valuable. You're being screened. Do you trust? Hill turned over her bracelet. Abraham, the unhappy wife from England, gave Marks's daughter-in-law a pair of earrings. You'll talk about your love life while the jewelry is appraised. Vent about your husband, your breakup. Finally, you've found someone who cares.

"I kept coming back because she was listening to me. I've never been able to get anyone to listen to me," Deveraux testifies.

But there's bad news. It turns out the jewelry is giving off evil vibes. This is going to take all night. "I have to pray on it," you will be told. Can you come back tomorrow? (Another test: Do you still trust? Or do you feel the hook sliding into your flesh?) You don't want to come back, you'll protest. You don't believe any of this, really. Such talk earns you a scolding. Your negativity is a problem. With this attitude, nothing can be done for you. You'll end up feeling kind of badgered into it, but you will leave your jewelry with her. And the next day, as instructed, you'll return.

"I wanted to get my bracelet back," Hill explains.

But when you come back, there's more bad news. Turns out you've been cursed. Centuries ago. In another life. This curse is the reason why your relationship ended, why you can't conceive a child. But there's good news. Marks and the family members who work under her can change things. "I can block this curse," Hill is told. "This is what I am here for. I can help you."

Best of all, she'll do it for free. This is her life's work, Marks says. This is her purpose. Doing right by you is how she gets right with God. You won't have to pay a cent, ever. You just need to take a $4,500 cash advance on your credit card, please. Money is the root of your problems, see? Money is evil.

This money—cash, of course—must be cleansed. Prayed upon. Stored in a dedicated drawer where it won't be touched until it's returned to you, free of bad spirits.

Now the hook is set. You're out thousands of dollars, and you want to get it back. But there is still evil plaguing you, it is revealed. More money needs to be cleansed. What's that? You don't want to give over any more cash? You need to get over your fixation on money! You need to trust the process, the work. We're talking about an ancient curse here! This is serious!

*   *   *

You continue in good faith, amazed at how much you've handed over, but telling yourself that it will return. That's what you are specifically, repeatedly told by Marks: All this money will come back to you. As instructed, you liquidate some bonds. You sell property. You cash out your retirement account, absorbing the painful tax penalty. We've come so far. It's not time to be timid or back down. You must give more money so more work can be done. Your boyfriend will come back to you. Your husband will leave you free to find the love and contentment you deserve. You'll have a baby. Everything will work out.

It seems ridiculous. Suckers, right? Anyone who visits a psychic deserves to be fleeced. Yet in the courtroom, on the stand, the victims don't sound stupid or deluded. One victim graduated from the U.S. Naval Academy; another is a lawyer. Instead, what they seem is all too human. At the time they first met Marks or a member of her family, they were lost and searching for peace. It's very easy to mock what happened to them, but it also becomes clear how something that started so innocently could spiral into a trap from which there was no escape. The victims, almost all of them women, were vulnerable. All of them were looking for hope.

Money is the root of your problems, says Marks. Money is evil. But she will pray upon your cash and cleanse it for you.

The cash rarely comes back. Marks told one client, Sylvia Roma, that hundreds of thousands of her dollars were lost in the 2001 attack on the World Trade Center. In court, the prosecution tediously documents where the $800,000 that Roma lost really went. "A St. Moritz 18-karat yellow gold watch," says a special agent from the Secret Service, flipping through a folder of property recovered at the waterfront mansion in Fort Lauderdale where Marks and her family relocated from Manhattan. "A Rolex watch with sapphires and 29 round full-cut diamonds." Photos of luxury cars flash on a video screen while the agent speaks. A Range Rover, white. A Mercedes coupe, black. A Mercedes SUV, black. A Bentley, a Ferrari, a Rolls-Royce and a Jeep. "A 14-karat gold key to a Porsche," says the agent, continuing until Judge Kenneth Marra cuts her off with an exasperated smirk.

Marks's eldest son, Ricky, sits in the gallery every day, his eyes boring into the backs of the prosecutors' heads. He pleaded guilty in 2013 to federal conspiracy to commit mail and wire fraud involving the same victims. Other family members join him when they can, seven more of them also having pleaded guilty to conspiracy or fraud charges. Fortunetelling is their business. Rose Marks, described by the prosecution as the family matriarch, is the only one who decided to take a chance on a court trial.

The last victim to take the stand is the author Deveraux. She's a small woman with an easy smile and a soft voice that hasn't lost its southern lilt. She starts with her basic information. That she was born in Kentucky in 1947. That she is the author of "happy little romantic novels." That a number of her books have appeared on the *New York Times* bestseller list and that she'd been doing "quite well financially" before she met Marks. Then, she had four properties in Santa Fe and an apartment in New York City, which is where she first found Marks, in the early '90s, before her divorce.

You will call Marks repeatedly, begging for the return of your savings. She's brusque. Abrupt.

They met in the usual manner. The walking past the Plaza Hotel, the sandwich board, time on her hands, a curiosity about psychics. The room with the chairs. A chance to vent about her love life. Her marriage, she reveals, "was horrific, terrible, very bad." Her husband, she testifies, was doing "everything to control me, make me feel as bad as he possibly could. It was brutal. He was screaming and yelling at me all the time." She felt that suicide was her only way out. Marks, according to Deveraux's polite and straightforward account, told her something that she deeply wanted to hear: "I can give you a peaceful divorce," Marks said.

"I wanted that," Deveraux matter-of-factly states in the courtroom. "A peaceful divorce."

* * *

The work began. Deveraux handed over one of her writing notebooks, for the energy it gave off. She also put up money. Twelve hundred dollars at first, with the usual promise that the cash would be returned when the work was done. Soon, Deveraux added "a few thousand here, a few thousand there, to give [Marks] more energy." That energy supposedly helped Marks telepathically enter Deveraux's husband's mind, to see what he was planning.

The work drew Deveraux in. She began to believe what she was told. And yes, what she was told does sound ludicrous. That her husband had sold his soul to the devil. That the peaceful divorce she was promised was more difficult to deliver than expected, so she should turn over a cool $1 million, which soon became a $1 million-a-year flat fee. In return, Marks became Deveraux's most trusted confidante, dispensing advice about all aspects of life. Advice that, in hindsight, could not have been worse.

For the split from her husband, Deveraux wanted to hire an experienced divorce attorney, but Marks steered her to a guy who had little background in divorce. That lawyer drafted an agreement giving Deveraux's husband too much, the property, the cars. And Deveraux would have to pay her former spouse's bills into the future, along with his future taxes. Marks pushed Deveraux to sign off on the settlement, explaining that the terms were irrelevant because her husband was "going to die very soon … within three years."

Twenty years later, he's still alive. Healthy. Very wealthy. Marks's advice was so destructive that prosecutors investigated the possibility she was working in league with the divorce attorney. (No evidence of collusion was found.)

Still, Deveraux stayed with Marks, even after the divorce. The novelist wanted a baby. Marks told her she couldn't have one without the psychic's help. She also told Deveraux that if she had a child, it would fall over her New York apartment's balcony railing. So Deveraux sold the apartment, giving Marks all the proceeds so that the money from the sale could be spiritually cleansed. "She was fierce about asking about it," Deveraux testified, referring to the hefty checks she regularly signed over to Marks. "Money was extremely important to her."

Deveraux suffered eight miscarriages. When she finally gave birth in 1997, Marks told her that she needed more money to keep the baby from harm. "I would have paid anything to protect my son," Deveraux explains. "Anything." The protection didn't work. Deveraux's young son died after being hit by a truck. Marks warned that he was going to hell without spiritual intervention. "I gave her some hair I had cut from my son, and she said all she saw were flames," Deveraux says, her voice wavering for the first time since she's been on the stand. "She said I had to write books. I was crying all day long. She said she had to have money to keep my son out of the flames."

With her son dead and her divorce still on her mind, the quality of Deveraux's books deteriorated, the author admits. The amount of money left to take from her dwindled in lockstep, and Marks became harder to reach, Deveraux says. That's pretty much the way these relationships conclude. There's a script for that too.

The end is so inelegant. All your money spent on those diamond-encrusted watches and sterling silver bracelets stashed at Marks's home. Also, it will come out, there's Marks's gambling addiction. Court testimony reveals that Marks poured millions of her clients' dollars into slot machines at the Seminole Hard Rock casino in Hollywood, Florida. You don't know this yet. You will call Marks repeatedly, begging for the return of your savings. (You'll be having significant financial problems by now, to say the least.) She used to take your every call. Now she picks up selectively. When you do reach her, she's brusque. Abrupt. She tries to talk you into showing more faith, sticking with it a little longer so she can complete the work. You ask, again, and then again, for your money. Finally, Marks cracks. "There is no money," she snapped at Andrea Walker, another client. "You want to sue me, sue me." She hangs up. The end.

Except now you're cooperating with the police. You're taping the phone calls. They will be played in court for jurors, who take less than five hours to deliberate and convict Marks on all 14 criminal counts. Marks, who opted not to testify, nods her head each time the foreman says the word *guilty*. That morning, she'd arrived at the courthouse in comfortable tennis shoes and pants, a clear change from the sharp outfits she'd worn throughout the trial. It's as if she can see the future, and she's ready to be

taken into custody, which is what happens. "I love you," she says to her distraught family as she's led away. "It's going to be OK."

* * *

Marks will likely receive up to 20 years in jail. Prosecutors have filed a motion to get $25 million of the victims' money returned, a maneuver unlikely to bear fruit, since her attorney, who was paid for his services in part with a used Rolls-Royce from the psychic, claims she no longer has any assets. That doesn't upset Deveraux. "I will accept no money from this [prosecution]," she'd earlier testified. "My only goal here is to make Rose Marks stop doing this." The guilty verdict is being appealed. Marks is too frail to survive incarceration, her lawyer insists. Even with a sentence as short as four years, "the wear and tear on her body from working since she was 8 or 9" would kill her. Regardless of her sentence, she has entered custody with a project to work on. She intends to write a book about her life, she has said. She believes it's a story people will want to read and, more important, buy. She thinks there's a way she can still make some money out of this.

Originally published in the March 2014 issue of *Reader's Digest* magazine.

In 2014 Rose Marks was sentenced to 10 years in federal prison but was released on Jan. 14, 2022. She is now 71 years old.

Humor Hall of Fame

During a training exercise, an Army unit was late for afternoon inspection. "Where are those camouflage trucks?" the irate colonel barked. "They're here somewhere," replied the sergeant, "but we can't find 'em."

—L. DOWNING

A lieutenant confronted a recruit and said, "I hear you're complaining about a little sand in your soup."

The recruit replied, "Yes, sir."

So the lieutenant asked the soldier if he had joined the Army to serve his country or to complain about the food. The recruit explained, "Sir, I joined the U.S. Army to serve my country—not to eat it."

—ROSE MILLER

"Could we move the pieces representing ourselves a little farther away from the battle?"

EARTH   MOON   MARS   VENUS

SPACE FORCE

BANX

At a reunion for my husband's Air Force bomber squadron, a man stood staring at me for the longest time. Finally, he came up to me and said, "I've got who it is you remind me of. I can't remember her name, but she was on *The Golden Girls*." "Oh, the little grandma?" I asked. "No," he said. "The dumb one."

—M.S.

A month into my stint in the Army, I was assigned to guard prisoners. The fact that I was very raw was made abundantly clear to me the first time I accompanied an inmate to the military prison. After we walked side by side for a few feet, the prisoner, who had a few years on me, pointed to my weapon and said, "You know, you should really walk behind me and have your rifle ready to fire in case I try to escape."

—HOWARD HEIN

Nightmare
in the Woods

by Derek Burnett

*Pamela Salant expected a quiet evening
camping near Mount Hood, Oregon —
then things took a horrible turn*

Day 1: It was shaping up to be the perfect weekend. Last July, Pamela
Salant, a 28-year-old preschool teacher, and her boyfriend, Aric Essig, 31,
who works for a sailboat company, had driven two hours east from Portland, Oregon, to camp overnight in the Mount Hood National Forest. They
planned to hike a mile and a half through the forest to Bear Lake, spend the
night, and walk back out on Sunday to attend a birthday party for two of
her students. It was sunny, clear and fine.

But during the hike, the subject of their on-again/off-again relationship
came up, and the tension between the two began to rise. By the time they
set down their packs at the campsite on the south shore of the lake, Salant
was blind with anger. "I'm sorry, Pam," Essig said.

"I'm going to see if I can find a better spot for us to camp," she told him,
stalking off along the western shore of the lake. It was 1 p.m.

Bear Lake is only about 100 yards long, hemmed in by trees, which
forced Salant to drift inland. With no trail to follow, she descended a
drainage basin, climbed up the other side and scrambled atop a pile of

*Salant moved to Portland, Oregon,
for the hiking. "Weekends are always
spent camping," she says.*

195

rocks. Where she expected the lake to be, she saw nothing but steep forest and, far beyond, a snowcapped peak. She began backtracking through the dense woods, but the farther she walked, the more confused she became.

"Aric!" she called. "Help!"

No response. She kept moving until she came to a stream. She knew that the creeks here flowed northward toward the Columbia River, several miles away. But what good was that when she didn't know anything else? She clambered up a series of cliffs to get the lay of the land, climbing a dangerous scree slope and topping out on a boulder. She scanned the horizon. Nothing but trees. She'd been hiking for six hours, and the sun would be setting soon. With a new panic, she began to descend. There, far below! A lake! But was it Bear Lake? It didn't matter—any lake ought to have trails or people along it. She picked her way down to the lower elevations, traversing the cliffs as carefully as she could.

When Salant awoke, the first thing she noticed was the cliff she'd fallen from looming 40 feet above her.

Then, a misstep, and darkness.

*   *   *

When Salant awoke a few minutes later, the first thing she noticed was the cliff she'd fallen from looming 40 feet above her. The second was that her left leg curved strangely outward below the knee. "OK," she told herself, "my leg's broken." Surprisingly, the injury was not excruciating—some primal part of her had taken over, allowing her to go into problem-solving mode: She was hurt and alone with night coming on and absolutely no gear. All she wore were shorts, a tank top, socks and boots. She could hear water trickling somewhere in the middle distance, probably a stream. She would sleep right here for the night, and in the morning she would follow the sound of the water to the creek.

*   *   *

Day 2: In the middle of the cold night, she awoke and felt that her left leg was wet. Hours later, at sunrise, she saw that the moisture was blood. She

In 2010, 4,900 people were rescued on or around Mount Hood.

had a deep gash on her right leg—a result of her fall—and it had bled all over her broken left leg. She could see its gleaming white bone with folds of torn and bloodied pink tissue above it. Once again, she processed this fresh horror with a strange detachment. "All right," she said to herself. "I need to get to the water. I'm thirsty, and I need to clean up this cut."

Dragging herself along in an awkward crab-walk, she found the creek a quarter-mile away. It took her an hour to get there, but she was upbeat. *Good*, she thought. *Either this will lead me back to Bear Lake or to the Columbia—either way, I'm saved.* She drank and washed out her injury. The water was pure and beautiful. *Magical*, she thought. She could feel it rejuvenating her. Salant took one last sip, then set out down the creek, scooting along on her butt.

Trees standing 150 feet tall made a helicopter rescue perilous.

* * *

The area to the west of Bear Lake contains some of the country's tallest timber and most inhospitable terrain. The stream Salant had chosen to follow is called Lindsey Creek, and it drops toward the Columbia River in a deep, waterfall-studded gorge so difficult to navigate that she may have been the first ever to attempt its descent. Still, she took a moment to admire it. The waterfalls, the ancient forest—they reminded her why she loved coming to this spot in the first place.

All day long she picked her way carefully down the gorge, clinging to the slopes at the edge of the creek. She moved methodically, plotting every step, crossing and recrossing the stream to avoid obstacles, and balancing on fallen logs or clinging to tree roots. She came to the top of an outcropping above the stream and stopped. There was seemingly no good way to go. Forward was too steep, backward was too steep, left was too steep. She could proceed down the opposite bank if she could cross the stream—but it was a 12-foot drop to the water. For an hour she sat and contemplated her plight. Then she jumped.

"I can't believe I'm doing this!" she screamed, hurtling down into the shallow creek. She landed on her right leg and pitched over onto her side, popping out of the water seconds later.

"OK," she said, panting and dragging herself out of the frigid water. "What's next?"

In the afternoon, she heard a helicopter. *Is that for me?* One swept overhead, but the firs obscured her location. *Maybe I should just sit in one spot and wait,* she thought. But no—she was too cold for that. Even though the day was warm, the V-shaped gorge was shaded, and she'd spent all day slipping into the cold water.

Around 4 p.m., just as the sun was hitting the gorge, Salant found a flattish spot between two trees and curled up to sleep, shivering. Use all your resources, she told herself. Her tank top had a built-in bra, which she pulled out and folded over her head for warmth. She removed the drawstring from her shorts, poked holes in her shirt and shorts just at the hips, and ran the string through to pull them together and seal in the heat. Then she peeled strips of dry moss from a nearby rock, covering her legs and stuffing her clothes with it.

She thought about Aric. He must have called for those helicopters. How stupid that their last exchange had been so nasty. It was Sunday evening now; she was supposed to be at her students' birthday party.

✳   ✳   ✳

Day 3: At the first hint of light, she arose, desperate to be moving again. She looked down at her legs. The gash on her right thigh still yawned fiercely, and the curve of her left leg made it appear vulnerable, pathetic. She felt that sudden strange detachment again and a kind of maternal responsibility toward her legs, as if they were children tugging at her sleeve. *God*, she thought, *can't you just take care of yourselves?*

She nursed them along down the gorge. Somehow it made her feel less lonesome to have someone to nurture, even if it was only her own legs. She washed out the wound on her right leg and wrapped it in her underwear. Later in the morning, she blundered through some thornbushes, and it occurred to her that she might use thorns to suture the cut. She stabbed at the folds of skin, trying to pin the laceration closed. But she could never do more than skewer one edge of the injury.

"OK," she said, dragging herself out of the frigid water. "What's next?"

Helicopters flew overhead once in late morning and again in early afternoon, but Salant was never in enough of a clearing to flag them. So she pushed on. She came across a familiar-looking green bush studded with pink berries and thought she remembered Aric identifying the plant as salmonberry. She nibbled at one of the fruits and spit it out. She waited a while, then sampled another. Satisfied that the berries weren't toxic, she gorged on them.

At nightfall, she tried to sleep, but pain and fear made that impossible. As she lay awake, visions of her childhood came to mind. Random scenes—church on a Sunday morning with her family, trotting around the running track as a high school athlete.

She so wanted to be with Aric and her family. She wanted to hold them and shout how much she loved them. There were things she still wanted to do—learn to play the fiddle and have children. But in the black of night, she recalled a dear friend, Luke, who had died two years earlier. *If I don't make it,* she thought, *at least I'll be with Luke somewhere.*

* * *

Day 4: When the sun rose Tuesday morning, Salant gritted her teeth. "I've had enough of this," she said. "I'm going to be found today. Or I'm going to die. But the journey is coming to an end." She made her way to a flat rock with a clearing overhead—a good place to be spotted. For three hours, she waited, shivering, starving, thirsty. No helicopters.

She scooted uphill a little to sit in the sun. A fat green caterpillar shrugged along nearby. She picked it up and bit into it. It cracked apart, spurting a metallic flavor into her mouth. Ugh! Then she spied a meaty-looking slug. She'd always wondered what one might taste like, and after plopping it into her mouth she knew. Never in her life had she tasted anything more repulsive. She spit it out and scooped up handfuls of water in a vain attempt to erase the awful gluey film on her tongue.

A chopper passed overhead. Salant tried to stand but toppled back onto the rock. The helicopter flew off.

Thwup, thwup, thwup.

Helicopters! She skidded back down to the flat rock where she'd spent her morning. A chopper passed overhead. Salant tried to stand but toppled back onto the rock. Then the helicopter flew off.

Did they see me or not? she wondered. Across the stream was another

Salant's survival plan was simple: Follow the creek.

salmonberry bush. *I'll count to 500, and if they don't come back, I'll go over there and eat some berries.* She counted as slowly as she could. *Four hundred ninety-nine, 500. Hell.*

She was crawling to the berry bush when she heard "You must be Pam."

*   *   *"

"What are you guys doing out here?" Salant asked.

Four members of a volunteer alpine rescue team called the Hood River Crag Rats had spent the day descending Lindsey Creek. They had been in radio contact with the Oregon Army National Guard helicopter that had spotted her. "I can't believe there are people who do this. I love you," she cried.

Salant says she'll continue to camp: "I do like that solo connection to the earth."

Half an hour later, a medevac chopper arrived. With no place to land, and with some of the Douglas firs stretching 150 feet in the air, the Blackhawk crew had to stage a daring cable rescue, lowering flight medic Ben Sjullie from 300 feet into a drop zone the size of a pickup truck. Ten minutes later, Salant was dangling from the cable above the treetops in Sjullie's bear hug. Safe inside the helicopter, Sjullie closed the door. "Are you OK?" he asked. And for the first time since her ordeal began, Salant broke down and cried.

* * *

"I just don't know if she could have made it past the point [where] we'd found her," says Tom Scully, one of the Crag Rats who rescued Salant. "There was a waterfall above and a waterfall below. Another day and she probably would have stayed right where she was." Scully is in awe of Salant for covering such terrain with broken bones. He calls his descent of Lindsey Creek—aided by ropes and climbing gear—"one of the burliest hikes I've ever been on. It wasn't even a hike. It was survival. There's nothing out there but nothing. We were all soaked and scraped up. And she had been at this for days without gear or clothes. She's amazing."

Salant reached Aric on his cellphone from her hospital room in Portland. He had spent the weekend camped out at Bear Lake helping the search effort, and now he was speeding toward Portland. "Aric?" Pamela said through her tears. "I'm OK."

"Thank God. Thank God. I'm on my way." When he stepped into her room, neither of them could find the right words, so they hugged instead.

Pamela Salant left the hospital after a week. In addition to the laceration on her right leg and the tibial plateau fracture just below her left knee, she had suffered compression fractures in her spine and abrasions all over her body. But all she could think about during her convalescence was the forest—how peaceful it had been out there, how much a part of it she had felt, like any other animal suffering along through nature.

As soon as she was able to use crutches, she and Aric camped again. "Are you sure you really want to do that?" her friends asked.

"Are you kidding?" Salant said. "It's all I want to do."

Originally published in March 2012 issue of *Reader's Digest* magazine.

Love's Last Refrain

by Jen McCaffery

This musician calms the dying and soothes their families

W hen Freddie Fuller arrived to perform in the hospital room in Temple, Texas, Pam Golightly worried it was already too late. Her stepfather, Dennis Strobel, was dying.

At 88, Strobel had just been moved to the palliative care unit. After spending five days by his side, Golightly could tell that something had changed in the Korean War veteran. He had become agitated, and a nurse had told her Strobel's time was near.

"You're probably wasting your time," Golightly told Fuller.

But Fuller, wearing a cowboy hat and toting a Taylor acoustic guitar, shared with her what medical professionals had told him time and time again over the years: Hearing may be the last sense to go.

"Let me go in and play," Fuller said. "It's as much for you as it is for him."

Fuller, 68 and a full-time musician, is known professionally as the Singing Cowboy. With two albums, the country and folk musician has performed all over the United States, as well as overseas for American troops. He also delights schoolkids with a one-man show called "History of the Texas Cowboy 1850-1900."

Growing up in Salado, Texas, Fuller heard gospel music all the time from his mother. She even sang as she hung clothes on the line. And she

"Oddly enough, I feel comfortable around people at the end of their life," says Fuller.

encouraged her young son's musical talent.

When she was dying of cancer, in 1987, he put their love of song to its greatest use. He would crawl into her hospital bed with his guitar and sing her favorites: "Amazing Grace," "Just a Closer Walk with Thee" and "I'll Fly Away." His mother seemed to relax, a peaceful look crossing her face.

"That moment allowed her and I to connect like we used to when I was singing as a kid," Fuller recalls. It emphasized to him the power of music. Consciously or subconsciously, people allow it to go to deep, sacred parts of their hearts and souls, Fuller believes.

So when he heard about a nonprofit organization called Swan Songs, he gave them a call. Since 2005, Swan Songs has arranged more than 800 free musical last wishes—bedside performers from bagpipers to mariachi bands—at hospitals, hospices and private homes in and around Austin, Texas. Fuller signed up on the spot.

Since then, he has performed dozens of musical vigils. Sometimes they're almost festive, with terminally ill people surrounded by family, including one patient who sang along and danced gingerly with her walker. Other times, they're quieter, as Fuller's experience with his mom was. And sometimes they feel a bit like a miracle.

That was the case with Golightly's stepfather. He enjoyed country music, and Swan Songs sent Fuller. When Fuller arrived at the hospital that day last February, Strobel seemed ready to say goodbye. Golightly and her sister, Paula Guerra, watched their stepdad's every breath, each holding one of his hands. Fuller played some Willie Nelson, Merle Haggard and Jackson Browne songs. After 45 minutes, Golightly asked for just one more song. Fuller chose "Love, Me," a country ballad by Collin Raye. "I played the last song, sang the last note, and hit the last guitar chord, and he took his last breath," Fuller says.

"She, her sister and I looked at one another, saying: 'Oh my gosh, we just experienced one of the most magical moments in our lives.'"

"It was a gift for us all," Golightly says of Fuller's singing. "At a really sad time, it was beautiful."

Originally published in the November 2018 issue of *Reader's Digest* magazine.

Smart People Do the Dumbest Things!

A high IQ does not exempt anyone from super screw-ups

JOURNALISTS

Every so often, the wordsmiths who suss out the news are subject to a very public form of execution: the corrections page. Here are some of the better goof-ups.

This post originally quoted photographer Tom Sanders as saying it takes him five years to get on the dance floor. It takes him five beers.

—slate.com

Norma Adams-Wade's June 15 column incorrectly called Mary Ann Thompson-Frenk a socialist. She is a socialite.

—*Dallas Morning News*

[We] wish to apologize for our apology to Mark Steyn. In correcting the incorrect statements, we incorrectly published the incorrect correction.

—*Ottawa Citizen*

Correction to the article "These Are the 100 Most-Read Female Writers in College Classes."

The original version of this included Evelyn Waugh, who was a man.

—*Time*

BOSSES

As the business magazine Inc. *discovered, all that the following company-wide emails from executives accomplished was ticking off employees.*

Subject: Computer Course After much consideration, we have decided to cancel the training for our new computer system on the grounds that once people learn the system, they usually leave.

Subject: System Failures It has come to my attention that the email system was down yesterday. From now on, I have requested that the system manager send a group message to everyone next time the system goes down.

Subject: Company Picnic We will have our first company picnic next week, which we have dubbed "Morale Builder." The picnic will feature carnival rides and all-you-can-eat hot dogs and beans. A menu of steak and lobster is available for executives.

Subject: Recognizing Employee Contributions After several months of strong sales, we have decided to print new Employee Appreciation T-shirts! These shirts will be on sale starting next Monday.

GAME SHOW CONTESTANTS

Jeopardy! is the game show for the brainy set. As you likely know, the show supplies the answer, and the contestants respond in question form. In these cases from the past several years, they responded in questionable form.

Answer: By the fourth century A.D., Rome had 28 public ones stacked with rolls of papyrus.
Contestant's response: What are public toilets?
Correct response: What are libraries?

Answer: A Christian hymn and a Jewish holiday hymn are both titled this, also the name of a 2009 Tony-nominated musical.
Contestant's response: What is "Kinky Boots"?
Correct response: What is "Rock of Ages"?

Answer: Paul III roared at him, "I have waited 30 years for your services. Now I'm pope, can't I satisfy my desire?"
Contestant's response: Who is Lady Godiva?
Correct response: Who is Michelangelo?

POLITICIANS AND BUREAUCRATS

Government has never been accused of being a well-oiled machine, as this headline from the Independent *suggests: "U.S. government memo on the danger of leaking to media has been leaked." Here are examples of the bureaucracy running mighty creakily.*

1. File these recent National Institutes of Health (NIH) expenditures under "Did we really need to study these?"

$230,000: The money an NIH-supported group spent to find out that the color red made female monkeys amorous.

$5 million: Amount granted to Brown University researchers for a study that reported, in part, on whether fraternity and sorority members like to drink more than the average undergraduate. (Answer: They do!)

$150,000: Sum that went to the National Science Foundation to investigate why we're so stressed out by politics, when most every American would have gladly supplied the answer for free.

—Sources: *2017 Wastebook* by Arizona
Sen. Jeff Flake; *National Review*

2. Not to be outdone by the NIH, the Department of Defense bought camouflage uniforms for members of the Afghan army to help them blend in with dense forests. First problem: Only 2% of Afghanistan is covered in

trees. Second problem: The uniforms were up to $28 million more expensive than the desert camouflage best suited for Afghanistan's arid terrain.

3. The United States has some very good laws; the ones that look askance at murder leap to mind. But national politicians have pushed through others that seem—how shall we put this?—less essential.

If you sell liquor, it is illegal to advertise wine in a manner that suggests it has intoxicating qualities. (It'll be our secret.)

If you've followed the above law, don't mess up by selling wine with a brand name that includes the word *zombie*. That's forbidden too.

You know what goes well with non-zombie-branded wine? Onion rings. But the government says they'd better not have been made from diced onions without saying so.

After eating all those fried onions, you may want an anti-flatulent. You'll know what that is because by law the bottle must note that flatulence is "referred to as gas."

4. Washington, D.C., may be the bonehead capital of America, but it hasn't cornered the market on dimness. In Placerville, California, the pothole situation got so bad that residents took to spray-painting rants and even explicit pictures near the worst cases to get the city's attention. It worked; the city sent out work teams. They removed the graffiti—but left the potholes.

—Source: fox6now.com

5. It's not just American politicians who mess up. A foreign leader had his private email hacked because he used 12345 as his computer password. One would think that dictator Bashar al-Assad of Syria would have known better.

—Source: mashable.com

LAWYERS

Lawyers may have gone to graduate school, but their rigorous education hasn't stopped them from asking these bizarre questions of witnesses in court.

How many times have you committed suicide?

Was it you or your brother who was killed?

Do you have any children or anything of that kind?

Without saying anything, tell the jury what you did next.

Was that the same nose you broke as a child?

Were you alone or by yourself?

Now, Doctor, isn't it true that when a person dies in his sleep, he doesn't know about it until the next morning?

—Source: *The Dumb Book* (Reader's Digest Books)

NUTTY PROFESSORS

The Ig Nobel Prize is a tongue-in-cheek honor bestowed by the periodical Annals of Improbable Research—at an event at Harvard, no less!—for incredibly trivial research. Here is how they toasted the winners.

Psychology Prize To researchers in Belgium, the Netherlands, Germany, Canada and the United States for asking a thousand liars how often they lie, and for deciding whether to believe those answers.

Literature Prize To the etymologists in the Netherlands, the United States, Spain, Belgium, Australia and Canada who discovered that the expression "Huh?" (or its equivalent) seems to exist in every language—and weren't completely sure why.

Economics Prize To the Bangkok Metropolitan Police for offering to pay police officers extra cash if they refused to take bribes.

ROCKET SCIENTISTS

While most dummies aren't rocket scientists, these are!

David Atkinson devoted years of his life to designing an experiment to measure the winds on Titan, Saturn's largest moon. In 1997, the probe was launched by the European Space Agency. Eight years later, on Jan. 14, 2005, Atkinson and his team waited anxiously for the first data to arrive. And then waited and waited some more, to no avail. An investigation revealed that a receiver for the measuring equipment hadn't been turned on before takeoff. The glitch delayed analysis of the data by a couple of days; much of it was later recovered by radio telescopes.

In 2004, a NASA probe was returning to Earth after collecting solar particles. As it reentered the upper atmosphere, rapid deceleration was supposed to trigger the deployment of two parachutes, allowing the probe to gently float back to terra firma. Instead, the capsule slammed into the Utah desert after the parachutes failed to open. It turned out the deceleration sensors had been installed upside down.

Astronomers using an Australian radio telescope believed they might have discovered evidence of alien life when they picked up a distinctive signal at the same time every day. Seventeen years later, in 2015, they learned its source: The signal was coming from a microwave oven used by staff members to heat up their lunches.

—Excerpted from *1,000 Unforgettable Senior Moments: Of Which We Could Remember Only 254* by Tom Friedman (Workman Publishing), © 2017.

CORNER-OFFICE WANNABES

Over the years, the human resources consulting firm Robert Half has collected résumés and cover letters from job hunters who were just a little too smart for their own good—and for their hiring prospects. Check out these examples of tortured verbosity from aspiring employees.

"Able to remedy posterity and proficiency to the desired cumulus within the work arena. Once expounding upon these various constitutional elements, affinity is achieved, and I sequester the cultivation essential for yielded efficiencies."

"[My goal is to] find a career that will allocate dexterity from preceding experiences to perform a job to superiority. In addendum

to facile and ardent task force will alleviate the
work environment of unethical work habits."

THE CRIMINAL "MASTERMIND"

*Folks who break the law and think they can talk
themselves out of trouble sit very close to the
confluence of smart and stupid. Behold people
bedeviled by their own silver-tongued excuses.*

The issue: A Missouri heroin dealer appealed his conviction, insisting he
should never have been arrested.

The excuse: His rights were violated because he was a student of mysti-
cism and the founder of his own religion. As part of his religious duty, he
distributed heroin to the "sick, lost, blind, lame, deaf and dead members of
God's kingdom."

—Source: *Washington Post*

The issue: Over 40,000 cases of confiscated wine were illegally consumed in
police stations in the Indian state of Bihar.

The excuse: Police insisted that rats had bitten through the tops of confiscated wine bottles and had drunk the booty.

—Source: rt.com

The issue: A man was pulled over for driving 10 mph over the speed limit
in Australia.

The excuse: "The wind was pushing me."

—Source: metro.co.uk

The issue: A California driver was fined $478 for driving alone in the car-
pool lane.

The excuse: He wasn't alone. He had the articles of incorporation for his
business with him. Since the Supreme Court regards corporations as people
in First Amendment cases, so should traffic court.

—Source: rd.com

The issue: A Canadian woman was pulled over for driving nearly double the speed limit.

The excuse: She told the officer she was speeding in order to make it to her nearby cottage in time for sunset. It was 8:20 in the morning.

—Source: CTV News

The issue: A Wyoming college student was arrested on charges of shoplifting.

The excuse: It was a homework assignment—she was researching a term paper on kleptomania.

—Source: Associated Press

WHY DOES DUMBNESS STRIKE?

We Take Life Too Seriously *A few years ago, China's* People's Daily *cited an article proclaiming North Korean dictator Kim Jong Un the Sexiest Man Alive. The article stated, "With his devastatingly handsome, round face, [and] boyish charm, this Pyongyang-bred heartthrob is every woman's dream come true." What the* Daily *didn't grasp was that the article was the brainchild of the satirical website theonion.com. The site's mockery often makes credulous readers cry out in shock, as these comments indicate.*

Headline: Red Cross installs blood drop-off bins for donors' convenience

Response: "That is absolutely ridiculous. I would hate to see how they draw their own blood let alone the containers they put it in. It's not like a pair of shoes, just can't throw them in there."

Headline: Maybelline introduces line of injectable makeup to enhance appearance of internal organs

Response: "They don't get it. I don't care what a woman's innards look like. It speaks to me of massive vanity."

Headline: Engineers unveil new driverless car capable of committing hit-and-run

Response: "So, our time is spent building cars that commit crimes on their own? Great job, world."

Headline: Busch Gardens unveils new 9,600-mile-long endurance coaster
Response: "Is this for real? I'm sooooo doing this."

Headline: 42 million dead in bloodiest Black Friday weekend on record
Response: "How sad. What is wrong with people. So sad and all they were doing is shopping."

Our Nerves Get the Better of Us *A sense of helplessness and giddiness explains why the IQs of expectant fathers plummet once they enter the delivery room. Popsugar.com asked mothers for the mind-boggling things their husbands uttered as their children were born.*

I asked him to talk to me while I was getting a C-section (to distract me from that fact). The first thing he says to me is, "OK, they just cut you open."
—Sarah Connor, *Livermore, CA*

When I asked my husband who our newborn baby looked like, he said, "Kinda reminds me of the dog."
—Stephanie Elsner, *Granby, CT*

Husband: Are you going to seduce my wife?
Doctor: Not in her current condition.
Me: Induce, honey, induce!
—Brenda Moar, *Queensland,*
Australia

"It's missing parts!" We were told the whole time that we were having a boy, but then the doctor pulled her out!
—Charlene Kidd, *Surrey, British Columbia*

We Get Carried Away by Love *Romance can frazzle any brain.* Cosmopolitan *and datingfails.com asked readers to describe the moment they realized their significant other wasn't a genius.*

My boyfriend and I were holding hands when he looked at mine and said, "Your hands are so small! How can you swim?"
—Ashley Marie

One night I was leaning on his stomach and he told me, "Babe, get up. You're hurting my ovaries."
—Christine

A girl told me that I seemed like a great guy but I reminded her of the actor Edward Norton. And since she hated his character in some movie that she couldn't even remember the name of, it would never work out between us.
—Josh

My hubby and I were eating salad when he picked up one of those big crunchy pieces and asked, "Is this what celery is made from?"
—Samantha

Originally published in the October 2017 issue of *Reader's Digest* magazine.

GRANDFATHER FOR LIFE

I grew up in a small town alongside the Rhine River in Germany. One summer day, a few weeks after my third birthday, I was feeling sad because I didn't have a grandfather. (One of mine had died and the other lived far away.) So, I decided to go get one.

I skipped to the little park close to our house and the river where several retired boat captains were reminiscing about the good old days on the water. One of them made a great impression on me with his lovely smile. I walked up to him and said, "Would you like to be my grandfather?" His face lit up and his smile broadened. He said, "Honey, I would love to be your grandfather!"

We met every day. He read me fairy tales and explained the pictures in the books. He bought me ice cream and chocolates. Some days he spent hours telling me about the cargo on the ships and where those ships would unload. Other days he took me to a puppet show.

But when I started kindergarten, I could no longer go to our daily meetings. I saw my grandfather only occasionally, and then not at all.

Life went on for me. I finished school and moved to the United States. As often as I could, I traveled back to Germany to visit relatives and friends. On one of these visits, I was in an elegant hotel in my hometown celebrating my birthday. An older gentleman tapped me on the shoulder and asked, "Is your name Ruth?" I told him it was, and he said, "My father was your beloved grandfather." He told me that my adopted grandfather spoke of me until his dying day. As he left, this stranger said, "Thank you for bringing so much joy into my father's life." I would like to tell my grandfather today that he still brings joy into mine.

—Ruth Moos, *Sewickley, PA*

Cherry Blossoms

Spring has sprung! The arrival of March means the blooming of cherry blossoms, and for 40 years, this city—with its more than 350,000 Yoshino cherry trees—has celebrated the season with an annual festival the locals call "the pinkest party on earth." The park pictured here plays host to many of the main events and now shares its name with the festival's founder, Carolyn Crayton, who also organized the planting of many of the trees around this area, referred to by congressional records as the Cherry Blossom Capital of the World. Where is it?

    A. Washington, D.C.

    B. Macon, Georgia

    C. Aiea, Hawaii

    D. St. Louis, Missouri

Answer on page 281. *Photograph by Sean Pavone/Getty Images*

TOUGH TIMES

During a time when money was tight, we had to cut back on all excess spending. Colleen, my daughter who was 6 at the time, came to me with an envelope and asked me to mail it for her. She'd received a letter from her grandmother the day before, and she handed me the same envelope with the flap crudely sealed with tape. She had scrawled across the front, "RETURN TO SENDER." "What's this?" I asked. "I'm saving money on a stamp." With tears flowing, I hugged her hard.

—Sharon Haiste, *Prince George, BC*

LOVE MATTERS

Both my husband and I had lost our jobs the month we got married. It was a tough time financially. I managed to secure employment, and my husband went back to school to become a teacher and coach. With Christmas around the corner, we were going to have a plain holiday, just the two of us. Our gift giving, we decided, would be only one gift each and only cost $10. It turned into an adventure—what could I get for my husband to convey my love for only $10? I decided to go the practical route. Living in the Midwest during the winter, we got a lot of sleet, snow and cold. He really needed some sturdy gloves, along with a hat and scarf, which I got with my trusty coupon. On Christmas Day, I got a big bear hug and an appreciative kiss from my husband. Then I held my breath—what gift did my husband get me? I opened the hand-wrapped package and gasped. It was a simple, sewn tote bag in my favorite colors. There was a lady at school where he student-taught that sewed. He asked her to sew me a bag and, every week, he sacrificed one dollar from his budget to pay for it.

—Monica Darga, *North Jacksonville, FL*

The Almost Perfect Murder

by Robert F. Howe

Detectives believed Donnah Winger had died at the hands of a deranged stranger. Then they took another look.

Donnah Winger couldn't have been in brighter spirits. The 31-year-old operating room technician was with her husband, Mark, at his Illinois Department of Nuclear Safety office to show off 3-month-old Bailey, the little girl they were in the process of adopting. Mark's co-workers fussed over the baby and remarked how the popular couple now truly seemed complete. "She always wanted a family," says Donnah's stepfather, Ira Drescher, who notes that a medical condition had prevented her from having biological offspring. "This was something she had dreamt about."

Later that afternoon, after the proud parents had returned to their modest brick home on Westview Drive in Springfield, Mark headed to the basement for a workout. He was jogging on his treadmill when he heard a loud thump upstairs. Alarmed, he bolted up the basement steps and, hearing his baby's cry, turned right through the bathroom and into the bedroom. Finding Bailey alone on the bed, Winger snatched up the .45 semiautomatic he had hidden in his nightstand and sped toward the dining room.

There, he witnessed a stranger kneeling over his wife, wielding fierce blows with a claw hammer. The assailant paused to glance up at Winger, and then raised the hammer to strike again. Winger took quick aim and shot him twice in the head. Frantic, he then phoned 911.

When police arrived, they found Winger bent over Donnah, who lay face-down in an inky pool of blood. An officer, who had his own camera in his car, snapped three quick images of the crime scene as medics attended to Donnah and her attacker, who both still had feeble pulses. Police then led Winger into his bedroom, where, his voice quaking, he detailed what he'd seen. When an officer informed him that a driver's license identified the intruder as Roger Harrington, Winger burst out, "That's the man!"

> *A stranger knelt over his wife, wielding fierce blows with a claw hammer.*

He explained how Donnah had met Harrington when she returned with Bailey the previous Wednesday, Aug. 23, from a visit to her parents' house in Florida. She had booked a van to get her home from the St. Louis airport. Harrington, 27, was at the wheel. He had terrified her by speeding down the highway, describing how a menacing spirit named Dahm sometimes urged him to hurt people, and boasting about orgies staged at his trailer in rural Sangamon County.

Winger said that he was at a business conference in Chattanooga, Tennessee, when Donnah called and described her harrowing ride. He instructed her to write down what had happened, and then phoned Harrington's employer to complain. A few days later, he also personally called the driver, then on suspension, to warn him to steer clear of his family.

As Winger was wrapping up his chilling recitation, Donnah and Harrington were rushed to the hospital, where they died within the hour. Meanwhile, investigators checked out Winger's story. On the refrigerator, they found Donnah's note about her frightening drive with Harrington. Running checks on him, they established that he was a divorced high school dropout who had previously been arrested for battery and had also had a brief stay in a mental health facility. They learned that he'd told many people about his evil spirit Dahm—his name for a Halloween mask he kept in his trailer. Police were soon convinced the Wingers had fallen victim to a psychopath.

The Almost Perfect Murder

All the officers were in agreement, save one. Detective Doug Williamson, relatively new to homicide, was reluctant to contradict his more seasoned colleagues but was privately troubled. "Winger would turn on and off emotion rather easy, yet there were never any tears," recalls Williamson, now a sergeant with the Springfield Police. "That wasn't normal."

There was another thing. Winger claimed to have cradled Donnah's head as she lay on the dining room floor fighting off death. Yet Williamson says he noticed Winger had blood on the back of his right hand, but none on the palm. Plus it seemed strange that a loving husband would comfort his wife as she gasped for breath, and then lay her facedown, as she was found, on the gore-smeared carpet.

Outside the Winger home, Williamson had run a check on a brown 1988 Oldsmobile Delta parked conspicuously on the wrong side of the street. As he suspected, it was Harrington's. Inside the car, something caught his eye. On the front seat, he found a blank bank deposit slip. Written on the back was the Wingers' address, Mark Winger's name and, strangely, a time: 4:30, just about the time of the killings.

The day after the deaths, Winger met again with detectives, who were already wrapping up their investigation. They asked if there was anything unusual in the house, and Winger mentioned a mug and a pack of Marlboro 100s that had been left in the dining room. Detectives concluded the items belonged to Harrington, but Williamson found it peculiar that a killer would bring his smokes along.

Williamson said he wanted to chase down new leads, but his superiors were convinced that Harrington was the culprit. "They're great detectives—they really are," says Williamson, who didn't press his misgivings. "But for whatever reason, they misinterpreted the facts." The evidence, including all the bloodied clothes, the gun, Donnah's note, the deposit slip found in Harrington's car, and the photos, were all filed away. Case closed.

Winger's family and friends gathered to comfort the distraught husband. A graduate of the Virginia Military Institute and an Army veteran who had become an engineer, Winger expressed his appreciation in a letter

225

to the local paper: "On behalf of Bailey and me, as well as Donnah's parents and siblings and mine, I want to publicly express our thank-you to the people in this community whose concern and understanding at this difficult time will long be remembered."

When the notice was published in October 1995, it seemed a gracious final gesture in a horrifying case. Yet there would be much more to come. Williamson couldn't shake his doubts, and eventually others came to sense that something was amiss.

* * *

For the first few nights after Donnah's death, Winger stayed at the home of Rabbi Michael Datz and his wife. They were friends who were expecting a baby and had a nursery that Bailey could use. Deann Schultz, one of Donnah's closest friends and a surgical nurse, also slept at the rabbi's that first night. "Deann stayed at our house presumably because she was a nurse and had kids, so she would know how to handle Bailey," recalls Rabbi Datz. But he adds, "We had no clue what was really going on."

Within a few months, Winger had hired nanny Rebecca Simic to care for Bailey. Simic and Winger soon became involved, marrying in October 1996 and moving to a farmhouse in nearby Pleasant Plains. Together, the couple would have three more children.

Winger kept in close touch with investigators over the following years. "Mark kept injecting himself," says Williamson. "He kept calling, and he'd say, 'Hey, I'm getting married,' or 'Hey, I'm coming in to get my gun back.'" He called often enough for Williamson's partner, Detective Charlie Cox, to grow suspicious, wondering if Winger wasn't double-checking to make sure detectives had really dropped the case. After that, Cox and Williamson rarely spent a free moment together without discussing the killings. "There are always cases that leave lingering questions," says Williamson. "But if we were having a beer or going on a fishing trip, this is the one we'd talk about."

* * *

In early 1999, police got their break: a call from an attorney saying Deann Schultz wanted to talk. Schultz had fallen into such despair since her friend's death that she'd attempted to take her life four times. Finally, her psychiatrist persuaded her to divulge her terrible secret. The story she told began a few weeks before the slayings. Shortly after confiding in Donnah that she was unhappy with her marriage and considering going back to a former boyfriend, Schultz received a call from Winger, who said he was attracted to her. In a matter of days, they began their affair at an Illinois hotel, and later got together in Winger's red pickup truck near a local playground.

A psychiatrist persuaded Deann Schultz to divulge her terrible secret to police.

Schultz stated that shortly after she began seeing Winger, he led her to believe that they would someday be together. In one of her most telling recollections, he had said, "It would be easier if Donnah died." And there was more. The Wingers had told Schultz and her husband about Donnah's wild ride with Harrington, so Deann said she knew exactly who Winger was referring to the day before the murders when he said, "I need to get that van driver in my house."

When she first came forward, Schultz spoke freely with police, but she later received immunity so her trial testimony could not be used against her. Detective Jim Graham, who spoke several times with Schultz, laments that despite all that Winger had said to her, "She didn't do anything to stop it."

Schultz had failed to prevent the crime, but her story was all police needed to reopen the case. Investigators' first step was to retrieve the bloodied clothing that had been taken as evidence at the time of the crime and send it off to a bloodstain pattern expert. The expert reported back that he found blood spatter from Donnah on Winger's clothing, but not on Harrington's. In addition, he observed that the castoff of Donnah's blood on the dining room wall was inconsistent with Winger's description of the killing.

Police then scrutinized the crime-scene photos, which had been sealed away without ever having been looked at. They showed Harrington's body in a position completely different from what Winger had described.

Investigators reviewed the 911 tapes. Winger had placed the 911 call but hung up midway through it. "In the background, Harrington is moaning," says State's Attorney John Schmidt. "Then suddenly, Winger says, 'My baby's crying. I've got to go. I'll call you right back,' and click."

In light of the 911 tape, police placed new importance on an earlier statement made by Winger's neighbor that at 4:30 p.m., about the time Winger hung up on the call, she heard what she thought was a single gunshot. Winger insisted he fired two consecutive shots at Harrington, yet police now concluded that the shots were several minutes apart, the second one aimed to silence Harrington. In fact, blood patterns on the floor suggested that Winger rolled Harrington over onto his back before firing the second bullet into the man's forehead.

But perhaps the most persuasive bit of evidence had been in police possession from the start: the note found in Harrington's car. Winger claimed he called Harrington the morning of his wife's death to tell him to stay away from Donnah. But in new conversations with Harrington's friends, police learned, from three people who were at Harrington's trailer when the call came in, that he was summoned for a 4:30 meeting at the Winger residence—all of which Harrington wrote on a roommate's deposit slip.

It all dovetailed with an ominous call that Deann Schultz said she received early on the afternoon of the murder. It was Winger, and he asked, "Will you love me no matter what?"

Finally, prosecutors felt they had sufficient evidence to secure an indictment, and on Aug. 23, 2001, officers took Mark Winger into custody. He was then held on $10 million bail.

The most persuasive bit of evidence had been in police possession from the start.

During the trial, prosecutors painted an eerie picture of what they believed happened at the Wingers' home on the day of the murder. Harrington arrived as requested, unarmed, and set his mug and cigarettes down in the dining room before Winger ushered him into the kitchen, where the note Donnah had written hung on the refrigerator. Harrington may have bent over to read it, or perhaps was forced to his knees at gunpoint. Then Winger shot him once in the head.

The Almost Perfect Murder

When Donnah, who had been playing with Bailey in the bedroom, burst in to see what had happened, Winger swung the hammer into her head. She collapsed facedown, and he struck her at least six more times, showering blood onto the adjacent wall.

Jurors in last spring's trial found the state's case persuasive. On June 5, 2002, Winger, now 40, was found guilty of two counts of murder. He is serving a sentence of life without parole and, still claiming innocence and insisting that he was set up by a jilted Deann Schultz, has appealed the conviction. (Bailey and his three other children reside with his wife, Rebecca, who continues to stand by his side.)

One vital element in the case has yet to be solved to everyone's satisfaction: motive. Some observers believe it was the affair—that Winger feared Donnah would find out he was seeing Schultz, demand a divorce and take away Bailey. Others think Winger was motivated by greed. After Donnah's death, he received about $200,000 in insurance and another $25,000 from the state's fund for crime victims. In the end, investigators suspect he was motivated by a combination of factors. One thing is certain, says Ira Drescher, "My family was destroyed for a long time after this. He betrayed us all."

Originally published in the February 2003 issue of *Reader's Digest* magazine.

Mark Winger was sentenced to life in prison without the possibility of parole and is incarcerated in Western Illinois Correctional Center in Mount Sterling, Illinois. In 2007 Winger was convicted of solicitation for murder when he tried to hire another prisoner to murder Deann Schultz and Jeffrey Gelman, a wealthy child-hood friend who would not pay Winger's $1 million bail. Winger was sentenced to an additional 35 years in prison.

Season of Miracles

by John Pekkanen

They were just kids, but they were old enough to grieve and big enough to dream

As they listened to "The Star-Spangled Banner," 12 young ballplayers anxiously awaited the opening game of junior baseball in North Charleston, South Carolina. Feelings ran high among the 7- and 8-year-olds, members of the Steve Evans Reds.

One of them, Jason Ellis "E.J." Fludd, 8, hovered near third-base coach Sandra Evans. "Aunt Sandy," E.J. asked, "is Coach Stevie up there watching us?"

Sandy, 32, answered softly. "Yes, E.J. I think Steve's spirit is right here with us."

"Play ball!" the umpire shouted. Sandy, tears welling, watched her team dash onto the field. *This season is for you, Steve,* she thought, as her mind drifted back to a year earlier.

*　　*　　*

"Sandy, we have a dinner guest," Steve Evans called out as he strolled in the door. Home from baseball practice, Steve had with him a shy youngster called E.J.

Steve always had a soft spot for kids. An easygoing 34-year-old with reddish hair and a lanky frame, he had volunteered to coach the team. In the spring of 1991, he'd rush home from his job as an insulation installer to get to practice.

Patient and encouraging, Steve proved an ideal coach for the restless, diverse group of youngsters—some White, some Black, others Asian.

231

"Several come from troubled backgrounds," he told Sandy. "I'm coaching to help them feel better about themselves."

One boy, E.J., laughed harder—and played harder—than all the others. He lived with his mother, who worked long hours as a cook at the Charleston Air Force Base. Having little contact with his father, E.J. was lonely much of the time. After every practice, he would give Steve a bear hug and say, "Thanks, Coach Stevie."

At dinner that first evening, E.J. won over the entire family. Soon he was coming regularly for dinner, often staying overnight. Sandy became "Aunt Sandy." Steve would include E.J. in family softball games with his son, Timmy, 12, daughter, Stephanie, 10, and four nephews—Thomas, Steven and David Evans, and James Garvin. The four nephews played with E.J. on the team.

The only bad news that year was at the ballpark—where Steve's team lost game after game. E.J. would slump in dejection at every defeat.

During one losing game, Steve put an arm around the boy. "Hold your head up, E.J.," he said. "You don't have anything to be ashamed of."

Steve then pulled out an Atlanta Braves baseball card. "See this?" he asked. "One day your picture will be on one of these."

E.J.'s eyes lit up. "You mean I could play for the Braves someday?"

"Sure, as long as you keep working hard and don't give up."

Then, on June 17, 1991, Steve was killed when a chemical reactor exploded at the plant where Steve was working. When Sandy heard the crushing news, she slumped to the floor, all feeling draining out of her.

Sandy was 17, just out of high school, when she married Steve in 1976. Money was tight—but they had fun. Steve loved driving Sandy and the children to Florida's Disney World, or spending a day "tubing" on nearby lakes and rivers.

Now Sandy sat in the funeral home, numb with grief. Looking up, she saw Steve's team, in their uniforms, file slowly in. A few moments later, Sandy noticed E.J., tears pouring down his cheeks, as he sat with his mother.

"He hasn't stopped crying since Steve died," E.J.'s mother said. Sandy opened her arms wide, and E.J. climbed into her lap. As he wept, Sandy held his trembling body close, trying to give him the comfort she couldn't give herself.

After Steve's funeral, the team played its remaining games in a daze. They lost them all.

In the following months, Sandy's sister, Louann Ackerman, grew increasingly worried. Sandy was sinking deeper and deeper into her private grief. When her sister stopped eating and lost 40 pounds, Louann felt panic. "This may be her way of ending it all," she said to her husband, Ira.

Then early in 1992, Louann had an idea. "In Steve's memory," she told Sandy, "I want to sponsor this year's team for you."

"Funny," Sandy said, "I 'd been thinking I might sponsor the team myself as a way to honor Steve. He loved those kids." Sandy and Louann renamed the team the Steve Evans Reds, for Steve's red hair. When Sandy told E.J., he said, "I promise you, Aunt Sandy, we're gonna win all our games for Coach Stevie." Steve's friend Ron Gadsden agreed to become coach and continue as manager.

On a warm March afternoon, the Reds gathered for their first practice. Forming the nucleus of the team were E.J., Sandy's four nephews, and Ron Gadsden's son, Ryan. Because some of the previous season's players were over the age limit, new ones were added. Younger and smaller than the ones they replaced, some of the new boys had no idea how to catch or hit. *This is going to be a rough season*, Louann thought.

Coach Gadsden drilled the new kids on how to hold a bat and swing. E.J. coached them on the man for whom the team was named. "Coach Stevie took a lot of time with us," E.J. explained, his voice cracking. "He was always nice, and he made us laugh." Then E.J. told the team, "We've got to win this year for Coach Stevie." Slowly, the message sank in as the Reds approached their opening day.

In the first inning of the season's first game, the Charleston Apartments Giants took a quick two-run lead before the Reds came to bat. E.J. hit a home run to lead a four-run counterattack. By the bottom half of the final inning, the score was tied 8-8. Then Thomas Evans hit a home run. To everyone's surprise, the Reds had won.

When the Reds won again, Louann noticed changes in her sister. During the games Sandy, leaden and unemotional after Steve's death, started clapping and shouting. By the time the Reds won their third game, she began eating again.

"With this team," Sandy told Louann, "I feel that Steve's not gone completely. There's a piece of him still here with all of us."

The team was also changing. The youngsters began saying, "We can't be beat!" Sandy, worried that E.J. and her nephews were feeling too much pressure to win for Steve, called them aside. "Remember," she said, "it's just a game."

"You don't understand, Aunt Sandy," E.J. said earnestly. "We have to win for Coach Stevie!"

Sandy fought back tears. *If we ever lose*, she thought, *these kids will be shattered.*

The Reds kept on rolling. They took one game 16-7 and another 17-6.

Sandy drew strength from E.J. *Just look at this little boy*, she thought. *He's hurting so much, yet he's still so loving and joyful.* Sandy began looking forward to the games and practices with a gladness she feared she'd never feel again. She took the team for pizzas. She even found herself laughing out loud.

"It's a miracle we're winning," Louann told her husband. "But the real miracle is seeing E.J. help Sandy to heal. I'm getting my sister back."

*   *   *

Near the end of the season, the undefeated Reds stood at the top of the league. To win the championship they had to beat the Giants—the team the Reds had defeated by only one run on opening day, the Giants' only loss.

The day of the final game, May 23, the temperature soared into the 90s. The Giants took an early lead in the first inning with four runs. The Reds fought back, and by the end of the second inning, they were tied 4-4. Then the Giants went on a hitting spree and moved ahead 10-4. This was the first time all season that the Reds had been so far behind. "Come on, we can still win!" E.J. shouted.

However, the tension became too much for Thomas Evans, and he suddenly burst into tears. Sandy raced out and pulled him close. "It's OK," she whispered.

"We're gonna lose, Aunt Sandy!" Thomas said.

"Don't worry about losing," she assured him. "We've done our best."

Although the Reds reduced the Giants' lead, they couldn't catch up. The Giants went ahead 12-9 with one inning to go.

The Reds trotted off the field for their last time at bat. Suddenly, Thomas Evans knelt near the pitcher's mound, drawing in the red dirt with his finger. On the mound he'd written his uncle's name.

"I wanted Uncle Steve to know we were thinking about him," Thomas told Sandy. Word of what the boy had done spread quickly through the Reds' dugout. Moments later, however, reality set in. The Reds had two runners on base—but there were now two outs. The dugout went silent.

The Reds' last hope was David Evans, the smallest player on the team. As he walked toward the plate, Louann prayed silently. *Dear Lord, please, help these kids. And Sandy.*

David, not much taller than his bat, made up for his small size with a scrappy attitude. On the first pitch, he swung awkwardly and missed. Then he fouled off another pitch. *It's finally over*, Sandy thought sadly to herself.

With the next pitch, David made contact, but the ball headed in the worst possible direction—straight toward first base and the best player on the Giants' team. He reached down to scoop up the ball—but it squirted past him.

David raced to second base as one run scored. This cut the Giants' lead to two, and there were runners on second and third.

Thomas Evans, next at bat, sent the ball flying for a clean hit. Sandy waved two runners home. With the game now tied, the Reds traded high-fives.

The next batter, Ryan Gadsden, got another hit, and by the time E.J. got to the plate, there were three runners on base. On the second pitch, E.J. connected perfectly, and the ball sailed deep into right-center field—a grand slam.

His teammates mobbed him. Sandy jumped up and down.

The Reds now led for the first time in the game, and more hits followed. When the third out finally came, the Reds had pushed across 11 runs in all. "I've seen it, but I can't believe it!" Louann yelled.

Disheartened and exhausted, the Giants went down without scoring. The Reds had won the league championship, 20-12.

Eight days later, Sandy stood at Steve's graveside with E.J. and her four nephews. The date—May 31—would have been Steve's 36th birthday.

Sandy knelt and, on her husband's grave, placed a photograph of the Reds holding their team trophy. "The team won the championship for you, Steve," Sandy said softly. "And we know you helped them do it."

Originally published in the May 1993 issue of *Reader's Digest* magazine.

The Night the World Fell Down

by Sue Martin as told to Alan Burgess

The terrible earthquake at Agadir, Morocco, caused the deaths of 20,000 people. Here is the dramatic story of one who survived.

I was undressing in the hotel bathroom when the earthquake struck. Jerry, my husband, was playing with our year-old baby, Diane, in the adjoining room. The time was 39 minutes past 11 on the 29th of February, 1960, in a Moroccan town called Agadir.

Until that moment I had been completely happy. We were on a two-week vacation from the U.S. Air Force base in Morocco, where Jerry was a lieutenant. The seaside resort of Agadir was full of vacationers, bright lights and music.

Then it happened. The walls began to shake. Plaster fell from the ceiling. And finally, with a great subterranean groan and roar as if some giant entombed in the center of the earth had snored and stretched in his sleep, the world disintegrated, and I fell down through black and timeless space.

I was not aware of any impact, only that I was suddenly in complete darkness, pinned under an enormous weight. "Jerry!" I screamed. Then water began to sluice down. *Oh, God*, I thought, *it must have plunged us under the sea.* (The water actually came from broken plumbing; it drained away quickly.)

The earthquake in Agadir reduced buildings to rubble.

From somewhere near me, I heard Diane cry. Then I heard Jerry's muffled shout, "Sue, Sue, where are you?" I shouted back that I was trapped. "I'm OK," he called back. (He wasn't, but I didn't know it then.) "I'm loaded down with rubble, but I'm going to get to Diane."

He told me afterward that it was the sound of Diane's crying that gave him the strength to kick and hack out a small cavern for himself in the debris. When he reached Diane, he found that she was pushing with her baby hands in his direction. As soon as he clasped her she stopped crying. She was unhurt.

The realization that they had both survived brought an overwhelming sense of relief to me. Cautiously I began to see what I could move. My left hand and arm were free and I could force them up to my head, which was jammed back by debris. I managed to clear a space of about 2 inches above my nose and to get my head forward. My right arm was pinned down amid a mass of masonry. The bathroom door had fallen diagonally across me—probably saving my life. My feet were sticking out under the bottom and I could wriggle them just a bit.

I was frightened. It was pitch dark and I was buried alive, pinned down more securely than I would have been inside a coffin. And the weight above me seemed to be getting heavier and tighter. It needed all my strength of will not to shriek uncontrollably in horror.

In the silence, I prayed. "God will help us," I said to myself. But if I could have seen our hotel from outside, I wouldn't have thought much of our chances of getting out alive. The four-story building had concertinaed down like a squashed layer cake. Fifty of the 72 hotel guests had been killed when the earthquake struck. Our room, 240, had been on the third floor. Now I was at the bottom.

Jerry shouted that he was trying to work his way through to an outside wall, dragging Diane with him. There were bound to be rescue workers around by now, he said. I mustn't give up.

As the hours passed, however, other things didn't help my peace of mind. All through that night there were recurring earth tremors—little shuddering shocks that dropped plaster and dust from the 2-inch-high ceiling above my head into my hair and seemed to pack the rubble down even tighter.

Jerry was making progress. He shouted at last that he could see cracks of light through the rubble. It was dawn and he was close to the outside wall. His shouts abruptly became less enthusiastic. I could tell by his voice that something had gone wrong. Then he told me. He had reached the outside wall only to find that a steel girder still blocked his way.

That was the last I heard from him. He didn't call again, and he didn't answer when I shouted. As the minutes ticked by, and then the hours, I shouted again and again. There was no answer. I lay in the darkness in a half-twisted position, pressed down by that enormous weight, in a black pit of despair.

At last—it was long past noon on the day after the earthquake, I learned later—I began to hear the noise of an electric drill overhead and far away. Soon I heard picks and shovels and then French accented voices shouting in English: "Sue? Where are you, Sue? We're coming! Hold on!" Vaguely I wondered how they knew my name.

I shouted back as best I could, and hour after hour these shovels and picks and French voices forced their way down toward me, scooping out a sort of human mouse hole through masonry, concrete, twisted girders, hotel furniture, all manner of debris. One of the voices stood out. It was a lively young male voice. "Sue," it kept calling. "Where are you, Sue? Keep telling me where you are."

It was this young man who gave me the best news of my life: "Sue, your husband and daughter are safe! You hear? They are safe!"

He kept up a chatter of news as they worked closer. He and the others were from the French naval air base about 3 miles away. A vast rescue operation was underway: men from the base; sailors from the French fleet, which had been cruising offshore; American doctors, nurses and rescue workers from the U.S. air bases near Casablanca. Everybody. They had found my husband and little Diane and got them out. A Frenchwoman whose house had tumbled had rummaged in the ruins and found some clothes for Diane. My husband asked to remain at the aid station to await news of me rather than go to the hospital.

At last—it must have been midafternoon—the rubble began to move around my feet and I felt a hand touch my toes. Three or four men cleared a space at that end, and I could hear them discussing how to get me free. It was the door that covered all but my feet which balked them. They tried to scrape around either side, but I seemed to be hemmed in by solid blocks of masonry.

How did I feel, they asked. In spite of the sun, which was apparently blazing down up above, I told them I was shivering and my feet felt like ice. Almost immediately two wonderfully warm hands seized my feet and began massaging them. The lively young French voice introduced himself. His name was Hubert. He and the other men had tested each other and decided that Hubert had the warmest hands, so he held my feet while the others went to find a doctor.

As the second dawn rose, it was believed that in all Agadir I was the only person still trapped who was alive.

They were quickly back. They had stopped cars and drained hot water out of the radiators into wine bottles. These, wrapped inside a blanket, they put against my feet.

They tried again to extricate me, but without success. They were afraid to move the door for fear the rubble overhead might shift and crush me. So they had to go back to the roof and dig a second shaft, which would come out at my head.

Hubert was left behind to maintain my morale. I felt cold, depressed and weak. A doctor gave me two injections in the soles of my feet. The second night was approaching. Though the doctor said I shouldn't, I wanted to sleep.

Hubert wouldn't hear of it. I was to stay awake until they got me out, he said. He sensed that I was nearing the limit of my endurance and played his cards like a true Frenchman.

"Sue," he said, "you are very beautiful."

That warmed me a bit. "How do you know that when all you can see of me is my feet?" I asked.

"To have your courage," he answered, "you must be beautiful."

He talked about my unseen beauty for several minutes. Then he added, "It is a pity you are married, Sue. If you were not, I should marry you because you have so much courage."

I knew he was only playing a part, to keep me going, but it served the purpose. He told me that he was 19, that he lived near Paris. He asked me all about Jerry and Diane and where we lived in America. All the while his warm hands gently stroked my feet.

Sometime in the middle of the second night he asked me if I knew the meaning of *petit poulet*. I didn't know what it meant and I didn't care. My resistance had now shrunk almost to the vanishing point.

"It means 'little chicken,'" said Hubert patiently. "That is what you are, 'my little chicken.' Now listen, because I am going to teach you many French words, and you will repeat them all after me. Imagine how wonderful it will be when you emerge from this hole speaking perfect French!"

All through the rest of the night, in a dark hole under thousands of tons of rubble, this 19-year-old boy taught me French.

Overhead, at the mouth of my shaft, a crowd of U.S. Air Force and Navy men, rescue workers, correspondents, all sorts of people, were keeping a night-and-day vigil. As the second dawn rose it was believed that in all Agadir I was the only person still trapped who was alive. They wished me to be saved. It seemed that I represented some small rallying point of the human spirit.

In the dawn they burrowed down to near my head. Now they were using oxyacetylene cutting equipment. I could hear the hiss—and afterward I discovered they had singed my hair. Then at last a gentle hand was brushing my face, a light appeared, and I could see blackened faces and the whites of eyes and teeth as the rescuers murmured to me. They used automobile jacks to help lift the door; they scraped the masonry away from me. But even then my hips wouldn't come out. They eased and pulled—and suddenly, magically, I was sliding free! It was one of the most marvelous moments I have ever known. I thank God for courage and for the strength and perseverance of my rescuers.

I couldn't see their faces now, only hear their voices as they passed me from hand to hand. When I looked up the shaft they had made, it seemed miles to the top. But up I went, passed from strong arm to strong arm, climbing, climbing all the time, as if I were going up to heaven.

At the top of the hole I felt the sunlight on my face. People were crowding around. They were all cheering. They seemed to be crying. I think I was crying, too, with sheer happiness, as they put me on a stretcher and into an ambulance and rushed me to the French aid station where Jerry was waiting for me. I had been entombed exactly 39 hours.

Three months later when I went back to Agadir, I met Hubert. He was as handsome and lively as his voice had sounded. He kissed me on both cheeks, and my eyes brimmed with tears. For I knew that I owed my life to this young man who had held my feet and called me his little chicken and talked of love to me in a situation surely unique in all the world's history of lovemaking.

Originally published in the August 1963 issue of *Reader's Digest* magazine.

WHERE, OH WHERE?

Mama Mimi

Say hello to Mama Mimi. This gentle giant, the brainchild of Danish artist Thomas Dambo, took up residence here in Rendezvous Park last year. She's made of recycled and renewable materials that were sourced locally and assembled by the artist and a team of workers on-site. Her mane, for instance, is driftwood, and she wears a necklace of rope and stones. Mimi is the 80th in a family of troll sculptures Dambo has installed all over the world. Where is she?

    A. Bernheim Forest, Kentucky

    B. Aullwood Audubon, Ohio

    C. Jackson Hole, Wyoming

    D. Breckenridge, Colorado

Answer on page 281. Photograph by Thomas Dambo

Humor Hall of Fame

During a heartfelt chat with a friend about relationships, my wife sighed and said, "You know, if something happened to Lloyd I don't think I could ever marry again." Her friend nodded sympathetically. "I know what you mean," she said. "Once is enough."

—LLOYD G. YOUNG

My husband surprised me with a night out to celebrate the anniversary of our first date. I was reminded of the man I fell in love with. We arrived at the theater and learned the movie was playing at a different location a full hour earlier. I was reminded of the man I married.

—@GOODSHEWRITES

The Good Divorce

by Wendy Swallow, from the book *Breaking Apart*

Though it went against everything in her,
the writer had to help her ex-husband
be a parent to their sons

When I was agonizing over whether to leave a marriage that had long been tense and distant, I took out books on children of divorce, on custody and single parenting. Most of what I read said that kids of divorce are angrier, sadder, more likely to be depressed or unable to have satisfying relationships.

One night in the supermarket checkout line, I skimmed an article on grown children of divorce. "A hole in the heart is universal," said one expert. I looked at the two little faces gazing up at me from the cart. *I can't do it*, I thought. *I don't want my children to have holes in their hearts.* Not holes carved by my own hand.

Still, my marriage continued to be full of fear and anger. Within it, I could not weave a cocoon of love and care around my children. In a letter I told my husband, Ron*, that I needed a divorce. I offered him generous visitation, weekend time and one night with the boys per week. Ron was agitated.

"I want joint custody of the boys," he said. "I don't want to 'visit' with my kids." He spat the word at me. "I want to be their dad. I want them half the time."

I honestly had never suspected that Ron would want custody or seek it.

I thought of my sons—David, 5, and Jesse, 3—living away from me for half the time. Hyperventilating, I rushed out of the room, unable to bear to look at the man who would take away my children.

Names have been changed to protect privacy.

245

*   *   *

Ron hired a lawyer who struck me as combative and hostile. My own lawyer seemed timid and conciliatory. I had no choice but to agree to a trial of joint custody—three months. David and Jesse would spend a week with each parent but spend Wednesday nights with the other parent.

Ron and I had vowed to tell our sons about this together, but by that point we were so hardened to each other we didn't even try. I told the boys in the car, outside the building in which I'd rented an apartment. They sat in the back, two confused little birds blinking at me in the dark as I explained why they were going to live with Mommy in a new place, then go back to Daddy for a while.

When I said that Mommy and Daddy didn't love each other anymore, David started to cry. I quickly tried to reassure him that we would always love them, that divorce didn't change how parents felt about their kids, but he didn't seem mollified. Jesse said nothing until the very end, then he pulled his thumb out of his mouth. "What's divorce?"

The first week on my own with them, we were too numb to do much more than watch videos and hug on the sofa. The second week, when they went to Ron's, was when the nightmare began for real. At night I would lie on their beds among their stuffed animals and cry myself to sleep.

When it was finally Wednesday and my turn to have them for a night, I went to pick them up at the day-care center. Jesse ran to the playground fence and said, in a cry of amazement, "You came back!"

All my explanations and reassurances had amounted to nothing. All he knew was what he felt, and it felt to him as if I had gone to the moon. Later, I mentioned the incident to a psychologist we were working with, and she shook her head. "No, he didn't think you went to the moon. He thought you had died."

Now I knew how people got holes in their hearts.

*   *   *

Relentlessly I questioned our joint-custody arrangement. David, overwhelmed by both a new school and a new living arrangement, was chewing holes in the sleeves of his sweatshirts. Jesse was suddenly kicking other children at day care and drawing stick figures with blood spurting from them.

I didn't know what was happening in Ron's house, but I could tell he was struggling to adjust. I fretted about how often the sheets were changed, whether Ron was giving the boys enough milk. I knew that sometimes he lost his temper, and I worried myself sick over the fact that I couldn't protect my sons anymore.

One Sunday evening I went to Ron's to pick up the boys, and found Ron pacing nervously on the sidewalk, the kids already in their car seats in the Volvo, which we traded back and forth with them.

Something was amiss. "I'm sorry," Ron said, breathing hard. He started to cry. "I just slapped Jesse. He did something bad, but there's no excuse."

I went over to the car. Jesse looked up at me, silent, ashen. A red mark was on his cheek. David was crying.

"He pushed a stone down the air vent of the car," Ron explained, "even though I told him not to. It made me mad and I guess I lost it. I'm really sorry. I can't believe I did that."

"We don't hit our children, Ron," I said, my voice rising. "We have an agreement about that."

"I know. It won't happen again. I promise." Ron leaned down and told Jesse he was sorry. Jesse turned away.

"If you can't take care of them without hitting them," I said, "then I am going to have to reconsider my agreement about joint custody." I got in and drove away, leaving Ron standing on the sidewalk, his head down.

I decided I needed a different lawyer. I chose a woman who sounded no-nonsense and tough on the phone.

"Do you have any idea what it takes to fight for custody?" she said when we met at her office and I laid out the details of my case. "It takes thousands of dollars. And you could end up the visiting parent."

"I can't risk that," I croaked, near tears. "I have to be in their lives."

"If I were you," she said, more gently now, "I would agree to joint custody and then do everything I could to help Ron be the best parent he can be. He wants to care for his kids. Is that such a bad thing?"

I staggered out onto the street, dazed by the sunlight and the harsh truths of this process. The thought of becoming a visiting parent had sent ice water through my veins—and I knew Ron had been facing that fear for months. No wonder he was fighting me.

I called him and said I would agree to joint custody on a permanent basis if we worked with a counselor. He agreed, and then wept with relief.

*   *   *

A little more than a year after our separation, I had the kids and was angry with them about some typical childlike failure. Ron called and, hearing the frustration in my voice, asked what was wrong.

"Oh, I'm just tired of having the same fights with them. And I'm mad at myself, because I'm getting too angry over this." I had trouble admitting my failures to him, but at the moment I was too overcome to hide what was happening.

"Well, what I do when I'm angry with them is put myself in timeout."

"What?"

"I put myself in timeout," he said. "It really surprises them and gets me to calm down. Then I can go back out and talk rationally."

It turned out that, with the help of the counselor we'd been working with, Ron had devised a series of tricks for managing his frustration and anger. David told me on another occasion that his father sometimes got down on his knees when he started yelling. "When Daddy is on his knees he isn't as big, and so he isn't as scary," David said. "Also, he usually starts laughing. He looks silly."

I was astounded. I had told Ron that he needed to learn to manage his anger once and for all or he was going to lose the boys, just as he had lost me. Now he was trying to get better, without my help. He was doing it for the boys.

Ron and I have a relationship today that most people find puzzling. On the surface we get along, which makes many wonder why we can't get back together. My children will probably always hope we do. But despite the dire predictions in the books, the boys appear to be doing fine. They're sweet and friendly. They're doing better in school than I expected. They're usually respectful and always loving, and busy with buddies and sports. I've learned that the statistics don't have to be manifest destiny, that with hard work Ron and I can make them untrue.

My children know that they live inside a web of loving bonds, and that their father and mother are woven together, for better or for worse, as long as they live. I pray that my boys will grow and thrive and remain wholehearted.

Originally published in the June 2001 issue of *Reader's Digest* magazine.

Kidnapped—and Buried Alive!

by Andrew Jones

His abductors had entombed him in a flimsy wooden box in the middle of nowhere. As days ticked by, hope began to fade.

"**I**f you don't give them $75,000, they will kill me. *These people mean business.*" There was a click, and then the hum of a dead line. Benny Baucom, founder and president of Bebco Industries, an electronics company in La Marque, Texas, had been called to the phone in his office on Sept. 22, 1982, a Wednesday. The voice that came faintly over the wire belonged to his 21-year-old son, Michael.

Baucom fought back panic as he realized that his son had been kidnapped. He asked Sherry, his daughter and secretary, if she knew who had asked for him on the phone. It had been a man.

On the way home to tell Mike's mother, Benny's mind kept racing around in a vortex, at the center of which was a former Bebco salesman, Ronald Floyd White, who had quit his job that spring. He had seemed to Benny to be a sort of con man, a gun nut who liked to refer to himself as a "mercenary."

Suddenly it all fell into place. Benny had been wondering about the $75,000 ransom demand. Why that amount? A few months earlier he had sold some property for $80,000. White knew about this sale and must have reasoned that his former employer had that much money readily available.

* * *

At 9:30 the previous evening, Mike Baucom was watching television at his home in Santa Fe, 7 miles from his father's plant. When he heard three raps on the door, he opened it—and found himself looking down the barrel of a .357 Magnum. The man with the pistol had long hair and was about his own age. Behind him was a man with jet black hair holding a shotgun.

They bound Mike's hands, blindfolded him and gagged him with duct tape. Then they walked him out to his own truck and backed out the driveway.

They drove through Houston and then north for half an hour to a secluded, heavily wooded area in an abandoned oil field. There the abductors made Mike repeat two separate messages into a tape recorder. The first: "Dad, I'm in trouble. These people are tough. If you don't give them $75,000 ..."

The second message contained instructions: "Drive to the San Jacinto monument east of Houston. Take the Lynchburg ferry across the ship channel. Follow the road to Junior's Minute Man, the grocery store at Interstate 10, and wait at the parking lot phone booths for a call."

When the taping was done, the two men walked Mike across a field to a hole in the ground. At the bottom of the hole was a flimsy plywood box, 8 feet long, 24 inches wide and 14 inches high. "We're giving you half a loaf of bread and a plastic bottle full of water," one said. "Be cool. If everything goes right, we'll be back in a couple of days to get you out."

They forced him to a lying position in the box, placed a lid on top, jammed in four lengths of ¾-inch plastic pipe for breathing tubes, and started shoveling in dirt to fill the hole. Then they drove away.

* * *

After conveying the bad news to his wife, Glendell, Benny Baucom called Chief Bryan Lamb of the Santa Fe police and mentioned his suspicions about White. Lamb told him to return to the factory.

On the way to the factory, Benny swung by Mike's house and saw that the yard was empty. He concluded that the kidnappers had taken him off in his own truck. Giving way to fury, he checked in at Bebco, then he drove to a sporting-goods store and bought two boxes of ammunition for the deer rifle he had placed in his trunk before leaving home. He loaded the rifle and headed for Ron White's trailer in Houston. "If Mike's truck had been there," he said later, "I'd have killed everybody in the place." But the truck was not there, so Benny settled down to wait. No one came. Finally, around 5 p.m., he called his factory. He was put through to an FBI agent.

In conjunction with local police, the bureau had taken over. There were to be agents at the Baucom home around the clock, and at the factory a small army of lawmen had set up a command post.

In his isolated tomb 80 miles to the north, Mike had found a way to turn over onto his stomach. From this position he discovered a gap between the end of the box and the sides. The more he worked on the end board, the looser it became. He was on his stomach, propped on his elbows, when the end board came free, letting the lid of the box with its burden of earth sag onto his head. He had time just to grab a scrap of lumber left in the box and jam it between the lid and the floor to avoid being crushed. Now he was pinned to the floor, facedown.

At 4:30 the next morning, Thursday, the phone rang in the Baucom home. Once again Benny found himself listening to Mike's voice—the same tape he had heard before. He broke in on it this time. "Tell me how you want the money!" he shouted. At the end of the transmission, a man's voice came on. "You've got two days to get the money." Then there was a click, followed by the dead-line hum. The conversation had lasted 25 seconds, not long enough for the FBI men to trace it. And they still had no delivery instructions.

That afternoon Benny picked up the ransom money with the lawmen. They made up a package of $5,000 in $10 bills wrapped around a wad of fake bills, with an electronic tracking beeper at the core.

Finally, on Friday evening, the call came to the Baucom house. A man's voice told Benny to go back to the factory and wait for instructions.

Preparations were fast and thorough, for the factory was a perfect place for an ambush. The two agents who would act as Benny's bodyguards fitted him with a bulletproof vest and put a tape recorder in his side jacket pocket and a radio transmitter in his shirt pocket. If Benny should get out of voice range, he was to talk into the transmitter.

When they drove up to the factory, the agents moved inside quickly, turning on lights, securing the building. Then they called to Benny to come in.

At 10:30 p.m. the phone rang. Benny picked it up and heard Mike's voice on tape: "Drive to the San Jacinto monument east of Houston ..."

At the end of the instructions Benny blurted, "Hey, I want to talk to my son! I've got your damn money. Where is Mike?" He was talking to a dead line.

Thus began the longest night in Benny Baucom's life. With the agents crouched on the floor of the car's backseat, covered by a sleeping bag, he drove to the monument and boarded the ferry. A two-way radio kept the agents in touch with other bureau personnel in the area—in cars, spotter planes, even a powerboat trailing the ferry.

They drove to the market where Benny was to receive the kidnappers' call. Its parking lot had four phone booths near the curb. With the money satchel in his hand, Benny stepped out of the car. One of the phones began ringing. "Is this Benny?" a voice said. "Get on I-10 and drive west to the Exxon station at the Uvalde Street exit. Wait by the two phone booths for further instructions."

They heard Mike's voice, very weak: "I'm out of water. I need more water." But the two men walked away.

At Uvalde Street, Benny pulled into the gas station and parked beside the phone booths. After two hours, one of the phones finally rang. It was a woman's voice this time: "Drive back to the minute market, park under the lights and open all the doors of your car. Then wait for further instructions."

Benny would now have to go it on his own. Shortly after 2 a.m., en route to the market, he let out the two agents. At the market Benny switched off his engine and opened all the car doors and trunk—and waited. Finally, at 5 a.m., an FBI agent came up to him and said, "It's off. They phoned your house a few minutes ago and said it's been called off for tonight."

Kidnapped—and Buried Alive!

*   *   *

On Saturday night, two men visited the burial site. When they shone a flash-light beam down one of the breathing tubes, they heard Mike's voice, very weak: "I'm out of water. I need more water." But the two men walked away.

*   *   *

Despite the massive FBI effort, hope was beginning to fade. Then a break occurred totally unconnected to their operation. At 12:30 a.m. on Sunday, the sheriff's office in Montgomery County, 40 miles north of Houston, received a call from a resident reporting a suspicious vehicle parked at a darkened Jiffy Stop convenience store. Deputies Jim Hall and John Orr responded. They saw a man with black hair beside a beat-up car filling plastic bottles from a faucet. The man told Hall he was replenishing the water supply for a camp back in the woods. Orr had been shining his flashlight around the interior of the car. Suddenly he shouted, "Look out, Jim, there's a pistol on the front seat!"

After frisking the man, they searched his car. They found a shotgun on the backseat and in the trunk a semiautomatic machine pistol, a bag of ammunition, a tape recorder, wire and rope, and a briefcase containing a passport for Ronald Floyd White. The name meant nothing to the deputies; indeed, they had no knowledge of the Baucom case. The suspect in hand said he was Timothy Connelly. His story: He had been picked up by two men who offered to pay him if he'd get some water for their camp. He didn't know where the camp was—they had told him they would come back to get him. While he was talking, the deputies spotted a slip of paper between the car seats. It contained a series of driving instructions with orders to wait for telephone calls. One line read, "You'll see Mike alive again if ..."

Hall and Orr called their dispatcher and asked for a statewide check on White. The reply came back fast: He was wanted down south—as a suspect in an ongoing kidnapping! While Hall and Orr were booking Connelly, they heard over the radio that colleagues had spotted a campfire in the woods. They raced to the scene, arriving just as two new suspects were being taken into custody: a bearded, long-haired man named Mark Oler, and a young woman, Debbie Williams. There was no sign of Ron White.

In the course of questioning by Jim Hall, Oler admitted that White had been at the camp that evening. Hall still did not know the name of the kidnap victim—all he had was "Mike" in the ransom note—and he was grilling the suspect largely on bluff. "Look, Oler," he said, "we know you've got Mike, and it looks like White has walked off and left you holding the bag. So far as we're concerned, you're the kidnapper, and if anything happens to the victim you'll face a murder rap."

The bluff worked. Oler led the police to the middle of an abandoned oil field. Stepping out into the pre-dawn cold, Hall shouted, "Mike?" He heard a voice, muffled and faint. He shouted again, and again, the barely audible voice replied. The police began digging frantically, using their bare hands. They found a hole and Hall reached down into it as far as he could. He felt a hand seize him by the wrist in a steely grip that would not let go.

*   *   *

At 7:30 that morning Benny Baucom heard the front door open. "We have Mike," Chief Lamb told him. He had a police car waiting and drove Benny and Glendell to Montgomery County Courthouse. Mike had lost 23 pounds but, apart from a rash of insect bites and dehydration, seemed to be in good shape. Minutes later, freshly showered, Mike himself walked in.

Mike told law officers of his five-day ordeal. Speaking in a steady voice, he recalled his panic when the wooden lid of his box began to sag. Ants were biting his hands and eyelids, and he had hallucinations about being chewed down to a skeleton. Finally, he heard someone calling his name and a hand in a hole above his head. He seized it and pulled.

Three days later, Ronald Floyd White was captured after a high-speed chase near Rio Hondo, Texas. White, Connelly, Oler and Williams were all later convicted of aggravated kidnapping.

Originally published in the September 1984 issue of *Reader's Digest* magazine.

Now happily married, Mike Baucom is CEO of Bebco Environmental, an offshoot of his father's company, and has suffered no lasting ill effects from his ordeal.

The Moment I Knew I Was in Love

Was it that shy glance, the clever line—
or an offer to fix a clogged sink?
As our readers' stories attest, lightning
often strikes when you least expect it.

This younger guy used to follow me around like a puppy when we were stationed at Lockbourne Air Force Base. I convinced myself I wasn't interested—he was like a kid brother. One day, we were driving in a snowstorm and ended up on the median. He was soaked and cold after an hour spent pushing the car free, so I said he could shower at my place. When he finished, he yelled out, "Honey, where are the towels?" My heart melted with that one word, and 43 years later, he still calls me "honey."

—Lynn Timon, *Charlotte, NC*

We were driving down the road when a rabbit ran out in front of us. He swerved to avoid it. Although I was pleased by his show of compassion, he won my heart when he called it a "bunny."

—Mary Lou McCowan, *LeRoy, NY*

One day in junior high, I went to the movies. I sat with friends behind a row of boys from our class. The boy in front of me turned around and

Christa Parry with her love

planted a kiss on me. When I got home, my parents asked me about the movie. I drew a blank. I couldn't remember anything after the kiss. I've been happily married to that boy for 41 years.

—Donnalou Baner,
Gridley, IL

A week after I met my future husband, we visited the Illinois State Fair with his family. At one point, someone yelled out, "Does anybody know what time it is?" At the same exact moment, we shouted back the Chicago lyric, "Does anybody really care?" I knew it was love.

—Christa Parry, *Mediapolis, IA*

On one of our first dates, my wife-to-be hopped on my motorcycle and took off, riding around my parents' yard as if she'd been riding all her life. Unfortunately, we hadn't gone over the fine art of stopping, and suddenly— BOOM. She was off. But up she bounced, announcing, "That was fun!" Then and there, I knew this was the girl for me.

—Dale L. Hall, *Chagrin Falls, OH*

I had been dating an airman. His buddies told me that while eating in the chow hall, he'd write my name in his mashed potatoes. I figured that must be love.

—Nancy Louise Amazeen Whitlock,
York, ME

Nancy Louise Amazeen Whitlock and family

Being part of a conservative Indian family, my parents and I put in many years searching for a suitable match for me. On that journey was a friend who stood by me through thick and thin. In the 14 years that we went from classmates to best friends, I never once consciously thought of him as a lover. I tried remembering the exact moment I'd fallen for him by reliving all those moments that had made us laugh, fight, cry and ache for each other. Try as I might, I could not recall it. Then it came to me at the altar on our wedding day. I had been in love with him all along.

—Priyanka Prasad, *Dumfries, VA*

Priyanka Prasad and her best friend

I was in the hospital having my tonsils removed. The guy I was seeing was going to pick me up after he got off work, at 5 p.m. But I was discharged early, at 3:15, and the nurse asked if someone would be picking me up. Just then, it hit me. "Yes, my boyfriend," I said, smiling. "He isn't supposed to be here until five, but he won't be able to wait that long. He'll get here early because he'll be worried about me." Sure enough, he was there 15 minutes later.

—Traci Stout, *Beaverton, OR*

The moment I knew I was in love with my now husband was every time I'd call him at work just to hear his voice. Now, 18 years later, I still find things to call him about just to hear his voice.

—Jeanne Hammer, *Bettendorf, IA*

Previous dates brought me red roses, candy, even jewelry. Instead, he brought food—Looney Tunes frozen dinners, to be precise. He said, "I looked in your fridge; it was pretty empty." How could I not fall in love?

—Suzie Berberich, *Dryden, MI*

My boyfriend of three weeks was helping my roommate and me move back to college for our senior year. While unpacking, I listed all the things I loved about my new apartment: "I love my new room, I love my bathroom, I love our kitchen, I love our living room, I love my boyfriend ..." As soon as I'd uttered those words, I wanted to stuff them back into my mouth. My beau just laughed, and we both knew that what I'd said was true. Five years later, we're now married and getting ready to celebrate our first daughter turning 1.

—Michelle Plantier, *Raleigh, NC*

Michelle Plantier with her beau

I moved next door to a kind family whose son was serving in Vietnam. They showed me his pictures, shared his letters and talked about him all the time. The fact is, I fell in love with him well before I ever met him. We've been married 49 years this month.

—Patricia Lucas, *Reno, NV*

Sitting alone at a coffee shop, working the Sunday *New York Times* crossword, I got stuck on a clue. An attractive guy peeked over my shoulder and said, "Trireme: a Roman galley. It's the answer to six across." Thirty-two years later, we compete to see who can complete the crossword fastest.

—Sher Garfield, *Bellevue, WA*

Pam: I was intrigued by the football player who sat behind me in trigonometry. It was January, and I'd heard that his mom had died in a car crash a few days before Christmas.

Chris: I was devastated by my mom's passing. When school resumed, I found myself sitting behind a short, cute blond girl in trig who kept turning around to talk to me. "Are you the one whose mom died?" she boldly asked.

Pam: He was amazingly honest about what had happened.

Chris: No one else knew how to talk with me about my mother.

The Moment I Knew I Was in Love

Pam: It began a months-long conversation at my parents' dining room table while we were ostensibly doing homework.

Chris: I found myself opening up to her more than I'd expected.

Pam: Sometime in the spring, my dad asked if the reason I was studying so hard was because I was falling behind in trigonometry. I thought about it, then smiled as the truth dawned on me. "I don't think it's about the trigonometry anymore," I said.

Chris: We've been "doing homework" together now for 25 years.

—Chris and Pam Longston, *Seattle, WA*

My life as a children's storyteller did not work like a fairy tale. Weekend bookings and looking for gigs proved challenging for any prospective love interest. Then one day, I was performing the tale of the frog prince at a festival. At the moment when I pantomimed the princess about to bestow her kiss, I was distracted by a blond woman in the audience. She wore a beret and had pale yet powerful blue eyes. As I stood there with lips pursed, I found myself thinking wistfully, *There's someone I'd like to kiss*. Fortune smiled upon me when we married two years later. And, yes, her kiss transformed me!

—Jonathan Kruk, *Cold Spring, NY*

I fell in love as soon as I saw her in the Pullman Pie restaurant. It took me about a month to ask her out, and I was shocked when she said yes. I still can't figure out what she saw in me. She was so beautiful. To me, it was like beauty and the beast.

—Andrew Ronquillo, *Prescott, AZ*

Andrew Ronquillo with his beauty

She was my best friend throughout high school. I could tell her all my deepest secrets except for one: that I was madly in love with her. Sadly, she married another and we lost touch. Cut to many years later: We were both divorced and had become fast friends again. This time, I let her know how I felt about her. We got married 30 years after high school, and I'm living my dream.

—Brad Bumgarner, *Gahanna, OH*

Soon after I began dating Matt, I told him that I had multiple sclerosis. It wasn't bad, I said, but I explained how the disease might affect me. Matt didn't care. "If it gets so bad that you can't walk anymore, I'll be your legs," he said. "If it gets to where you can't see, I'll be your eyes. And if you can't talk anymore, I'll still know you love me because I know your heart."

—Barbara Wolf, *Lemoyne, PA*

On our first date, we went to a restaurant, where she ordered a steak with all the fixings, a fully loaded baked potato and a Budweiser. The waiter turned to me, and I simply said, "I'll have what she's having." It's been true love ever since.

—Thomas Miebach, *San Antonio, TX*

Dave's stepmom did not want us to get married. "Look at her mother," she said. "She's going to look just like her when she gets old." Dave shot back, "I like the way her mother looks, and I'll be proud to have her look like her mother." If I wasn't in love with him before, I certainly was then. We just celebrated our 58th anniversary, and, yes, I do look like my mother.

—Blair Covington, *Hollywood, FL*

He was 14 and I was 15 when our friend passed away. Waiting in line together at the viewing, I felt a squeeze of my hand. I turned to him, and he was crying. Right there, I fell in love. We are now in our 30s, and we often wonder aloud, "Is everyone experiencing this level of love?"

—Heather Fields, *Keyser, WV*

Originally published in the February 2017 issue of *Reader's Digest* magazine.

A SIGN FROM ABOVE

My husband had passed tragically, and unexpectedly, the evening before. I returned home in the morning, supported emotionally by my sister-in-law. We sat in the upstairs loft exchanging stories about a man who left us too young. I glanced out the window and noticed a woodpecker sitting on the roof. It appeared to be watching us. The bird, a species rarely seen here, sat for almost 20 minutes "listening" to us reminisce. I affectionately named the woodpecker after my late husband. It's been five years since he passed, and a woodpecker continues to appear at my weakest times.

—Shannon Neuhaus Rozewicz, *Sussex, WI*

CHEEKY BIRD

Early each morning, I go for a 2-to-3-mile run near my home. On Wednesdays and Fridays, as I pass a particular house, I hear a "catcall" of sorts, a loud whistle coming from the backyard. I'd rather not say whether or not I like it, but I'm not interested in changing my running route. So, not long ago, it was a bit windy and sure enough, I heard the whistle. But this time, the gate had blown open and I was able to see the charmer, the culprit, the admirer—it was a parrot.

—Jeffrey Molinari, *Sacramento, CA*

PHOTO OF LASTING INTEREST

Refugee Tent Kiss

Among images of Syrian refugees in a makeshift camp inside a Budapest train station, "it was the black-and-white photo that grabbed my heart. A moment of affection, tenderness and love, in the midst of months of chaos. In their love, their tenderness and their hope, there is hope for all of us."

Photograph by Zsíros István

Chosen by Omid Safi, director of the Duke Islamic Studies Center and onbeing.org columnist

Humor Hall of Fame

After a loud party in the apartment above, my friend asked the offender, "Didn't you hear me pounding on the ceiling?" The woman smiled. "That's OK. We were making a lot of noise ourselves."

—RALPH WARTH

A teacher displayed pictures her second graders had drawn after hearing about the Pilgrims' voyage and the first Thanksgiving. One drawing, by an Army child, a veteran of many Army moves, caught our attention. There, among the Pilgrims, Indians and turkeys, was a moving van with the name *Mayflower* written on it.

—MRS. H.R. TODD

Real-life horror movies

Love Your Enemies— It'll Drive 'Em Crazy

by J.P. McEvoy

A celebrated writer explains how to defang enemies of all types

Well, maybe it won't drive 'em crazy, but it'll certainly discombobulate 'em. You can waste a lot of energy being nasty to enemies. Wise old Ed Howe said it years ago: "If you attend to your work and let your enemy alone, someone else will come along some day and do him up for you."

But suppose your enemy won't let you alone? You can do what the man did who was walking the bounds of his new farm and met his neighbor. "When you bought this piece of ground," said the neighbor, "you also bought a lawsuit with me. Your fence is 10 feet over on my land."

Now this is the classic opening for a feud that could go on for centuries. The new owner smiled. "I thought I'd find some friendly neighbors here, and I'm going to. And you're going to help me. Move the fence where you want it, and send me the bill. You'll be satisfied and I'll be happy."

The fence was never moved, and the potential enemy was never the same. He went around talking, to himself. After that he was mystified but friendly.

There is an old saying, "There are no little enemies." Enemies may seem unimportant, but be careful. Don't give them cause to make a career of getting even with you. Don't tell off that snooty receptionist who blocks you off from getting in to the boss. One day she'll marry the boss.

There are all kinds of enemies, and one of the arts of living is to learn to tell them apart—so you can either plow around them the way a farmer plows around a stump, or get rid of them by making friends. A gardener once wrote to the Department of Agriculture: "I've tried everything I've heard about or read, including all your bulletins, on how to get rid of dandelions—and I've still got 'em."

By return mail, he received the last word on the subject: "Dear sir, if you have tried everything and you still have dandelions, there is only one thing left for you to do. Learn to love 'em."

But sometimes you run into a really big enemy—the kind that you can't go under or over or around and who doesn't want to be loved. Crossword puzzle experts know him by his three-letter name, SOB.

One of William Randolph Hearst's favorite editors came to him one day in a rage and said, "I can't go on like this. I've tried for years and I just can't get along with that SOB in the accounting department. He goes or I go."

Hearst had a deceptively mild way of speaking. "You're absolutely right," he said softly to his irate editor. "I'm not surprised that you can't get along with this man. Nobody can. He is that rare phenomenon, a one hundred percent SOB. But every organization must have at least one SOB. He's ours. You can be replaced. He can't." In this case the editor was the one who went crazy.

Besides the little enemies who can't wait to grow up to get even with you, and the big enemies—the icebergs that show only one-seventh of their nasty bulk above the surface of everyday life—there are the most difficult enemies of all, the "In-Betweens."

If you ignore the In-Betweens, they pursue you; if you turn the other cheek, they knock your block off. You can't lick 'em because there are too many of them and you can't join 'em because if you make friendly advances, they think you're afraid of them and they get twice as ornery. There isn't a thing you can do about them; they're crazy already.

Finally, there is the enemy who never meant to be an enemy at all. He's not mad at you; he's mad at the world, and you are wandering witlessly around on his lonely battlefield, stepping on land mines not meant for you.

Love Your Enemies—It'll Drive 'Em Crazy

Let me tell you about one of them. She was the dark-eyed daughter of our village barber: a small, stormy Gina Lollobrigida. Years ago, I brought my two girls up from Cuba in the late spring and put them in public school down the road. They talked a very peculiar language neither English nor Spanish— and their first- and second-grade colleagues gave them a hard time, naturally. Especially Lolla, who was older and the ringleader Terror of the Tiny Tots.

Pat and Peggy came home crying almost every day, so I decided to cheer them up. "Let's have a party," I said. Pat's and Peggy's tears dried magically. Right away they got creative: "Ice cream! Cake, big red balloons!" "And friends?" I said. The tears started again. "We haven't got any friends," Pat blubbered. Peggy wailed. "Nothing but enemies."

Then I had one of my rare inspirations. "Let's have an enemy party. Let's invite all your enemies—especially the worst ones—and we'll fill 'em up with ice cream and cake and give 'em big red balloons to take home."

Little Pat and Peggy exchanged knowing looks, and one of them said with an eloquent Spanish gesture, "*Que pasa al viejo?*" (What goes with the Old One?)

The Enemy Party was a merry success, and the best time was had by the biggest enemy, little Lolla, who rolled on the floor and shrieked with delight.

Pat and Peggy never came crying home from school anymore. Their biggest enemy had turned into their stanchest champion. Nobody dared lift a finger to them ... little Lolla would have broken it off, pronto.

One day Lolla's father dropped by to see me. "I come to thank you for asking my little girl to the party," he said. Then he added, mystified, "Why did you?"

"Why not?" I told him. "She's a solid little citizen and she likes ice cream, cake and big red balloons, just like any other little girl. Yes?"

"Oh, yes," he said, "but do you know something? Nobody ever asked her to a party before. Why?"

A good question. Are the Lollas left out because they are enemies, or do they become enemies because they are left out? There are several schools of thought working on this, but the Great Teacher settled it long ago. "Love your enemies, pray for them that persecute you, do good to them that hate you ..."

And it'll drive them crazy, because it works!

Originally published in the December 1957 issue of *Reader's Digest* magazine.

Crushed by Corn

by Nicholas Hune-Brown

For hours, no one knew that Arick Baker had fallen into a 137-degree grain bin and was slowly being squeezed to death

Ever since Arick Baker was a kid, his father had warned him: "If you go down in the corn, you don't come out."

The enormous grain bins that dot the Iowa landscape store enough dried corn to swallow up a body completely, squeezing the breath and life from a person in seconds. Accidents happen, and they're often fatal. In 2010 alone, 26 Americans were killed in silo accidents. For the firefighters of Iowa, more often than not, a trip to a grain bin isn't a rescue operation—it's a recovery mission.

On a Wednesday one recent June, however, 23-year-old Baker wasn't thinking about the risks. With his dad, Rick, getting older and the only other farmhand over 70, Baker was increasingly responsible for the farm's most unpleasant tasks. His first time cleaning out a dusty silo had taken all day Monday and Tuesday, and now he was just trying to finish the job.

That morning, while his father and another driver took turns hauling away truckloads of grain, Baker stood in the 60,000-bushel bin using a length of PVC pipe to try to break up the chunks of rotten corn that were blocking the flow. It was a sweltering day, and it was 137 degrees inside the massive cylinder of corrugated steel. Baker is asthmatic, so his dad had

Baker stands close to the spot where he was buried for four hours.

given him a battery-powered ventilation mask with a visor and a cloth that he tied under his chin. The mask didn't make oxygen, but at least it filtered out all the dust kicked up while Baker worked ankle deep in the corn.

Around 10:30 that morning, Baker's dad left his spot on the roof, where he'd been keeping an eye on his son, to turn off the auger, the rotating screwlike device that was churning at the base of the silo, moving the kernels of corn out of the bin and into the waiting truck. With the load complete, Baker's father drove off. Just seconds later, Baker felt the corn beneath his feet give way.

He didn't know it then, but he had broken through a chunk of rotten corn that had solidified into a bridge with a cavernous air pocket beneath it. That pocket was now filling up fast, drawing in the corn—and Baker along with it, until it was up to his knees, then his waist. He had a rope wrapped around his right arm, and he held on as tightly as he could, but it was useless. The corn was like quicksand, dragging him down, and

The pressure on his body was enormous. It felt like being strangled by a thousand boa constrictors.

he could only watch helplessly as the cord slipped out of his gloved hands. "Dad!" Baker yelled once. He took a deep breath. Darkness, silence. He was down in the corn.

Baker was stuck firm, his left arm pointed straight up, with just his fingertips poking out of the corn. The pressure on his body was enormous. For Baker, it was an awful sensation, to feel himself squeezed with equal force across every inch of his body. It felt like being strangled by a thousand boa constrictors. He tried to move his leg an inch, but the corn would rush back in to fill the void, packing him in even tighter. Every breath was exhausting. He was hyperventilating, which didn't help either. Still, he was breathing. His mask seemed to be doing just enough. But how long could the batteries last? Three hours? Then what?

My father must know by now I'm down here, Baker reasoned. *Surely he'd figure it out.* But a second thought kept gnawing at him: *What if the second driver came back and turned on the auger?* The gearbox was just inches from Baker's extended right foot. He'd be sucked into the machinery.

* * *

Hours crept by, and Baker kept himself from going crazy by thinking about everything he would miss. Just the weekend before, Baker and his friends had driven out to Lake of the Ozarks. They'd rented a pontoon and gone over to Party Cove. It was one of the best weekends of his life. And to think that now it could all be over ... He'd never get to talk to his friends, some of whom had moved away from Iowa and would learn about his death over Facebook. He'd never find out what might happen with that girl he'd just started chatting with—the girl who, at the very moment he was slowly suffocating alone, was texting him: "Did you die, mister, or are you just not talking with me today?"

At a certain point, Baker resigned himself to death. Filling his lungs seemed to take more strength than he had, the slightest swelling of his chest meeting the unbending resistance of the mountain of corn pushing in from all around him. He was tired of fighting, and he began drifting in and out of consciousness.

*   *   *

At 10:32 that morning, just moments after driving away, Baker's father had left his son a phone message: "Hey, Arick. Like a jackass, I forgot to wait to make sure you got out OK. Give me a call when you get this." Two hours later, when he still hadn't gotten a reply, Baker's dad called the other truck driver and told him to check on his son before restarting the auger. When the driver looked inside the silo, there was no sign of Baker, just his rope dangling limply from the top of the bin down into the corn. That's when he flagged down a passing state patrolman.

It was 12:45 when the Iowa Falls Volunteer Fire Department reached the farm. Fifteen-year veteran Tyler Prochaska and another firefighter, Jason Barrick, immediately lowered themselves into the bin. It was still. Silent. They scuffed through the stiflingly hot, gloomily lit structure for a few minutes before radioing back the bad news: "If the kid's in here, he must be dead, because I don't see him or hear him."

The firefighter said, "If the kid's in here, he must be dead, because I don't hear him."

Then, from down in the corn directly beneath their feet, a yell: "I'm alive, I'm alive, I'm alive!"

Prochaska and Barrick sunk to their knees and began digging like dogs. They could hear Baker beneath them, counting out loud for some reason, and they followed the sound of his voice. Prochaska was elbow deep before he found the young farmer's outstretched hand.

"Finally," Prochaska would say later, "I grabbed something that grabbed me back."

Knowing that Baker was still alive galvanized the firefighters, who piled into the bin to help. The digging, however, was slow, and Baker's initial euphoria at being discovered began to fade. With his head peeking out of the corn, it was clear that he was at the center of a funnel, the grain piled high and precariously around him. Five times, Prochaska and Barrick uncovered Baker's head, and five times something shifted and the grain avalanched down onto him, plunging him back into the terrifying darkness all over again. They dug again, working to the sound of the intermittent beeping coming from his mask as the batteries died.

The firefighters brought in the grain-bin rescue tube—a metal cylinder with detachable panels designed to contain the victim and relieve some of the pressure. It was only recently purchased, and now they were putting it to the test.

Prochaska and Barrick pushed sections of the tube down into the corn around Baker, forming a barrier, then climbed in with him, taking turns scooping out the grain with their hands, their helmets, whatever else they could use.

Prochaska wedged himself into the tube, using his body like a jack to keep the barriers from collapsing. Even so, one of the barriers buckled, letting grain trickle in, so Prochaska jammed his back against the leak. Paramedics urged Barrick and Prochaska to take a break after working for two and a half hours in the broiling silo, but they refused to leave Baker's side. *If we move, he's gone*, Prochaska thought.

Meanwhile, more than 120 volunteer firefighters from across the county as well as local farmers gathered around the bin, ready to help. Using saws and torches, they cut holes into the base of the bin to try to empty the container, though the grain only trickled out. Volunteers took shifts shoveling out the grain that pooled beneath the openings. It was slow going until Baker's dad, who'd arrived earlier, used a neighbor's bulldozer to clear the debris.

The rescue was in its third hour, around 4 p.m., and Baker was still skeptical he would make it. And then it happened. In one swift motion, rescuers freed his leg and pulled him up and out of the rescue tube, alive, where he collapsed onto Prochaska. Baker sobbed as the two men hugged and then fell to the ground, too exhausted to support their own weight.

*   *   *

A month later, the Baker family held a dinner for the rescuers. Remarkably, Baker had recovered over two days in the hospital without lasting damage. Doctors had pumped him full of liquids and extracted corn kernels embedded in his skin. His heart had been pushed to the limit, they told him.

"They said if I had been five years older, my heart would have exploded," says Baker. "If I had been five years younger, I would have been crushed."

At the dinner, Baker and Prochaska shared hugs and tears before diving in to pork loin and comparing notes on the ordeal. Between the toasts, Prochaska had a question: "Why were you counting out loud?" he asked Baker. "Were you timing us?"

Baker laughed. "I wasn't counting anything," he said. "I just didn't have anything else to say."

For the most part, Baker has put his experience in the silo behind him, as if it were a surreal dream rather than the actual near-death experience it was. Keeping the memory smooth and tidy, the edges rounded off.

Sometimes, though, a heavy feeling comes over him, and he'll slump under pressure and an awful helplessness. For a second, he'll be there—back in the darkness, down in the corn.

Originally published in the May 2014 issue of *Reader's Digest* magazine.

Arick Baker took over the family farm after his father, Rick Baker, died in 2019. Married with a son and daughter, he has no lingering issues from his time in the silo and remarked recently that "just last week I finished cleaning out the very same grain bin I was trapped in."

Goodbye, Childhood

by Joan Mills

One of the longest of all our voyages can happen in a moment

I can tell you the month (October) and the year (1935), and I am very sure of the day. It was the one on which I learned poignancy and regret, and something new about happiness.

I was 9: fat, freckled, viewing life astigmatically through thumb-printed spectacles. I had grown just old enough to care that on me hair ribbons draggled, dresses assumed odd shapes, socks crawled down at the heel. Yearning for patent leather Mary Janes with silver buckles, I wore instead blunt brown oxfords. I hated them. It is the scuffy toes of those plain, practical shoes that I see now, kicking up a rustle of October leaves as, in customary solitude, I walked home from school.

What with the fat and the freckles and such, it was my habit to beguile away the commuting time with make-believe. The lesser players in my imaginary extravaganzas varied.

If Tarzan didn't suit my mood ("Me Jane"), if I didn't feel like oven roasting a wicked witch, then I would conjure up a pride of golden lions, tame them and let them follow me.

But I was the star—magnificent, omnipotent, gowned in gossamer and gilt. Seeing me plod earnestly by, you would not have guessed that you had glimpsed a spy in splendidly effective disguise, or that, by flapping my

arms, I could soar like a lark. Nor would I have told you. It was a private, wonderful world I made, in which nothing was impossible. Especially me.

So. There was the day, brilliant with autumn, and I, unseeing, passing through it as usual, lost in my make-believe.

But at the turn into my street, when I slowed to admire my Mary Janes, they were brown oxfords. Alarmed, I looked at my gossamer gown, and saw lumps and buttons.

Never had fantasy so failed me. I stopped at once to consider the strange unease I felt. Try as I would—and I desperately did—I could not summon the certainty that I was gowned in gossamer, and capable of flight. No lions padded softly in my footsteps. In a flood of frightened understanding, I discovered that I had outgrown my magical world. I knew that from that moment I would see it only from a distance, as grown-ups do. The realization brought me almost to tears. For the first time, I felt that most poignant of adult emotions—regret at the irrevocable passing of a part of one's life.

It surprises me now that I recognized all this so precisely. But I did—and I felt the weight of the occasion. *I must remember this*, I thought. Rubbing my stomach, where the sorrow seemed to sit, I looked about to fix memory with details of the day.

Only then did I notice how fine a day it was. Before me, trees were letting go of leaves, quietly, one by one. The ground beneath, the path ahead were layered in autumn's cheerful litter. The circle of the sun made me blink, so yellow-white it was in a sky of perfect clarity. I grew dizzy with looking upward, trying to see through the blue translucence to something I had heard about—infinity.

Nearer to Earth (under my nose, in fact), invisible motes of leaf smoke flavored the air. I put out my tongue and tasted them. I sniffed apples—the season's first falls beneath a neighbor's tree—and the ranker odor of frost-nipped mums. A breeze blew lightly, and skittering leaves crackled like paper.

Mistrustful as I am of others' total recall, I hear, see, smell, taste, feel exactly how it was to be me, in that place, at that time, more than 30 years ago. It is out of a child's well-remembered awareness that I report what happened next.

The real world impacted on me. In fragments and pieces, I had realized it before: the fragility of flowers, the raucousness of crows, the sidewise scuttling of baby crabs had all, at one time or another, enchanted me. Tucked into a comfortable hollow of tree roots, I had relished the softness of moss under my hand and the green shade sheltering me.

But not until that day had my every sense been so thoroughly broached. It seemed that I shared with a foraging squirrel the eager lightness with which it leaped down from its tree; that the lift of air on which a leaf drifted supported me; that silence was alive with sound. I saw that the street on which I lived was dazzling.

A queer happiness flowed into me. It settled upon the confused ache that lingered in my middle. I felt sorrow, loss—and love for everything beautiful in the world.

I ran home, raked up a hasty pile of leaves, and burrowed into it to think. Leaves make lovely child nests—weightless, warm and comforting. The light within is dimly, pleasantly mysterious. There are faint, friendly noises. (Leaves drying? Bugs exploring?) The smell is good—earthy, clean. A child curled under leaves itches a little, but children enjoy a slight itch. I nestled in. The darkness and the shelter soothed me, and for a while I did not think of anything.

When I was ready, I thought. Wistfully, I thought about being very young (which seemed a long time ago), and growing up (to which I tentatively resigned myself). I considered how nice it was to hide among leaves. Then, cautiously, I thought about the curiously beautiful day outside. Had it changed?

I poked a tiny peephole in my nest. It was only a scrap of lucid sky that I saw, but it reassured me. *How lucky I am,* I thought, *to be me in the world right now!*

That's all I remember, but I'm glad I remember it well. One door had shut gently behind me, but another had opened to show that reality can be as magical as dreams and wishes.

It was solace to be 9 and know that. It is solace to be 42 and remember it. I have never gotten over wishful thinking—have you?—but I've never gotten over marveling at life, either.

Few of us can fully communicate to another our moments of being surprised by this world's sudden joy, but surely we all share them. That unspoken sharing went out from me to my youngest son not long ago when I believe I saw him make his own bittersweet approach to growing up.

Toward dusk of a raw winter day, Chris trotted past the corner of the house, hailing forward a brave band of imaginary companions. "To the fort, men!" he called, and he tunneled into a snowbank, happy as a mole in summer soil.

I stayed at the kitchen window for the pleasure of watching our last and littlest, enjoying what a funny guy he is, marveling that he could be so blithe about the cold. A flush of pink upon the snow diverted me; rare glory was spreading across the sky. I tapped on the glass and signaled Chris to look.

Goodbye, Childhood

He popped with a shout from his bunker (frosted like a cupcake, snow even on his lashes) and ran to the top of the bank where the view was grandest. There he slowly circled, seeing it all, his upturned face radiant. Beyond and above him, the whole sky blazed.

Then that roaring, boisterous boy child of mine sweetly amazed me. He stretched forth his arms, as if in them he could embrace the universe. It was a moving gesture, generations old, of absolute appreciation.

Thus the ancients worshiped the sun; thus my son stood until the last flare had faded. He lowered his arms, and then himself, and sat in the snow. Chin in hand, he remained, contemplating the early dark.

Chris came quietly to supper, wearing an inward look. I wanted to ask: Was this the day reality happened? I wanted to say: "I know how it is. I know."

I said nothing. When I filled his plate, I patted him casually and left him to his thoughts. Poignancy, regret and happiness—if that's what he felt—go along with growing. And growing up is something we must do alone.

Originally published in the May 1968 issue of *Reader's Digest* magazine.

CREDITS AND ACKNOWLEDGMENTS

"Why We Forgive" from *The Book of Forgiving* by Desmond Tutu and Mpho Tutu. © by Desmond Tutu and Mpho Tutu; *Reader's Digest*, July 2014

"Song of Defiance" by Fergus M. Bordewich; *Reader's Digest*, April 2003
Photograph on page 4 by Barbara Alper/Getty Images; page 9 by Michael Melford

"'My Family Is Dying!'" by Sheldon Kelly; *Reader's Digest*, April 1990

"Four-Wheel Dives" by Roz Warren, Humoroutcasts.com (Jan. 9, 2017), © 2017 by Roz Warren; *Reader's Digest*, October 2018
Illustration by Joanna Avillez

"The Arrow That Saved My Life—Twice" by Donna Barbour; *Reader's Digest*, July/August 2020
Photographs courtesy Donna Barbour

"What Became of the Airlift Orphans?" by Karen Walker Ryan; *Reader's Digest*, May 2000
Photograph on page 28 courtesy Karen Walker Ryan; page 33 by Breton Littlehales; pages 34 and 35 by Michael Carroll

"The Coldest Case" by Mary A. Fischer; *Reader's Digest*, September 2005

Photo illustration on page 38 by Anastasia Vasilakis, photos courtesy of Los Angeles District Attorney's Office; pages 43 and 44 by Anne Cusack/Los Angeles Times via Getty Images

"The Gift of Understanding" by Paul Villiard; *Reader's Digest*, June 1965

"Grizzly on the Nature Trail!" by John and Frankie O'Rear; *Reader's Digest*, July 1973
Photograph by Don White/Getty Images

"I Married a Pack Rat" by Mary Roach; *Reader's Digest*, January 2005

"Rescue at Mogadishu" by Malcolm McConnell; *Reader's Digest*, July 1992
Photograph on page 65 by ForeverPhotographer/Getty Images; page 66 Hum Images/Universal Picture Group/Getty Images

"Changes of Heart" by Cathy Free; *Reader's Digest*, January 2009
Photographs © Dan Lamont

"The Inanity Defense" by Andy Simmons; *Reader's Digest*, November 2009
Illustrations by Zohar Lazar

"When Amy Met Duane online" by Doug Shadel and David Dudley; reprinted from the June/July 2015 issue of *AARP The Magazine*, © 2015 by AARP, all rights reserved; *Reader's Digest*, June 2016

"'Not in Our Town!'" by Edwin Dobb; *Reader's Digest*, November 1994
Photograph by Michele Westmoreland/Getty Images

"Hot. Thirsty. Lost." by Kenneth Miller; *Reader's Digest*, September 2012
Photographs by Tom Spitz

"Giving Creatures Comfort" by Juliana LaBianca; *Reader's Digest*, May 2016
Photograph by Mike McGregor

"Attacked by Pirates" by Donovan Webster; *Reader's Digest*, April 2006
Photograph by Lynsey Addario/Getty Images Reportage

"How Sweet It Is" by Andy Simmons; excerpted from *Now That's Funny!* by Andy Simmons © 2012 Reader's Digest Association

"Mission Impossible" by Tim Hulse; *Reader's Digest* International Editions, 2017
Photographs on page 128, 135, 138 by Bergwacht Bayern/Getty Images; page 132 courtesy Roberto Antonini

"'I Turned In My Son'" by Charles Hurt; *Reader's Digest*, December 2000
Photograph courtesy John Cook

"The Boxer and the Boys" by Meera Jaggannathan; *Reader's Digest*, June 2015
Photograph by Ross Mantle Photography

"The Woman Who Wrestled a Cougar" by Mary Murray; *Reader's Digest*, May 1993
Photograph on page 151 © Evgeny555/Getty Images; page 154 courtesy Beth McLellan

"Man in the Crowd" by Joni Rodgers; *Reader's Digest*, June 2013
Illustrations by Edwin Fotheringham; photographs on pages 158 and 160 right by Matthew Mahon; page 160 left courtesy Joni Rodgers

"Swept off Mount McKinley!" by Peter Michelmore; *Reader's Digest*, May 1991
Photograph by Eastcott Momatiuk/Getty Images

"Fox in the Kitchen" by Avril Johannes; *Reader's Digest*, December 1998
Photograph by James Capo/Getty Images

"A Lobster Tale" by Julie Powell; excerpted from *Julie and Julia*, © 2005 by Julie Powell, published by Little, Brown and Company; *Reader's Digest*, October 2005

"The Psychic, the Novelist and the $17 Million Scam" by Robert Andrew Powell; *Reader's Digest*, March 2014
Photograph on page 185 by PixHound/Getty Images; page Tamer Soliman/Getty Images; page 189 Andrew Brookes/Getty Images

"Nightmare in the Woods" by Derek Burnett; *Reader's Digest*, March 2012
Photographs on pages 194 and 202 by Robbie McClaran; page 197 Design Pics/Craig Tuttle/Getty Images; page 198 Cavan Images/Getty Images; page 201 Nick Wiltgen/Getty Images

"Love's Last Refrain" by Jen McCaffery; *Reader's Digest*, November 2018
Photograph by Bret Hartman

"Smart People Do the Dumbest Things!" by the editors of *Reader's Digest*; *Reader's Digest*, October 2017
Illustrations by Zohar Lazar

"The Almost Perfect Murder" by Robert F. Howe; *Reader's Digest*, February 2003

"Season of Miracles" by John Pekkanen; *Reader's Digest*, May 1993
Photograph by CHUYN/Getty Images

"The Night the World Fell Down" by Sue Martin as told to Alan Burgess; *Reader's Digest*, August 1963
Photograph by Reporters Associe/Gamma Rapho/Getty Images

"The Good Divorce" by Wendy Swallow; excerpted from *Breaking Apart* by Wendy Swallow, copyright © 2001. Reprinted by permission of Hachette Books, an imprint of Hachette Book Group, Inc.; *Reader's Digest*, June 2001

Where, Oh Where? Answers 20: D, Alton Bay, New Hampshire. 52: B, Wooden Shoe Farm, Oregon; 126: D, Laguna Beach, California (the exact location is Victoria Beach). 220: B, Macon, Georgia. 242: C, Jackson Hole, Wyoming (the three other choices are also home to Dambo's troll sculptures).

"Kidnapped—and Buried Alive!" by Andrew Jones; *Reader's Digest,* September 1984

"The Moment I Knew I Was in Love" by the editors of *Reader's Digest; Reader's Digest,* February 2017
   Photograph on page 256 top courtesy Christa Parry; page 256 bottom courtesy Nancy Louise Amazeen Whitlock; page 257 Priyanka Prasad; page 258 courtesy Michelle Plantier; page 259 courtesy Andrew Ronquillo

"Love Your Enemies—It'll Drive 'Em Crazy" by J.P. McEvoy; *Reader's Digest,* December 1957

"Crushed by Corn" by Nicholas Hune Brown; *Reader's Digest,* May 2014
   Photographs © David Purdy – USA TODAY NETWORK

"Goodbye, Childhood" by Joan Mills; *Reader's Digest,* May 1968
   Photograph by Ekaterina Goncharova/Getty Images

Cartoon Credits

22 John Caldwell/Cartoonstock.com; 51 John Atkinson/Wrong Hands; 98 Dave Carpenter; 99 Kim Warp; 125 Harley Shwadron; 171 Toro/CartoonCollections.com; 192 Paul Noth/Cartoonstock.com; 193 Jeremy Banx/Cartoonstock.com; 244 Frank Cotham from The Cartoon Bank; 262 Gemma Correll